D1508492

THE KURDS

CONFLICT AND CRISIS
IN THE
POST–COLD WAR WORLD

THE KURDS

STATE AND MINORITY IN TURKEY, IRAQ AND IRAN

James Ciment

☑®
Facts On File, Inc.

The Kurds: State and Minority in Turkey, Iraq and Iran

Copyright © 1996 by James Ciment

Facts On File, Inc.
11 Penn Plaza
New York NY 10001

Library of Congress Cataloging-in-Publication Data
Ciment, James.
    The Kurds: state and minority in Turkey, Iraq and Iran / James Ciment.
        p.   cm. — (Conflict and crisis in the post-cold war world)
    Includes bibliographical references (p.   ) and index.
    ISBN 0-8160-3339-0 (alk. paper)
    1. Kurds—Politics and government. 2. Middle East—Ethnic relations. I. Title. II. Series.
DS59.K86C56   1996
323.1′19159—dc20   95-9595

Cover design by Vertigo Design

Printed in the United States of America

MP FOF 10 9 8 7 6 5 4 3 2

This book is printed on acid-free paper.

For
Vera Beaudin Saeedpour
American Citizen, Jewish Scholar, Kurdish Patriot
and
In Loving Memory of
Doug Blum

CONTENTS

LIST OF MAPS   ix

PREFACE: CONFLICT AND CRISIS IN THE POST–COLD
    WAR WORLD   xi

CHAPTER 1: INTRODUCTION   1
    The Mid-1990s   3
    Issues   7
    Participants   15
    Tactics of War   28
    Negotiations   32

CHAPTER 2: A HISTORY OF KURDISTAN   36
    To World War I   36
    Turkey   43
    Iraq   52
    Iran   63

CHAPTER 3: KURDISTAN AND THE KURDS   75
    Topography and Climate   75
    Demography   76
    Kurdishness   78
    Tribes and Tribal Confederations   79
    New Affiliations/New Identities   92

CHAPTER 4: NATION-STATES   106
    Turkey   106
    Iraq   113
    Iran   120
    Middle East and International   127

CHAPTER 5: ISSUES, TACTICS AND NEGOTIATIONS   135
    Issues   135
    Tactics   155
    Negotiations   167

CHAPTER 6: KURDISTAN SINCE THE GULF WAR   176

   Iraq: Establishing the Safe Haven (1990–1991)   176

   Turkey: War Against the PKK (1990–1995)   187

   Iraq: Civil War in the Safe Haven (1994–1995)   192

   Update: Turkey and Iran (1995–)   197

   Kurdistan into the Twenty-first Century   201

GLOSSARY   209

BIBLIOGRAPHY   213

INDEX   215

LIST OF MAPS

1. Middle East   2
2. Turkey   107
3. Iraq   114
4. Iran   121

PREFACE: CONFLICT AND CRISIS IN THE POST–COLD WAR WORLD

The eminent British historian E. J. Hobsbawm has recently declared the end of the "short twentieth century," delimited by the two great Russian revolutions of 1917 and 1991. If that is so, then this series might be considered among the first histories of the twenty-first century.

Whatever date we care to assign the beginning of the new century, we carry into it a lot of baggage from the past. The Cold War may be over, but just as the two global struggles of the first half of the twentieth century left a legacy of troubled peace, so has the great confrontation of the second half.

Conflict and Crisis in the Post–Cold War World explores that legacy. Each conflict described in these volumes has been a place where the Cold War turned hot.

The confrontation between East and West, however, did not ignite these conflicts. Each one has a history that stretches back to long before the atom bomb was dropped on Hiroshima or the wall was built in Berlin. Most of them, in fact, are not products of the Cold War so much as they are legacies of the European imperial order of the last several hundred years, and, in the case of Kurdistan, of a struggle that goes back a lot farther than that.

Similarly, these conflicts have had important indigenous and regional components. The great delusion of the Cold War, that all conflicts were essentially superpower confrontations by proxy, has been exposed in the post–Cold War era for the myth that it was. Ethnicity, religion and the animosity between settler and indigenous societies are, in varying measures, at the root of the very different conflicts examined in this series.

But that is not to let the Cold War off the historical hook. The struggle between Washington and Moscow exacerbated, extended and exaggerated each of these conflicts, and many more. Both East and West offered support in the form of money, weaponry, intelligence and military training to their favored clients. Worst of all, they provided an ideological force-field that deflected potential negotiations and peaceful solutions.

The books in this series examine the roles of pre–Cold War history, the Cold War, and indigenous and regional factors in these conflicts.

They are intended as introductory volumes for the reader acquainted with but not versed in the stories of these wars. They are short but comprehensive and readable reference works. Each follows a similar format and contains similar chapters: an introduction and overview of the conflict; its history; the participants, both those in power and those struggling against it; the issues, tactics and negotiations involved; and a final chapter as update and conclusion. (The volume on Israel/Palestine contains an additional chapter on the larger regional conflict between Israel and the Arab nations of the Middle East.) Each book also contains several maps, a glossary of names and terms and a bibliography.

THE KURDS

1

INTRODUCTION

*Level the mountains, and in a day
the Kurds would be no more.*
                    ——Kurdish adage

*In Arabic, the words for "wolf" and "Kurd"
are synonymous.*
                    ——Arab linguist

The Kurds are a nation without a state, if by nation we mean a people who are ethnically distinctive and who have written for themselves a history of political and military struggle to achieve self-rule and cultural autonomy. In fact, since the breakup of the Soviet Union, the Kurds have become the largest ethnic group in the world that occupies a geographically compact area and has no nation-state of its own. The obstacles to Kurdish nationhood, however, have been as formidable as the determination of the Kurds themselves.

The Kurds have the misfortune of occupying lands ruled by three aggressive and repressive states: Turkey, Iraq and Iran.[1] Competing nationalisms, regional power struggles and international politics have continually thwarted Kurdish efforts at self-determination and cultural autonomy throughout the twentieth century, indeed, back to early Mesopotamian civilization. Imperial, republican, military, dictatorial and theocratic regimes alike have sought to subjugate the Kurds for strategic purposes, to gain access to economic resources, to establish administrative hegemony and to build independent nations. In short, the Kurds have had many enemies for many reasons, and they have had them for a long time. Yet not least among the obstacles to Kurdish independence have been the Kurds themselves.

The Kurds are a mountain people. The isolation and impenetrability of their mountain homeland have long protected them. From this fastness, the Kurds have defended their autonomy and their distinctive way of life from the authority of lowland regimes throughout history. The mountains are where the ancient Kurds fled Babylonian hegemony and where the guerrillas of the Kurdish Workers' Party (PKK) fight the current Turkish regime in Ankara.

But the mountains have also been the Kurds' worst enemy. They have isolated them and kept them ignorant of political, economic and social

1

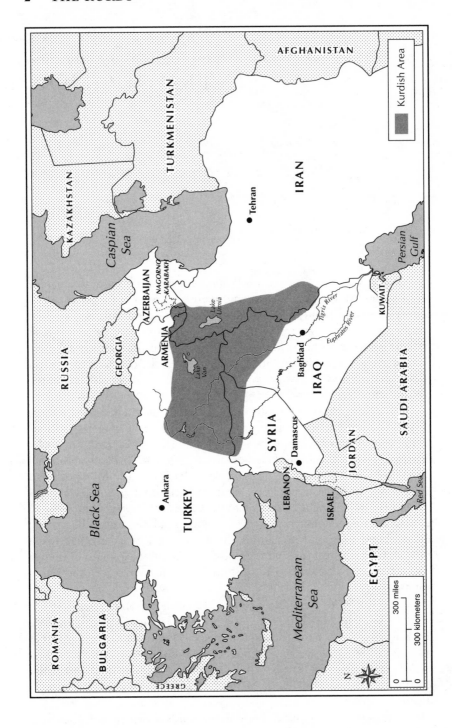

developments in the larger Middle East. They have also kept the Kurds divided into hostile and mutually suspicious factions. They have permitted local tribal chiefs, warlords and political leaders to maintain an ironclad grip on their subjects. And in the twentieth century, the mountains have helped retard political and social change, preventing the Kurds from coming to terms with the wave of nationalism that swept the Middle East, until it was too late.

This study will try to answer several questions: What makes the Kurds a nation? What kind of political status do they seek and what are they willing and likely to settle for? And, finally, what has prevented them from achieving this political status? The answers cannot be found in the Kurdish mountains alone, nor solely in the corridors of power in Ankara, Baghdad and Tehran. Occupying one of the most strategically situated regions of the modern world, Kurdistan has long been the object of imperial and superpower interests.

The Kurdish struggle, then, is a world issue. Its long and volatile history, profoundly affected by imperial expansion in the nineteenth century and Cold War politics in the twentieth, is likely to continue into the immediate post–Cold War era and beyond. As one journalist has noted, any lasting settlement in the Israeli-Palestinian conflict will leave the Kurdish struggle as the most significant and potentially explosive ethnic flash point in the post–Cold War Middle East.

THE MID-1990s

TURKEY

Since 1984, the Turkish military and various branches of its internal security forces have fought a low-intensity conflict against PKK guerrillas in the southeastern provinces of the country, an area unofficially known as Turkish Kurdistan.[2] The PKK is a militant Turkish Kurd organization which is often labeled Marxist-Leninist but in fact is more nationalist than communist. The war has followed a predictable pattern. During the warm season, roughly from April to November, government forces try to pin down PKK guerrillas and engage them in running firefights. Each winter, when heavy snows render roads in the Kurdish highlands virtually impassable, the military retreats to its bases and makes strategic plans for the upcoming season. The Kurds, meanwhile, use the hiatus to recruit, rearm and regroup. Militarily speaking, the Turkish government has been forced to reinvent the wheel every spring.

Ten years after the war began, during the winter of 1994–1995, the pattern was broken. Turkish military forces maintained their offensive through the snowy season in the hopes that continued pressure might break the back of the PKK. The unusual winter offensive marked but the latest step in the gradual intensification of the conflict. Over the past several years, the Turkish military has expanded and intensified its counterinsurgency tactics. Several thousand villages have been depopulated and the country-side denuded of crops and forests. The logic behind the strategy is obvious: to deny civilian support and natural cover to the Kurdish guerrillas.

In March of 1995, the Turkish military escalated its efforts against the PKK in another theater of the war: northern Iraq. Over 35,000 troops, supported by attack helicopters and fighter jets, crossed the border to attack PKK guerrilla bases that Ankara claims have been the launching points for raids into Turkish territory for over a decade. The operation, initiated on March 20, continued until early May, and then resumed in July. Turkish and Kurdish sources offer wildly different accounts of the operation's successes.

But whatever the successes in the field, the invasions represent a significant setback for Turkey in the international arena. Member governments of the European Union, a political and economic bloc Turkish leaders are eager to join, have vigorously protested both the legality of the operations and their impact on Iraqi Kurd civilians. The United States, Turkey's largest source of military aid, expressed early cautious support for the invasions, accepting Ankara's promises that the invasions would be limited in both geographic scope and duration. However, protests from European and NATO allies such as France and Germany, as well as the mounting evidence of civilian casualties, caused the Clinton administration to back off its earlier support and urge a quick withdrawal of Turkish troops in May.

The Turks face a double quandary. Domestic support for the war is uneven, and elements within the government are divided over the efficacy of a strictly military approach to the Kurdish struggle. But to give in to Kurdish demands for autonomy and cultural rights would require a sea change in the Turkish government's official line on the Kurds since Turkey's establishment as a republic after World War I: that the Kurds are not really a distinct ethnic group requiring a special status within the republic. In fact, Ankara continues to insist that the PKK is seeking independence for Kurdistan, a demand just as insistently denied by PKK leader Abdullah Ocalan.

Internationally, the Turks committed themselves in the wake of the Gulf War to protecting Iraqi civilians from Saddam Hussein. The no-fly zone over northern Iraq was defended by allied jets stationed at Turkish air bases. In addition, their active participation in the war to end the Iraqi occupation of Kuwait situated them squarely in support of the principle of the inviolability of national borders in the Middle East. The invasion of northern Iraq and the resulting civilian casualties contradict Ankara's public statements and activities in support of both Operation Desert Storm and

Operation Poised Hammer, the Gulf War Coalition's postwar, anti-Baghdad defense of the safe haven, an area of northern Iraq consisting of three provinces and the bulk of the Iraqi Kurd population.

IRAQ

One explanation for the Turkish invasion of northern Iraq has been the anarchic situation on the ground there. Since the spring of 1994, the two major Kurdish parties in northern Iraq, the Kurdistan Democratic Party (KDP) and the Patriotic Union of Kurdistan (PUK) have been engaged in a Kurdish civil war. The Turkish PKK has taken advantage of the resulting chaos, operating more bases there and conducting raids on Turkish territory with increasing impunity.

Following a series of terrorist bombings and assassinations in 1993 and early 1994, violence both the KDP and the PUK officially attribute to Saddam Hussein, the two sides openly attacked one another across a broad front on May 1, 1994. For over a year, the civil war engulfed much of northern Iraq, although the bulk of the fighting was centered in the KDP stronghold in the northwestern portion of the safe haven, near the Turkish and Syrian borders.

The internecine fighting has been intense and bloody. As in most civil conflicts, battle lines have not been clearly drawn between civilians and combatants. Estimates by the Western press place the total number of dead at over 5,000, a total greater than the number of Kurds killed over the same period by military forces in Turkey, though how many are civilians and how many are combatants has not been determined. Both sides continually downplay the ferocity of the conflict for fear of bad publicity in the West, upon which both parties rely for protection from Baghdad.

Nearly a year into the fighting, a temporary cease-fire was declared in April 1995 and extended on June 1. It has largely held, though the safe haven remains split into rival areas of KDP and PUK control. In late spring 1995, however, some tentative signs of a resolution to the fighting emerged. The Iraqi Kurdish regional assembly, evenly divided between KDP and PUK representatives, met on May 27 after a five-month hiatus (it was originally formed after elections in May 1992), and voted to continue its activities for another year.

In August and September, the two parties met in Ireland for peace talks, with the United States presiding. After more than a month, however, little progress had been made, other than a temporary agreement to extend the cease-fire. The civil conflict in northern Iraq has both short- and long-term causes. The immediate source of the fighting involves patronage and finance. Despite its symbolic significance, the Kurdish regional assembly has had little say in the running of the safe haven. Real political power lies with the KDP and the PUK. These two political parties maintain armies of *peshmerga* (traditional fighting forces; literally "those who stare death in the face") which enable them to exact taxes, collect customs duties and siphon off foreign aid.

But the longer-term causes of the conflict are steeped in Kurdish history. Despite their democratic-sounding names, the Kurdish Democratic Party and the Patriotic Union of Kurdistan are, in fact, tribal confederations garbed in the rhetoric and trappings of democratic political institutions. Their leaders maintain the firm yet personal obedience and loyalty of their troops and supporters, who are often related to the leaders by clan and family affiliation. Both KDP leader Mahmoud Barzani and PUK head Jalal Talabani are members of prestigious clans with an ancient heritage of leadership. As tribal confederations, they are suspicious both of political rivals and of the democratic process. As a beleaguered minority in a state with a 60-year history of despotic and totalitarian rule, the leadership and supporters of the KDP and PUK find it difficult to grasp a key concept of liberal democracy, that of the role of a loyal opposition.

IRAN

In contrast to southeastern Turkey and northern Iraq, Iranian Kurdistan has been relatively quiescent in the mid–1990s. Since 1992, however, the Kurdish Democratic Party of Iran (KDPI)[3] has established bases in the safe haven. The Tehran government asserts that Iranian Kurd guerrillas have launched repeated attacks against Iranian territory from these bases. The Iranian government has also charged that KDPI forces are receiving arms, training and sanctuary from Iraqi Kurd groups in the safe haven and has hinted that the Iraqi Kurds may be merely acting as a conduit through which arms from Turkey and the United States reach KDPI guerrillas. This claim is backed up by the eyewitness accounts of several Iraqi Kurds who have reported that Turkish arms were "accidentally" left behind near KDPI bases during previous incursions in 1992 and 1993.[4]

The Iranian government has not stood idly by. Throughout 1993 and as late as November of 1994, Iranian jets launched bombing raids against KDPI camps. In October 1995 the KDPI also claimed that Tehran had executed at least ten rebel Kurds. Tehran has at various times charged Saddam Hussein, non-Kurdish Iranian opposition forces and Iraqi Kurds with aiding and abetting the KDPI in northern Iraq. Meanwhile, Tehran has launched a diplomatic offensive to isolate the KDPI. Since 1992, Iran, Turkey and Syria have sought to negotiate an agreement ending cross-border governmental support of Kurdish rebels in all three countries. Iran has long charged Turkey with supporting the KDPI, while Turkey has charged Syria and Iran with the same vis-à-vis the PKK.

While the fighting between Tehran and the KDPI remains on the shadowy fringes of the Kurdish struggle in northern Iraq, two facts clearly stand out. First, KDPI resources and military action remain marginal, a fraction of those of the PKK at the other end of the safe haven. The KDPI, which was receiving help from Saddam Hussein, was nearly destroyed by Iranian offensives during the final year of the Iran-Iraq War. Second, relations between the Iraqi Kurds and the KDPI are very different from those between Iraqi Kurds and the PKK. Whereas both the KDP and PUK have agreed to patrol their territory against PKK guerrillas, they have openly announced their support of the KDPI. This is partly for ideological reasons—the PKK is far to the left of either the KDP or the PUK—and partly for strategic ones. The KDPI, many observers have noted, has become a tool of the Iraqi Kurds, while the PKK remains fiercely independent and even hostile toward them.

ISSUES

The Kurdish struggle against the central administrations of the region is an ancient and complex one. Over the past century, a variety of grievances has provided rallying points for Kurdish discontent and resistance in all three countries. They range across the social, economic, cultural and political spectrums, and include issues as diverse as the right of parents to give their children Kurdish names to demands for a larger share of revenues from the vast hydrocarbon reserves beneath Kurdish soil. This broad range of issues, however, can be catalogued under three general headings: cultural, political and economic.

TURKEY

Cultural issues
Until 1991, it was illegal to speak Kurdish or display symbols of Kurdishness in Turkey. The 1991 lifting of the ban against linguistic and cultural expression, however, was only a partial one. Kurdish can now be spoken in the privacy of the home, but the language remains taboo in public discourse and on the broadcast media. Education in Turkish Kurdistan, conducted strictly in the dominant language, remains a tool of Turkish nationalist indoctrination; Kurdish students are taught that their culture and language do not have an existence independent of the Turks'. Most displays of Kurdish identity are still punishable by fines and/or imprisonment. Kurdish place-names have been expunged from all maps, and parents are forbidden from giving their children Kurdish names.

Political parties with a specifically Kurdish agenda, or even having the word Kurd in their name, are prohibited. The Kurdish-dominated provinces are rarely referred to as Kurdistan in public discourse, and the Kurds themselves are officially referred to as "mountain Turks who have forgotten their language." In short, given this assertion of hegemony by the state, the

Kurdish struggle in Turkey has taken on the trappings of a cultural war. The very assertion of Kurdishness or even the existence of a Kurdish people in Turkey can be and is construed as a political crime.

Kurdish politicians and their Turkish supporters emphasize the need for a reassessment of the ban on Kurdish culture, and they demand the legalization of the public use of Kurdish, including a lifting of the ban on Kurdish broadcasts and publications. They ask that the prohibition on Kurdish dress and other public displays of Kurdish culture be annulled. But most importantly, they insist that the Turkish government officially recognize the existence of the Kurdish minority and the reality of a distinct Kurdish ethnic identity within the Turkish polity.

The government has responded cautiously and, according to Kurdish activists, reluctantly. The lifting of the ban on the use of Kurdish in the home, they say, was motivated by international criticism and attention during the Gulf War. Whatever the reason, there has been progress on a number of fronts. Turkish newspapers now routinely discuss the Kurdish issue and refer to the Kurds by name in print, though technically this still flouts Turkish law, and numerous periodicals have been closed and their editors fined and/or imprisoned for violating these statutes.

The government's defense of its nonrecognition policy toward the Kurds rests on state security, internal order and national cohesion. The Turkish Republic, founded in the wake of World War I on the ruins of the Ottoman Empire, has a long tradition of culturally motivated politics. Kamal Ataturk, founder of the modern Turkish state, viewed cultural autonomy by national minorities, along with Islamist politics, as the two greatest threats to his vision of a modern, Western-oriented, secular Turkey. Turkish leaders continue to maintain that cultural autonomy for the Kurds threatens the unity of the Turkish state and is a means by which foreign powers might divide Turkey into its constituent parts, as they did to the Ottoman Empire. Kurdish demands, it is also widely believed, would open up a Pandora's box whereby Turkey's 25 other minorities might demand further concessions.

Political issues

Given the 70-year-long history of cultural suppression, it is not surprising that the latest and most radical of Kurdish insurgencies, the guerrilla war led by the PKK, has insisted until recently on total independence and complete sovereignty for Turkish Kurdistan. Since the Turkish state was established on and organized around the principle of Turkish nationalism, it could be presumed that Kurdish cultural autonomy necessitated a separate Kurdish state. Thus sovereignty became the key political plank in the PKK's platform. The government counters that separation is not only undesirable, but impossible. So many Kurds have moved to the urbanized western half of the country that a separate Kurdish nation, if it ever existed at all, is no longer a viable political entity.

Meanwhile, Ocalan has scorned reformist Kurdish politicians and their efforts to ameliorate Turkish nationalism and adjust Turkish policy to allow for cultural autonomy and limited Kurdish self-determination. Ocalan's disdain has not been entirely unfounded, given the reformers' extremely limited progress and the punishment they have received for their efforts. Not only have no concessions to self-determination been made by the Turkish government, but the southeastern provinces have been periodically placed under military rule, and the vast majority of administrators appointed to serve there are of Turkish origin. Moreover, the internationally criticized brutality by which the Turkish government has historically squashed Kurdish protest has fueled separatist sentiments among the masses of Kurdish people, a fact even members of the military have admitted to, at least after they have retired from service.

Given the Turkish government's attitude toward more modest Kurdish demands for cultural autonomy, its harsh repression of separatist actions should not come as a surprise. Government spokespersons routinely refer to PKK guerrillas as "Marxist terrorists" and "bandits." During the 1980s, Ankara insisted that the group was organized, armed and even manned by foreign powers such as Iran, Syria and the former Soviet Union. More recently, however, the government has admitted that the PKK is largely a Turkish Kurd organization, with most of its resources and personnel coming from within the country. For their part, the guerrillas have made concessions in recent years as well. Since the early 1990s, PKK communiqués have dropped the absolute insistence on immediate independence, opting instead for a multistaged process of separation beginning with a Turkish form of federalism.

Economic issues

Turkish Kurdistan is an impoverished region, even by the developing-nation standards of the Middle East. On nearly every socioeconomic index, from infant mortality to literacy, to savings and investment, Kurdistan lags behind other regions of Turkey, sometimes by extremely wide margins. Kurdish politicians and intellectuals attribute this gap to a peculiarity in Turkish economic development. Kurdistan, they argue, represents an internal colony, its natural resources plundered by Turkish and foreign firms with little invested in return. Its agricultural land has largely been bought up by outsiders and a small Kurdish bourgeoisie, turning a once-independent peasantry into an exploited rural proletariat or agricultural wage earners. Its people are forced to migrate to Turkish and European cities where they work, if they work at all, at dangerous and underpaid jobs.

The Turkish government, for its part, points to the progress of the Greater Anatolia Project (GAP) whereby massive infusions of government funds have led to the development of new infrastructure and industries, including dams and roads. These developments, however, do not placate Kurdish critics, who say that the roads are primarily defensive in nature, allowing the government to move troops in and around Kurdistan, and the dams are there to supply western Turkish cities and industries with electricity. The PKK demands Kurdish control over economic resources, while Kurdish reformers in parliament insist on a fairer distribution of the income from those resources. The government insists that the resources of Turkey are as indivisible as the nation itself and that government investment in Kurdistan far outstrips tax revenues collected there.

The PKK, however, is not merely nationalist, but socialist-leaning as well. Among its most important economic priorities is land reform, though the specifics of this demand have evolved over the years. From a hard-line socialist platform of the 1980s, with its insistence on collective farms and collective ownership of the means of production, the PKK has lately promoted a more reformist and populist line. Private ownership and foreign investment will be welcomed in any Kurdish political entity, say recent PKK communiqués; land reform will mean the breaking up of the largest estates, with compensation to the owners, and the distribution and sale of land, financed by subsidies and low-interest loans, to landless agricultural workers.

IRAQ

Cultural issues

It has been said that Turkey wars with the Kurds because they are Kurds, but Baghdad does so because they are rebels against the state. There is some truth to this observation. The Kurds of twentieth-century Iraq have never known the kind of blanket prohibitions on their culture and language suffered by their Turkish cousins. Iraqi Kurds have been free to display cultural symbols, speak their language and refer to themselves as a distinctive ethnic group. Since independence in the early 1930s, the government in Baghdad has periodically formalized Kurdish cultural rights in law.

Still, there are restrictions, but they do not apply only to the Kurdish population of Iraq. The Baath regime, in power under Saddam Hussein's leadership since the late 1960s, has created what may be the Arab world's most totalitarian state. Until the creation of the safe haven in 1991, Kurdish language newspapers and Kurdish language broadcasts were heavily censored by the government in Baghdad, though these restrictions usually concerned political content rather than cultural expression.

Nevertheless, the almost continual state of warfare that has existed between Baghdad and the Kurds since the early 1960s has led to gross violations of Kurdish human rights, which crested with the *anfal,* or "spoils of war," campaign in the wake of the Iran-Iraq War, a campaign intended to punish Kurds for their support of Iran and to prevent further Kurdish uprisings. While the distinction may be lost on the Kurdish victims of Baath policy, there is a difference between Iraq's and Turkey's approach to the

Kurdish struggle. In Iraq, the campaign against Kurdish culture is a result of political rebellion. In Turkey, it's the other way around.

There are several reasons why Baghdad has been less prone to attack Kurdish cultural expression. One has to do with the Kurds themselves. In the post–World War II era, that is until the 1980s and the rise of the PKK, they have been a far more militant and formidable foe of the state than their Turkish brethren have been. In addition, Iraqi Kurdistan has always been economically better integrated with, and thus more crucial to, the Iraqi state. Allowing cultural expression has been seen by Baghdad as a reasonable price to pay for peace in a region rich in agriculture and oil. From the Arab perspective, history and culture have played their part too. Unlike the Turks, the Arabs have no imperial tradition of ruling over Kurds, at least not in modern times. None of the ethnocentric baggage accumulated by centuries of imperial rule has weighed down the Arab regimes in Baghdad.

Nevertheless, ancient traditions count for less in this equation than modern history. Since the 1920s and 1930s, both Turkey and Iraq have been engaged in the process of nation-building, but of two very different kinds. It is in these differences, and in the different Kurdish responses to them, that the fullest explanation can be found for the very different characters of the Turkish and Iraqi Kurdish struggles for cultural autonomy.

Political issues

Turkey's effort at nation-building in the wake of the Ottoman Empire's collapse was based on the idea of an indivisible Turkish people and culture. In Iraq, a state created out of three Ottoman *vilayets*, or provinces, by the victors of World War I with no regard for ethnic divisions embarked on a different form of nation-building. Since there was, and arguably still is, very little Iraqi nationalism, the idea of an Iraqi nation had to be woven out of whole cloth. Over the years, the leadership in Baghdad, with the partial exception of certain pan-Arab elements in the military, has opted for an inclusive form of nationalism, embracing the various minorities of Iraq as distinct but integral components of the Iraqi nation. Even the current totalitarian Baath regime emphasizes this inclusive approach to Iraqi nation-building.

Moreover, unlike Turkey, where virtually all traditional Kurdish political and social leaders and institutions were eliminated in the interwar era, the great Kurdish tribal confederations have been left intact in Iraq. Rather than destroying them, the regimes in Baghdad have chosen to work with or co-opt them. While the PKK owes little to previous organizations and tradition and is therefore free to embrace an extreme form of nationalism and even socialism, Iraqi Kurdish political parties remain hitched to more traditional forms of Kurdish separatism. These include a willingness to engage in a give-and-take dialogue with Baghdad when necessary or advantageous. They also include the traditional Kurdish strategy of pressing any advantage they have over the central regime when they sense it is weak and unable to maintain effective control of its Kurdish areas.

Thus, Kurdish nationalism in Iraq has been limited to the goal of separation rather than both separation and social revolution, as with the PKK in Turkey. It has also been riven by tribal divisions and power struggles, allowing Baghdad, at times, to use this limitation to its advantage by playing off one group against the other or by making strategic concessions to Kurdish leaders.

In the years since the establishment of the safe haven, two mutually exclusive political forces have been at work. One has been the effort of the Iraqi Kurds to press the issue of a Kurdish state, despite very mixed messages of support from their international allies. By holding elections in 1992 and establishing a provisional government, the Kurds attempted to create a *fait accompli*, a Kurdish state with all the trappings of Western-style democracy. At the same time, the Kurdish "political entity" has succumbed to the age-old problems of tribal rule, chaos and civil war.

Economic issues

In a backhanded compliment to the Iraqi government, two scholars write that "one can argue that the Kurds of Iraq have been given a reasonable share of the country's wealth, at least as much as the Arab countryside has received from an essentially negligent Baghdad."[5] This is not an entirely fair assessment. Despite its political repressiveness, the Baath regime has arguably done more to improve the educational, health and financial well-being of its citizenry than the government of any other heavily populated country in the Middle East. And while Iraqi Kurdish leaders may dispute the numbers, Kurds there have received a fairer share of the proceeds of their region's resources than have their compatriots in Turkey and Iran. Socioeconomic indices point to the smallest gap between the dominant population and the Kurds of any country in this study. According to one economist, Iraqi Kurdistan is blessed with the finest infrastructure of any Kurdish region in the Middle East and is comparable to the best of the developing world. Of course, the impact of the Gulf War and of United Nations postwar sanctions has undone many of these accomplishments.

In the 1920s, Iraqi Kurdistan, then under British rule, was the site of one of the first major petroleum strikes in the Middle East. The presence of that oil has been a key factor in the Kurdish struggle for self-determination. Since the end of the 1920s, Kurdish leaders have complained that they have not benefited equally from the exploitation of this resource. At the same time, they have envisioned an independent Kurdish state, made viable by the inflow of petrodollars. Needless to say, Baghdad has refused to relinquish any control over this valuable resource, though it has periodically offered to review the way the proceeds have been distributed.

Iraqi Kurdistan is a wealthy region above ground as well as below. Well watered and fertile, northern Iraq has long been one of the breadbaskets of Iraq and indeed of the Middle East as a whole. Yet despite this wealth, the safe haven is nearly bankrupt today, with international politics partially to blame. Like much of Iraq, Kurdistan was devastated by the air offensive aimed at destroying the nation's infrastructure during the Gulf War. In addition, Iraqi Kurds today face double sanctions, those imposed by the UN on Iraq as a whole and those placed on the north by Baghdad.

Other problems lie with the Kurds themselves or, more precisely, with their political institutions and leaders. Virtually the entire market for food and other goods is controlled by the two tribal confederations that rule over their respective spheres of influence. Most foreign goods smuggled in or permitted to enter legally under UN guidelines, as well as many domestic products, are sold in urban areas on the black market, which itself is controlled by the KDP and PUK, and which is regulated by their *peshmerga*.

IRAN

Cultural issues

While the Kurds of Iraq and Turkey insist on their ethnic, linguistic and even racial distinctiveness from their Arab and Turkish neighbors, Iranian Kurds acknowledge their affinity with the Persians.[6] Indeed, Kurds are more closely related to Persians than to any other ethnic group in the Middle East. Both trace their lineage, with a certain imprecision, to the ancient Medes, people speaking an Aryan language who descended on the region around 2000 B.C. Kurdish is a close linguistic cousin of Farsi, the language of the Persians and official tongue of modern Iran. Thus, while cultural autonomy plays an important role in Iranian Kurd politics, the intensity of the conflict between the official culture and Kurdish culture never approaches that of Turkey or even Iraq, where the Kurds and Arabs maintain a certain disdain for each other.

Under the shah's regime, restrictions on Kurdish cultural expression were moderate in comparison to Turkey's, and Kurdish language media was permitted, albeit heavily censored for political content. Kurdish language instruction was permitted in primary and secondary schools, but only as an adjunct to the general course work, which was conducted in Farsi. The official attitude toward Kurdish cultural autonomy has not changed dramatically under the theocratic regime in power in Tehran since 1979. Nevertheless, practical efforts to achieve linguistic uniformity have faltered somewhat. The current Iranian government has not been effective in asserting its control over the isolated and far-flung Kurdish provinces. And, of course, the establishment of an overtly religious state has exacerbated tensions between Iran's Shiite Muslim majority and its Kurdish Sunni minority.

Several factors play a role in the more muted struggle for Kurdish cultural autonomy in Iran. Some concern the Iranian state; others lie with the Kurds themselves. Unlike Turkey and Iraq, Iranian nationalism did not have to be created in the aftermath of World War I. The Persian state was not broken up like the Ottoman Empire, and its ancient history provides a stronger common identity than that of Iraq. Persians, it is said, have always lived in a multicultural empire, where they form but a large minority. Thus, it is argued, the government of modern Iran is more comfortable ruling over a multicultural state and has not felt the Turks' need to foment an exclusive and hegemonic nationalism.

For their part, the Kurds of Iran have cultivated a dualistic identity. They simultaneously identify themselves as Kurds apart from other Persians and as Iranian Kurds apart from other Kurds. This dual identity has both ancient and modern roots. For thousands of years, the borders between the empires of the Middle East have divided Iranian Kurds from their brethren to the west. Because of their close linguistic and cultural affiliation to Persians, Iranian Kurds were able to form alliances with Tehran. In the twentieth century, the Kurdish Democratic Party of Iran has pursued a policy of independence from and nonintervention in the affairs of Iraqi and Turkish Kurds.

Political issues

Despite their linguistic and cultural affinity with Persians, the Iranian Kurds were the first Kurds in modern times to establish an independent state. But the Mahabad Republic, which was formed in the immediate aftermath of World War II and lasted for one year, came into existence through a fortuitous set of circumstances, including a very powerful ally, the Soviet Union, and a temporarily incapacitated foe, the young shah Reza Pahlavi of Iran. Its precipitous collapse was due not just to the withdrawal of that ally and the regrouping of Iranian forces, but also to internal Kurdish disagreements.

Thirty-three years later, in the wake of the shah's overthrow in 1979, the Kurds once again established a quasi-independent state. And again, the political entity was short-lived, brought down by a rebuilt Iranian army, internal Kurdish divisions and the military offensives of the Iran-Iraq War. The *peshmerga* were broken up, with resisters reduced to small armed bands. Today, Iranian Kurdistan is quiescent, especially in contrast to the Kurdish regions of Turkey and Iraq. The KDPI operates bases in Iraq and launches periodic, inconsequential raids against Iranian forces, but it fails to put forward a political program beyond self-serving tribalism. With the elimination of their urban leadership through assassination, Iranian Kurds lack both organizing potential and the broader vision of earlier Iranian Kurd nationalism. Nevertheless, Iranian Kurd leaders still insist that their goal is autonomy within a *federal* Iran, not independence.

Economic issues

As in Turkey, the economic relationship between Kurdistan and the heartland of Iran is an internal colonial one. Oil is the only significant resource in Kurdistan, and it is extracted by the state with a disproportionately small amount of the revenue being reinvested in the region. Iranian Kurdistan is desperately poor, with a per capita income significantly below that of the rest of the country. The shah's much-heralded "white revolution" and land reform of the 1960s were supposed to alleviate Kurdish poverty, but did not. Landlord resistance and corruption limited the scope of the reforms. And while the Khomeini government rose to power in part by rhetorically addressing the economic discontent of the Iranian poor, including the Kurds, who participated heavily in the revolution, it quickly moved to the right on economic issues and failed to undertake serious land reform.

Given this history, it is not surprising that the Kurdish rebellions of the 1940s and 1970s were led by socialist leaders appealing to the frustrations of the landless peasantry. Nevertheless, the destruction of Kurdish autonomy, the Khomeini regime's economic conservatism, the new tribal leadership of the KDPI and the widespread economic decline of an internationally isolated Iran have both crippled the Kurdish economy and dampened the prospects, at least for the moment, for land reform and general economic change.

PARTICIPANTS

Western-style political organizations generally do not exist in Kurdistan, though Turkey and Iran present partial exceptions to the rule. This fact of Kurdish political life is due in part to the governments of the three countries where most Kurds live, and in part to the nature of Kurdish political institutions. In Iraq, alternative political parties to the Baath have not been permitted in recent years. In Turkey and Iran, where limited forms of democracy exist, parties based on ethnic affiliation are banned, though in both countries parties that promote Kurdish issues are permitted if they are very circumspect about it. Thus Kurdish political organizations are the revolutionary guerrilla type, as is the case with the PKK in Turkey, or tribal confederations calling themselves political parties, like the PKK and KDP of Iraq, or a little of both, like the KDPI.

If there are no recognizable political parties in Kurdistan, neither are there recognizable democracies in Turkey, Iraq and Iran, though the departure from democratic norms follows a different path in all three. The Turkish government is heavily influenced by the military, especially in affairs relating to Kurdistan. Iraq is a totalitarian state, controlled by an omnipresent and virtually omnipotent Baath Party and government. And while democracy exists in Iran, legislative initiatives are restricted by Koranic principle and a theological judiciary. In none of the three states is there anything remotely resembling a free exchange of ideas, a respect for human rights or a fully functioning democratic process.

TURKEY

The Kurds

Democratic Opposition   There are two kinds of Kurdish political organizations in Turkey: those that operate within the framework of limited parliamentary democracy, and the PKK, which has chosen armed resistance to the state since 1984. Of course, only the banned PKK and nonmilitant but equally banned Socialist Party of Kurdistan openly call themselves Kurdish political organizations. All other parties that participate in Turkish elections are either mixed parties of Kurds and Turks, or Kurd-dominated parties that are not officially chartered as Kurdish parties. Any party that openly advocates Kurdish self-determination is in contravention of the Turkish constitution's provisions concerning threats to the "territorial integrity" of the nation. Moreover, the government and right-wing politicians frequently insinuate that legal pro-Kurdish parties support the PKK, a treasonous act under Turkish law and one of the reasons offered by the government for its periodic bans against them.

The boundaries between political legality and illegality are vague, and numerous parties and politicians have unwittingly stepped over the line in recent years. As a result, they have been banned and their leaders and members fined and imprisoned. In addition, a new wave of political violence by death squads against pro-Kurdish party facilities and organizers has been widely reported in the international press since the late 1980s. It is widely believed that these death squads are connected to Turkey's internal security forces.

Nevertheless, numerous political parties continue to vie for Kurdish votes in national and local elections among Kurds both in Kurdistan and in western Turkish cities. In general, election turnouts in Turkish Kurdistan are similar to those in the rest of the country, though this participation is questioned by the PKK, which says that frequent banning of pro-Kurdish parties, the mass relocation of Kurdish civilians by government forces, voter intimidation, the long-standing "emergency" situation and the 300,000-plus soldiers in the region make a mockery of the electoral process.

PKK   Whether the electoral process in Turkish Kurdistan is vigorous, as the government claims, or shackled into irrelevance, as the Kurdish opposition asserts, the dominant factor in Turkish Kurd politics remains the PKK. Founded in 1978, the PKK has been an illegal underground organization from the start, and was forced to establish much of its organizational infrastructure, including guerrilla training bases, in Syria and the Syrian-controlled Bekaa Valley of Lebanon.

In 1984, the PKK began its military campaign against the Turkish army and security forces. Unlike the equally militant Kurdish organizations in Iraq, the PKK is not affiliated with any tribal confederation or tribal leader, though it tries to cooperate with and win local chiefs over to its cause. When Kurdish men and women (approximately 10 percent of PKK guerrillas are women, a momentous departure from Kurdish tradition) join the PKK, they are breaking away from old affiliations and loyalties based on tradition. The PKK is both antitribal and, until the last few years, anti-Islamic and anticapitalist.

Today, the PKK is estimated to have approximately 20,000 armed guerrillas scattered about the southeastern provinces of Turkey, northern Syria, Lebanon and northern Iraq. Its early radical agenda alienated the PKK from much of the Kurdish peasantry through its antireligious rhetoric as well as its habit of assassinating the family members of Kurds it considered collaborators with the state. Government efforts to paint the PKK as a tool of Moscow during the Cold War also had an effect on the organization's support. The end of the Cold War and the PKK's efforts to tone down its rhetoric and turn away from its anticivilian tactics have gained the guerrilla movement wider support both in the Kurdish countryside and in Kurdish enclaves in western Turkish cities. But the biggest aid to the PKK's cause, say observers, has been the government's systematic and destructive counterinsurgency campaigns against the guerrillas and their suspected civilian sympathizers.

The Turks

The Government   Turkey is a republic, at least in name and, to a degree, in practice. Under the 1982 constitution, parliamentary representation is based proportionally on a party's nationwide vote, while elections for the president are separate and based on a nationwide popular vote. From 1983 to 1993, the country was ruled by the centrist Motherland Party (ANAP). Since the 1993 death of Turgut Ozal, president since 1987, President Suleyman Demirel and Prime Minister Tansu Çiller of the center-right Correct Way Party (DYP) have been in control of the government. In addition, Turkey is a member of NATO and an applicant to the European Community.

Though founded as a republic in the 1920s, Turkey's political history has been a rocky one. There have been three military coups since World War II. The Turkish polity has been sharply divided between right and left through much of its history. Clashes between the two and escalating political crises set the stage for the military takeovers of 1960, 1970 and 1980. In 1983, direct military rule gave way to civilian rule when the new parliament was elected and Ozal became Prime Minister, though coup leader General Kenan Evren was appointed to serve as the new president.

Evren's appointment highlights a fundamental problem with Turkish democracy; the inordinate political power wielded by the military. Most opposition politicians and outside observers concede that Turkish democracy is flawed. Routine legislation is in civilian hands, but crucial national questions, most especially the war in Kurdistan, are decided by military leaders. The current president, Suleyman Demirel, is an old man and largely a figurehead, while Prime Minister Tansu Çiller is politically weak. The press is partially censored, the judiciary is kept on a short leash and much of the Kurdish part of the country remains under "emergency rule," with justice dispensed largely by military tribunals.

Until the coup of 1980, the Turkish government's economic program was a statist one, with many heavy industries, most of the nation's infrastructure and the General Anatolia Project's massive network of dams and hydroelectric power stations under the control of government-owned corporations. Over the past decade, the country has embarked on a program of economic liberalization. Since the 1980 coup and the general international trend toward privatization, the Turkish government has sold off many of its enterprises.

On paper at least, the government maintains an extensive network of health, education and welfare institutions. But, in fact, these are usually underfunded and situated largely in urban areas. Its foreign debt burden, due in part to the war in Kurdistan and one of the largest in the developing world, has forced the government to cut back on many social services.

The Military   Increasingly since the 1980 coup, the Turkish military has appeared to back away from any overt role in the nation's politics. Following the establishment of the new parliament in 1983, the presidency reverted to civilian control in 1987, for the first time since the 1950s, with the election of Turgut Ozal. In that same year, martial law was lifted across the nation, though a slightly less constrictive "emergency rule" remains imposed on the southeastern provinces.

Despite this shift to the background, the military is still a major player on the Turkish political stage. While the vast majority of Turkish soldiers are conscripts serving two-year stints, the officer corps operates as a separate, self-contained and independent force. It often sees itself as "the guarantor of the Turkish nation," especially during the periodic political crises of the postwar era and most especially in the southeastern Kurdish provinces, where, say many Turkish and foreign journalists, it is "barely under civilian control." Turkey's growing importance to Western security in the wake of the Cold War (Turkey is now the number three recipient of US military aid) has only increased the power of the military in Turkish politics.[7]

Governmental efforts to ease restrictions on Kurdish cultural expression or open up the political process are vigorously opposed by the military, which usually gets its way. The one exception, President Ozal's partial lifting of the ban on spoken Kurdish in 1991, was followed by a military-supported antiterrorism bill that gave the army a free hand in its war against separatists and has led, according to the human rights organization Middle East

Watch, to a spate of human rights abuses by security forces. The military has also opposed Demirel's tentative peace feelers toward the non-PKK Kurdish opposition. In each case, Demirel, overthrown by the military twice before, has backed off.

The Non-Kurdish Opposition   While the military's role in establishing strict limits on Turkish politics should not be underestimated, within those confines, Turkey hosts vigorous and combative political debate. Parties from the far right to the far left participate, though the dominance of centrist parties over the past decade, as well as the fear of a military coup, has limited the kind of political street-fighting so common in Turkey in the 1960s and 1970s. Virtually all issues are debated and discussed in parliament, where members enjoy legal immunity from the antiterrorist laws (though the 1994 arrests of six members from the DEP party has undermined this protection), and in political campaigns. Nevertheless, there is a broad consensus behind the strict prohibition on dialogue with the PKK, as well as a strong commitment to economic liberalization.

Dozens of political parties competed for seats in the parliamentary elections of 1994. A small coalition of pro-Kurdish leftist parties took some 20 seats, though a minority of Kurds boycotted the election. In addition, a new political force, familiar to much of the Middle East but seemingly out of place in officially secular Turkey, has made itself felt. The Islamist Welfare Party took over 20 percent of the popular vote and won more than 30 seats, a fact that has stirred up Turkey's religious minorities.[8]

IRAQ

The Kurds

In May of 1992, the Kurds inside the safe haven went to the polls to elect a parliament for the first time in their history. The result was a virtual dead heat between the two major parties, the KDP and PKK. By the previously established rules of the contest, and arguably by democratic custom, there was supposed to be a runoff for the leadership position. This did not happen. The parliament's 105 seats were divided neatly: 50 to the KDP, 50 to the PUK, and five seats given to representatives of Kurdistan's Christian minority.

By late 1992, the alliance had frayed. Fears of violence canceled the scheduled October runoff between KDP and PUK leaders Mahmoud Barzani and Jalal Talabani. Two years after the initial election, violence did indeed break out in the safe haven between the KDP and the PUK and, though temporarily muffled by a cease-fire in force since May of 1995, may break out again at any moment.

The KDP and the PUK   Both of the major Kurdish parties are current manifestations of much older political alliances in Iraqi Kurdistan. The KDP, located in the northwestern part of the safe haven along the Turkish and Syrian borders, is led by a member of Iraqi Kurdistan's most illustrious hereditary clan, the Barzanis. The PUK, situated along the eastern reaches of Iraqi Kurdistan, adjacent to Iran and centered around the city of Sulimaniye, is led by another important clan leader, Jalal Talabani. Like the Barzanis, the Talabanis claim an ancient heritage based on the founding leadership of an important *shaikh*. Nevertheless, in the popular Kurdish imagination, no other name conjures up the glory of Barzani. Instead, the Talabani tribal confederation represents a coalition of forces in opposition to the Barzanis, since, despite the latter's prestige, Kurds fear the dominance of any single tribe.

Despite the intense electoral and military competition between the two parties, these organizations and their leaders bear a resemblance to each other in several ways. First, both are structured traditionally with a strict hierarchy of status and power reflecting the degree of kinship to the first family of the confederation. Second, both maintain their own *peshmerga* forces who enforce party decisions, exact party dues and maintain order in their respective spheres of influence. And finally, both Talabani and Barzani rely on their role as charismatic leaders, charisma being defined here in the anthropological sense. That is to say, both rely on their genealogy and traditional tribal role to command their followers through well-chosen words and deeds.

But there are differences as well, though these can often be difficult to define and mean one thing when interpreted by Westerners and another when understood by Kurds. The international press often describes Talabani's PUK as the liberal party and Barzani's KDP as conservative. This distinction is based mainly on the fact that Talabani is the more westernized of the two leaders in his education (he is a lawyer) and political style, while Barzani is seen as the leader possessing the old-fashioned integrity of the tribal leader. Moreover, Talabani is widely considered to have a more urban following, and in Kurdish politics and history, "urban" and "progressive" are often linked. Indeed, the communiqués that emerge from the two organizations reflect an ideological difference, with the PUK supporting what might be described as a more socialist-oriented development.

Still, too much should not be made of these ideological differences. In the current impoverished and war-torn conditions of Iraqi Kurdistan, neither party is in any real position to implement its programs and thus is not required to back up its rhetoric with substance. Significantly, on the most crucial issues facing Iraqi Kurdistan—its future sovereignty and relations with Baghdad—Talabani has proven himself more willing to compromise than Barzani. In short, the PUK is more radical in social rhetoric, while the PUK is more hard-line on the nationalist issue.

Other Kurdish Parties   A number of other parties, including the Kurdistan branch of the Iraqi Communist Party, a peasant-based populist party, an Islamist party and a party of Assyrian Christians also participated in the

1992 Kurdish parliamentary elections. None of them, however, attained the seven-percent threshold required for representation in the parliament. The Islamist Party came closest with five percent of the vote.

According to election rules established by a temporary coalition of Kurdish political parties, the Iraqi Kurd Front (IKF), the Christian minority voted on different ballots, with over 50 percent going to the Assyrian Democratic Movement. Given that only 12,000 Christians voted, their representation breaks down to one seat for every 2,500 votes, while Muslims have one representative for every 70,000. This discrepancy in representation may be due to the efforts of Kurdish leaders to placate their Western backers, who, they feel, are sensitive to the political rights of minorities, especially when they are Christian.

Since the parliament was soon rendered irrelevant by the peremptory decision-making of the two main tribal confederations and the ensuing civil war, the potential power wielded by the Christian delegates and their tiebreaking votes quickly evaporated. Instead, the only minor party to make its voice and power felt in the safe haven has been the Islamists. Situated in Talabani territory along the Iranian border, and influenced and supported by the regime in Tehran, the Islamists have challenged PUK control over territory and the right to collect duties on goods imported from the east.

The Baath government

Since a 1968 coup, Iraq has been ruled as a one-party state by the Baath Party. At first under the authority of a small coterie of military and civilian officials, the Baath Party and the Baath regime soon came under the control of a single leader, Saddam Hussein. The Baath, or Resurrection Party, considers itself the vanguard party of a uniquely Arab and Iraqi revolution. There is some truth to this. Having nationalized the Iraqi oil industry in 1971, the Baath has used hydrocarbon revenues to construct a modern infrastructure for the nation. In addition, the Baath instituted sweeping reforms in social legislation, particularly concerning the status of women, whom it partially liberated from Islamic restrictions.

The regime also took a revolutionary path in its foreign policy. Distancing itself from the United States and from Britain, its former ruler, Baghdad formed a close alliance with the Soviet Union in 1972. And despite its pro-Arabist rhetoric, Baath has gradually pulled Iraq away from earlier pan-Arabist leanings. Toward the Kurds, at war with Baghdad since 1961, the Baath took a radical approach as well. After initially seeking a military victory in a war it had inherited from previous regimes, the Baath government proposed a sweeping change in the political, cultural and economic relationship between Baghdad and the Kurds. The proposal, known as the March 11, 1970, accords, failed to resolve the fighting. The war between the Kurds and the government continued until 1975 and led to a resounding victory for the latter. After the post–Gulf War establishment of the safe haven, the Baath resurrected this initiative, but this effort too has failed to resolve differences with the Kurds.

As is the case with many one-party regimes, however, the Baath's efforts to revolutionize Iraqi society alienated many powerful interests whose representatives it ruthlessly purged from positions of authority in both the civilian and military sectors. The regime gradually established a totalitarian state in which dissent has been forbidden and a vast network of informers and security personnel keeps the populace in line. Censorship and torture have been routine in a state that one dissident Iraqi writer has labeled the "republic of fear."9

The current regime in Baghdad sees a total identity of interests among the leader, the party, the regime, the people and the state. A threat to any one of these is considered a threat to all. Thus Kurdish rebels, with their insistence on autonomy and their willingness to form alliances with internal enemies of the regime and external enemies of the state, most especially Islamist Iran, are seen as enemies of the Iraqi people, to be dealt with ruthlessly.

Non-Kurdish opposition

While the Kurds are the most determined, best armed and most successful of antigovernment groups, they are not alone in their opposition to the Baath regime. During the Iran-Iraq War, a number of groups opposing Saddam Hussein formed a front under the aegis of Libya and Syria. It included left-wing parties, most prominently the Communists, Arab nationalists, various ethnic parties and Shiites. With their armies of *peshmerga* and de facto control of much of northern Iraq, the Kurds dominated the front and, say their critics, threw their weight around in such a way as to cause the breakup of the alliance shortly after it was formed in 1983.

Since that collapse, only one group besides the Kurds has made its presence felt in Iraqi politics: the Shiites. While the leftist parties and their trade union base were destroyed by Baathist purges in the 1970s and 1980s, the Shiites continue to comprise some 40 percent of the Iraqi population (and a majority outside the Kurdish safe haven). Ensconced in their marshy redoubts on the Persian Gulf, the Shiite rebels were decimated by the Iraqi military in the wake of their rebellion following the end of the Gulf War. While the UN coalition has established a no-fly zone below the 32nd parallel to protect them from the Iraqi air force, it has not tried to keep ground troops out. Nevertheless, the Shiites maintain a sporadic armed resistance to the Baath regime.

Other groups troublesome to the Iraqi regime made themselves felt in the mid–1990s. Like the Kurds, many Iraqi Arabs maintain an allegiance to tribe and clan, though not nearly as intense. The Baath regime has tried to cope with these allegiances by sharing power and/or by pitting one clan against the other. This policy has kept the opposition from coalescing, but has brought grievances with and challenges to the state. In June 1995, military officers from the al-Dumaili clan mounted a small-scale mutiny from their barracks near Baghdad. The uprising was soon quelled by loyalist forces and the idea that it represented a serious threat to the state was dismissed by Baghdad as "wishful Western thinking."[10] Most outside observers consider Saddam Hussein's grip on power to be firm and not likely to be seriously challenged in the near future.

IRAN

The Kurds

The KDPI today is a shadow of its former self. Having once led the first independent republic in modern Kurdish history, the KDPI now operates from its exile in the safe haven and is largely controlled by Iraqi Kurd forces. The KDPI led a brief rebellion against the Shah's government in the late 1960s and participated actively in his overthrow ten years later. But the rebellion that engulfed Iranian Kurdistan in the first year of the Islamic revolution was largely a spontaneous affair, led by peasants, working-class Kurds returned from Iranian cities, and students influenced more by Maoist revolutionary thought than the KDPI's statist and democratic-socialist approach to political change. The KDPI also helped organize the Kurdish boycott of the referendum on the Islamic state in December, 1979. In 1980, however, the KDPI, allied with left-wing Muslim forces, or *mujahideen*, and the pro-Soviet Tudeh Party, felt the full brunt of the Islamist purge of left-wing revolutionary forces during the Islamist consolidation of power in the early 1980s.

The KDPI of the 1980s was different from Kurdish organizations in both Turkey and Iraq. Its secularism and nontribal organization were similar to the PKK of Turkey, but it was not a revolutionary organization of that kind. Its struggle has been largely nationalist, to create a democratic Kurdish homeland in Iran rather than the kind of revolutionary regime envisioned by the PKK. It has neither recruited nor maintained a separate guerrilla force but, rather, has relied upon local *peshmerga* and their tribal leaders. Thus, while it has tried to create a political entity that transcends tribal divisions, it has not been antitribal in the manner of the PKK. And as noted above, the KDPI, in contrast to Iraqi Kurd organizations, was largely independent of foreign entanglements until recently. While it received help from Baghdad during the Iran-Iraq War, the cooperation was not on the same scale as that of Tehran and the Iraqi Kurds, who actually launched joint offensives against Saddam Hussein in the final years of the war. Since 1992, however, the KDPI has come under the influence of Iraqi Kurds, especially the PUK.

The government

Since the February 1979 overthrow of Shah Mohammed Reza Pahlavi, Iran has been ruled by an Islamist government. Led by the charismatic Shiite religious leader Ayatollah Ruhollah Khomeini until his death in 1989, the Islamic government came to power as the dominant member of a coalition of anti-Shah forces which included, among others, left-wing political parties and various ethnic minorities. Legitimizing its role in a 1979 referendum on the establishment of an Islamist state, the religious wing of the revolutionary coalition quickly turned on its leftist, secular and ethnic minority allies, beginning with a war against the Kurds in the summer of 1979. Purges against left-wing parties, most prominently the Tudeh Party, followed, leaving the Islamists in sole possession of power in both the *Majlis*, or parliament, and the executive. Secular supporters of the Islamists, such as Prime Minister Abolhassan Bani-Sadr, were soon forced out by more radical religious elements.

The new Tehran government immediately embarked upon a radical political and social makeover of the Iranian state. Social legislation was enacted to bring the country into line with Islamic principles. The educational system was reformed, Western cultural products and media were banned or forced underground, and the symbols of Islamic patriarchy were placed in their stead. Political reforms quickly followed. The military and security forces were purged of suspected supporters of the shah or the democratic opposition and the judiciary was placed in the hands of Islamic judges, or *qadis*. And, of course, Iran's foreign policy was radically realigned. From a client state of the United States and the Western alliance under the shah, the Islamist government allied itself with radical leftist regimes, not only in the Middle East but throughout the world. Its anti-Western bias, however, was equaled by its hostility to the Soviet Bloc.

Unlike the Baath revolution, the Islamist revolution in Iran was a popular one. Iran did not experience a coup by a small coterie of military and civilian insurrectionaries. Instead, hundreds of thousands of people protested (and many died at the hands of the government) over several years, demonstrating not only their hostility to the shah but their support for the ayatollah. This popular support for the new regime permitted it to engage in a demonstration of democracy, though with a strong bias towards Islamist candidates and policies.

While there were many diverse elements in this mass demonstration of popular political sentiment, the dominant group, in influence if not in numbers, was the petit bourgeois retailers and factory owners, or *bazaaris*, who were furious with the shah's favoritism toward the rich and the comprador class affiliated with foreign capital. They allied themselves with religious leaders upset with the shah's program of secularism and westernization, and together took power. Not surprisingly, the economic reforms of the revolution have not matched the radicalism of the political and cultural agenda. The Islamist government has not instituted land reform, as it had hinted it would during the revolution.

The war with Iraq, which lasted from 1980 to 1988, contributed to this limit on reforms and to the increasing power placed in the hands of a small group of parliamentarians and advisors close to the ayatollah. Under the revised constitution of 1989, presidential powers were expanded and the office of prime minister eliminated. In addition, Iran suffered immensely from the war, with hundreds of thousands of casualties and billions of dollars in property damage and lost oil revenue. In the aftermath of the war, and the death of the ayatollah less than a year later, a group of more pragmatic parliamentarians, centered around then-Speaker of Parliament Akbar Hashemi Rafsanjani, have attempted to steer Iran back from the international political isolation, extreme cultural regimentation and economic stagnation of the Khomeini years. Neutral in the Gulf War, but still facing US-imposed sanctions, Tehran has recently begun making overtures toward the even more isolated regime in Baghdad.

Non-Kurdish opposition

The Kurds are not the only minority in Iran, nor are they even the largest. That distinction goes to a Turkic-speaking people known as the Azerbaijanis or Azeris, who live on the foothills and plains to the east of Kurdistan. Kurdish resistance to the Islamic regime, however, has been far more open, sustained and intense. This is due in part to the fact that while Kurds are closer to the Persians ethnically and linguistically than the Azerbaijanis, they are Sunni while the latter are mostly Shiite like the Persian majority.

Despite the post-Soviet formation of an independent Azerbaijan Republic adjacent to Iran, the Iranian Azerbaijanis have been relatively quiescent in recent years. Meanwhile, ideologically based opposition groups, particularly on the left, were effectively crushed during the early years of the revolution. A more recent opposition group of liberal secular nationalists, the Society for the Defense of Freedom, has been repressed in recent years for making accusations of governmental corruption.

OUTSIDE FORCES

Throughout their modern history, the Kurds have faced one incontrovertible fact of realpolitik: they have no predictable or permanent allies in the region. Because of this fact, they have often sought alliances with international powers. Over the years, the Kurds have looked for support from Great Britain, Nazi Germany, the Soviet Union, the United States and most recently the European Community and the United Nations Gulf War coalition (referred to from here on as the Coalition for brevity's sake). While Kurdish leaders and their followers have sought out regional and international allies for pragmatic reasons, these alliances have more often than not proved disastrous for the Kurds in the long run. Frequently, these alliances have come undone when the friendly power decided it was in its interest to drop the Kurds in favor of the regime they were opposing. Moreover, by seeking outside alliances, the Kurds have often exposed themselves to charges of being the agents of foreign powers, a serious charge in any part of the world but especially so in the heightened nationalist atmosphere of the post–World War II postcolonial Middle East.

Middle East Alliances

The recent history of alliances between the various nation-states of the Middle East and the Kurds presents a bewildering complexity. This history can perhaps best be understood by applying the rule that "the enemy of my enemy is my friend." Turkey has sought alliances with the Iraqi Kurds to fight its own PKK guerrillas. In addition, Turkey has been supporting Iranian Kurdish rebels since the Islamist revolution of 1979. Meanwhile, Baghdad has been in no position to support the PKK, given its preoccupation with fighting Iran in the 1980s and its expulsion from northern Iraq in the 1990s, although it offered help to Iranian Kurds in their war with Tehran during the Iran-Iraq War and did support Turkish Kurd rebels during their great uprisings in the 1920s and 1930s.

For its part, Iran has heavily backed Iraqi Kurds since the early 1960s. This support reached its zenith under the shah in the early 1970s and under Khomeini during the final years of the Iran-Iraq War. In addition, Islamist Iran has been accused by Turkey of supporting the PKK, a charge denied by Tehran. Despite recent talks between Turkey and Syria, Damascus continues to permit the PKK to operate bases from within its territory, though the extensive PKK bases in the Syrian-controlled Bekaa Valley of Lebanon appear to have been scaled back in recent years.

Farther afield, other Middle Eastern nations, including Israel, Libya and Saudi Arabia, have played the Kurdish card. Israel has supported both Iranian and Iraqi Kurd rebels with arms and intelligence, while it has politically backed Ankara, its most trusted ally in the Middle East, against the PKK. Libya's ties with Islamist Iran and its pre–Gulf War hostility to the Baath of Iraq explain why it hosted a conference designed to bring together Kurdish opponents of Saddam Hussein during the Iran-Iraq War. And the Saudis have funded a network of Islamic boarding schools in Turkish Kurdistan that allows Ankara to remove young Kurds from possible PKK influence.

Alliances Outside the Middle East

Kurdistan may not be the geographical heartland of the Middle East, but it does lie adjacent to it. The Kurdish highlands border on, as well as contain, parts of the fertile crescent, among the richest agricultural lands in the Middle East. Kurdistan's own oil fields, and its proximity to some of the richest reserves in the world, has added to Kurdistan's historical strategic value. No wonder then that virtually every major power of the twentieth century has become involved in Kurdish politics.

The first, of course, were the British. During the peace conferences following World War I, Britain gained for itself a mandate over Iraq, including Iraqi Kurdistan. In the 1920s, Britain formed alliances with Iraqi Kurds and funded Kurdish rebels in Turkey to keep Ankara off-balance and out of the oil-rich region. A decade later, with the formation of an independent pro-British regime in Baghdad, the British abandoned their Kurdish allies, giving exclusive control of the new state to the Arab majority.

In the wake of World War II, new international players in the Middle East became involved. Iran, for instance, was divided into Soviet and British spheres of influence in order to deny Nazi Germany any influence with the Kurds or the Persians. To secure its southern flank during the war and establish friendly pro-Soviet regimes in the Middle East, Moscow supported independence for both Azerbaijani and Kurdish peoples in Iran. But early Cold War pressure from the United States forced the Soviets to pull back.

From the 1950s on, the United States was the most important Western power in the Middle East and in Kurdistan. Until the fall of the shah, the US based its Middle East strategy on establishing Iran as the bulwark of Western interests in the Persian Gulf. In turn, Iran's policy was guided by suspicion of and hostility toward the Baath regime in Baghdad. To aid the shah, the United States helped fund his efforts in support of Iraqi Kurd rebels. When Iran achieved its desired territorial concessions from Iraq in the Algiers Accord of 1975, the shah and his US backers abandoned the Kurds.

A similar scenario played itself out in the early 1990s as well. In the aftermath of the Gulf War, the US and the Coalition urged Iraqi Kurds to rebel against Saddam Hussein. But when Baghdad turned its forces on the Kurds in March of 1991, the Coalition failed to come to the Kurds' aid, forcing them to seek refuge in Turkey and Iran. This time, however, international media attention was focused on the Kurds and influenced the decision to establish the safe haven.

Today, the US continues to lend support to its new strategic priority in the region, Turkey. Ankara's recent invasions of northern Iraq in pursuit of the PKK have been supported by the Bush and Clinton administrations. However, cracks appear to be forming in the Coalition. Under popular pressure from both their own citizens and Kurdish émigrés, several states of the European Union have openly criticized Turkish human rights violations in its war with the PKK. Germany, Britain and especially France have made it clear that the EU membership Ankara's leaders covet is predicated on the improvement of the human rights situation in southeastern Turkey. In addition, while the US insists on maintaining UN sanctions against Iraq, France, Russia and other powers appear to want them lifted.

TACTICS OF WAR

TURKEY

The Kurds

The PKK is a tightly organized and highly disciplined guerrilla organization. Its bases, both in Turkey and abroad, serve both as military training camps and political education centers. The Turkish government alleges that the PKK forcibly conscripts many of its fighters, a charge denied by PKK leaders who claim, to the contrary, that they are forced, for lack of arms and other resources, to turn away many recruits. In either case, most of the guerrillas are young men and women from the Kurdish countryside, though an increasing number come from Kurdish towns and Kurdish ghettoes in western Turkish cities.

Organized into small bands, the PKK inside Turkey live off the land. They receive food, clothing and shelter from villagers, though the government claims this is done at gunpoint. Equally important, the PKK relies on Kurdish villagers for information about the movements of Turkish security forces. Whether supplying information or food, the villagers take great risks aiding the PKK. In recent years, the PKK says it has tried to minimize its contact with Kurdish civilians by storing arms and other supplies in caves rather than in villages. As for the source of these arms, Turkey claims they are provided by foreign powers (the Soviet Bloc in the 1980s; radical Middle Eastern regimes today). The PKK offers a different explanation. Most of its arms are captured from the Turks or provided by Kurdish deserters from the military, it says, while much of the PKK's funds are collected from the large Kurdish communities in Europe.

Relations between the PKK and the civilian population of Kurdistan have undergone a dramatic change since the 1980s, or so the organization claims. During the early years of fighting, PKK guerrillas were known to target not just Kurdish government informants, security personnel and politicians, but their families as well. According to PKK spokespersons, this practice has been discontinued since 1990 because, they say, many Kurdish civilians are forced into performing security duties for the government.

For obvious reasons, the PKK eschews direct battlefield engagements with the Turkish army. Vastly outnumbered and outgunned, the Kurdish guerrillas prefer ambushes and raids, with an emphasis on isolated outposts and military convoys. When the government mounts its periodic large-scale offensives, the guerrillas usually retreat to mountain hideaways, fade into the general population, or head across the Iraqi and Syrian borders (or back into Turkey when the army invades northern Iraq). Finally, while Ankara claims the PKK engages in terrorist actions, and the PKK itself has threatened to do so, bombings and other terrorist actions both in western Turkey and Europe have been few and far between.

The government

In recent years, the Turkish military has emphasized denying the PKK civilian cover. To this end, the Turkish government has forcibly relocated the residents of some 3,000 or more Kurdish villages. Some have been settled in towns, others have been placed in camps and specially built villages, surrounded by barbed wire and isolated from the surrounding populace. The government has also uprooted crops and destroyed forests in the hopes of denying the Kurds food and shelter. Free-fire zones have been established in areas cleared of their civilian populations.

Denying the PKK access to the civilian population represents one half of the government's strategy. The other is a massive application of military firepower. Between 300,000 and 400,000 soldiers, not including national security forces and local police, patrol the southeastern provinces of Turkey. In addition, the Turks have established a system of village guards whereby civilians armed by the government patrol their immediate surroundings. Ankara insists the patrols are organized on a strictly voluntary basis, the lure of service being a fixed income from the government. The PKK claims the guards are recruited forcibly.

Since 1994, the Turks have upped the ante by attacking in winter, when the Kurds normally regroup, as well as launching the largest invasion of foreign territory in the republic's history. The military has changed its tactics in recent years as well. Large infantry columns and tanks have given way to rapid deployment forces convoyed by helicopter into PKK strongholds.

IRAQ

The Kurds

Aside from the 1991 Gulf War, northern Iraq has witnessed no fewer than four wars in the past decade and a half: the Iranian war against Baghdad (1980–1988); a spontaneous Kurdish uprising against Baghdad (1991); a Turkish-supported struggle against the PKK (1991–1995); and an internal civil war between Kurdish factions (1994–1995). Each war has been marked by different tactics.

During the Iran-Iraq War, Kurdish forces and the Iranian military launched large-scale invasions designed to penetrate and hold Iraqi territory. Supported by Tehran's airpower and artillery, Kurdish and Iranian forces invaded the northeastern provinces of Iraq, capturing cities as well as countryside. This was a tactic similar to the one employed during the last years of the 1961–1975 war between Baghdad and the Kurds, when the Shah provided heavy weapons support. In both cases, the strategy proved disastrous, for two reasons: first, it played to the government's conventional military superiority; and second, it depended upon continued support from Iran, which came to an abrupt halt when Tehran decided it was in its interest to negotiate with Baghdad.

The post–Gulf War uprising against Baghdad was as spectacular as it was brief. Across the length of Iraqi Kurdistan, *peshmerga* and Kurdish soldiers deserting the Iraqi military raided Iraqi military bases, took control of armories, occupied government buildings, and chased loyal Iraqi military units out of the territory. Within several days, Iraqi Kurdish forces held a larger area of Iraq, including areas where Kurds were not in a majority, than they had ever held in the past. Their position, however, proved vulnerable when the promised protection of the Coalition did not materialize.

During 1992 and 1993, the Kurds participated in anti-PKK military actions with the Turkish military. This Iraqi Kurd–Turkish cooperation came to an end when growing tensions between the KDP and PUK turned Kurdish attention toward internal struggles. The civil war between the two Iraqi Kurd factions witnessed a spate of terrorist bombings and attacks against Kurdish civilians, as well as direct military engagements between *peshmerga* battalions.

The actual fighting, however, was preceded by a growing factionalism within the provisional government. Under the agreements arranged after the first round of elections, governmental positions, ministries and resources were divided between the two factions. Increasingly, members of one party or another who held supervisory or administrative positions began to purge their staffs of members of the opposing faction. As tensions increased, fighting broke out. The aim was to capture territory belonging to the opposing party in order to establish facts on the ground, that is to say, control over potential voters and financial resources in order to maintain dominance within the Kurdish political entity.

The government

War between Baghdad and the Kurds has been almost continuous for over three decades, though there have been periods of relative quiet when armed engagements have been rare, as they are in the current safe haven period. Nevertheless, when the government has launched full-scale offensives against the Kurds, it has been ruthless in its tactics. In the wake of both the 1961–1975 War and the Iran-Iraq War, the government attempted systematically to depopulate large areas of Kurdistan, relocating Kurds to Arab cities and jerry-built settlements surrounded by barbed wire and armed guards. In the wake of the Iran-Iraq War, Baghdad launched its *anfal* ("spoils of war") campaign against Iraqi Kurds. This involved not only the displacement of tens of thousands of Kurdish civilians, but a systematic effort to render their homelands unlivable.

The *anfal* campaign was intended to break the back of Kurdish armed resistance. To do this, the military divided Kurdistan into sectors and then proceeded to drive the *peshmerga* out of each one. Villages were occupied and huge pincer movements were deployed to drive the *peshmerga* into shrinking enclaves where the army could engage them in direct firefights and bombardments, including chemical attacks.

The use of chemical weapons to turn back Kurdish offensives in northeastern Iraq, say Kurdish sources and Human Rights Watch, began during the last years of the Iran-Iraq War. This tactic was ignored by much of the world until the chemical attack on the Kurdish city of Halabja in the spring of 1988. During the 1991 uprising, Baghdad again threatened the Kurds with chemical weapons, but resisted using them, no doubt fearing Coalition reprisal.

Conflict between Baghdad and the Kurds of the safe haven has been sporadic since 1991. The Kurds have charged Baghdad with using long-range artillery, as well as making incremental incursions along the border between Iraq and the safe haven. In addition, the Kurds charge Baghdad with planting bombs in Kurdish cities and assassinating journalists and international aid workers. Baghdad denies these charges, claiming they are the result of conflicts between the KDP and the PUK. Baghdad, however, has clearly attempted nonviolent reprisals against the Kurds, including propaganda offensives and attempts at economic strangulation.

IRAN

The Kurds

Iranian Kurds have not engaged in the same kind of long-term armed resistance as their counterparts in Turkey and Iraq. Uprisings have tended to be brief and, with the exceptions of the Mahabad Republic in the 1940s and the post-Revolution struggle in 1979 and 1980, not particularly threatening to the government's control over Kurdistan. There are several explanations, both ideological and tactical, for this difference. First, Iranian Kurds do not have the same tradition of armed struggle as their Iraqi counterparts, nor do they hold the same intense grudges against the central regime. Second, Iranian Kurds have been divided in their allegiances. The political leaders of Iran's Kurdish rebellions have usually been urban and left-leaning, while the conservative *aghas*, or tribal chiefs, of the countryside have provided the military leadership. The agenda of the urban leaders has been seen as a challenge to the traditional authority, status and economic standing of the rural leaders, while the *aghas'* defense of the political and economic status quo has been dismissed as reactionary by the KDPI's urban cadres.

This rift between rural and urban leaders helped doom the Mahabad Republic and a short-lived uprising in the late 1960s. In the spring of 1979, however, Iranian Kurds rose up in a revolt similar to those of Iraqi Kurds. Thousands of *peshmerga*, students and workers returning from the revolutionary streets of Tehran and deserting government soldiers began seizing Iranian military posts and supplies. When the Iranian military returned in the summer, the *peshmerga* fought them both in direct engagements at military bases they had seized and guerrilla-style in the mountains. While Tehran was able to establish its control over cities and bases, it had not been able to pacify the countryside by the time Saddam Hussein launched his invasion in September 1980. Support from Baghdad, which helped the Iranian Kurds maintain their guerrilla units during the course of the Iran-Iraq War, was never on the scale of that provided by Tehran to Iraqi Kurds. This was not for lack of interest on Baghdad's part, but because Iran had launched effective offensives against Kurdistan early in the war. This forced the Iranian *peshmerga* into small groups and defensive positions high in the mountains, rendering the delivery of weapons and other supplies far more difficult.

In recent years, the Iranian KDPI and its *peshmerga* have turned to Iraqi Kurds for both logistical support and a territorial base from which to launch raids against Iran. While these raids have sparked retaliation by the Iranian air force, they are little more than a nuisance for Tehran. For the most part, the Iranian Kurds engage in small-scale hit-and-run tactics against border outposts.

The government

The Iranian government's response to Kurdish uprisings has usually been dictated by forces beyond its control. Soviet support for the Mahabad Republic kept the army at bay for over a year in 1945 and 1946. When the Soviets departed, the Iranian military met with little resistance when it moved in to reconquer the territory.

In the post-Revolutionary uprising of 1979, the military was at first hampered by serious internal divisions. Many of the officers were carryovers from the shah's military, and divided in their allegiance to the new regime. Only when Khomeini took personal charge of the effort, and launched battalions of *pasdaran*, or Revolutionary Guards, against the Kurds did the government make progress. The *pasdaran* were sent in to disable the Kurdish *peshmerga* permanently, and practiced wholesale executions of Kurdish prisoners.

Since the establishment of the safe haven, the Iranian military has employed its air force against KDPI bases in northern Iraq. This has been only marginally effective, failing to stop the KDPI raids on Iran and stirring up storms of protest by the Iraqi Kurds, the Iranian Kurds, and the international community. In the past several years, the Iranians have been negotiating with Turkey to try to stop what Tehran alleges is an indirect arms pipeline from Ankara to the KDPI, via the Iraqi Kurds.

NEGOTIATIONS

TURKEY

There have never been direct negotiations between the PKK and the Turkish government and, given the current state of war between the two, there are unlikely to be any in the near future. Both sides share the blame for the failure to resolve the conflict. Not surprisingly, each side holds the other responsible. Of the two, however, the government's lack of forthrightness is more egregious, for several reasons.

Until the presidential administration of Turgut Ozal in the late 1980s and early 1990s, the government's official Kurdish position was that the Kurds simply did not exist as a distinct ethnic and linguistic population within the state. Ozal, Turkey's most perceptive and strategically minded civilian leader in recent years, opened the door to possible negotiations with Kurdish representatives, but only slightly. He continued to give the Turkish security forces a *carte blanche* for extralegal actions and military offensives in the Kurdish provinces, and he continued to maintain his predecessors' opinion of the PKK as a Marxist-Leninist organization involved in terrorism and international drug-running.

The government has also brushed aside PKK offers of a truce. While the government's responsibility for the lack of negotiations is on public record, the PKK's responsibility can be understood as implicit in its demands. While PKK leader Ocalan has made recent pronouncements denying his organization's ambition to establish an independent Kurdish state, the PKK's own literature demanding Kurdish freedom and sovereignty belie his pronouncements. Moreover, public statements by the PKK as late as 1992 speak of establishing an autonomous zone within Turkish Kurdistan where the PKK would organize a provisional government. Clearly any such action in this direction would imply an organizational agenda for the establishment of an independent Kurdistan. The government of Turkey says it will never agree to a cease-fire with an organization intent on establishing an independent or semi-independent state within its borders.

IRAQ

Negotiations between Kurdish rebels and the Baath government have a long and tortured history. In 1970, Baghdad offered a wide-ranging proposal guaranteeing Kurdish cultural autonomy, Kurdish administrators, additional investment funds and other concessions. The plan failed to achieve peace and each side, of course, blamed the other. But in fact it was sunk by the atmosphere of mutual suspicion and recrimination that had plagued relations between the government and the Kurds since the beginning of their war in 1961. After the Kurds' 1975 defeat by the government, Baghdad unilaterally instituted a partial version of the 1970 protocols, but they were not effectively implemented. In addition, because control of Iraqi Kurdistan is divided between two mutually hostile parties, the Baath government has frequently attempted to make peace with one side, and even induce it to cooperate with the government, while it goes after the other side.

Yet another obstacle to negotiations and peace has been the intransigence, or at least the shortsightedness, of the Iraqi Kurd leaders. Historically tribal leaders practiced a wily form of negotiation with the central regimes. When the government was in a position of strength, the Kurds gave in, offering their allegiance and laying down their arms. But when they sensed governmental weakness, they attacked and kept attacking as long as the government seemed unable to respond. If war is statecraft by other means, then rebellion has been a form of Kurdish statecraft. Being necessarily weaker than their governmental opponents, Kurdish leaders have seen negotiation as a tactical maneuver not unlike war itself. When the enemy or negotiating partner has shown signs of weakness, the Kurds have expanded their demands. This has frequently produced a backlash within the government and military by those who see the current negotiators as ceding too much to the Kurds. Thus Kurdish intransigence in negotiations has often led to governmental frustration and renewed warfare.

Iran

In terms of hostility and intransigence, negotiations between Iranian Kurds and the Islamist government have fallen somewhere between those in Turkey and those in Iraq. Tehran has not shown the same uncompromising attitude as Ankara, nor has the KDPI, at least until recent years, thrown up the same obstacles as have the Iraqi Kurds. Despite this somewhat less hostile atmosphere, relations between the Kurds and the Iranian government remain tense.

Continuing guerrilla warfare and escalating tensions with Iraq forced the government to make major concessions to the Kurds in the first year of the revolution. The Kurds rejected these and made a proposal of their own, which the government rejected in turn, saying it would not offer any further concessions. As a showdown between the Kurds and the government loomed, Saddam Hussein invaded Iran. The confrontation between the Kurds and Tehran was temporarily postponed and when it finally came, it arrived as a massive Iranian military offensive designed to prevent Iranian Kurdistan from becoming an invasion route for Baghdad.

In the aftermath of the Iran-Iraq War, the KDPI sought negotiations, but the Khomeini government was in no mood to make any concessions. Having negotiated a draw with Baghdad after years of declaring that the war would not end until Saddam Hussein was driven from power, Khomeini decided to preempt any talks with the KDPI by having security agents, posing as negotiators, assassinate KDPI leader A. R. Ghassemlou in 1989. While the assassination only heightened Kurdish suspicions, Ghassemlou's successor, Sadeq Sharafkandi, remained open to negotiations with the post-Khomeini government of Akbar Hashemi Rafsanjani, which itself showed a greater willingness to settle the hostilities peacefully. These efforts were scuttled after Sharafkandi's assassination in 1992.[11] The current head of the KDPI, Mustafa Hejri, has not pursued any serious negotiations with Tehran despite the government's repeated offers to talk. Hejri cites past governmental duplicity as the main obstacle.

NOTES

[1] There are small Kurdish populations in Syria, Armenia and Azerbaijan, as well as a substantial number of emigre Kurds in Western Europe, particularly Germany. This study, however, focuses on the three states with the vast majority of Kurdish citizens.

[2] It is illegal in Turkey to refer to the region as Kurdistan and the people living there as Kurds.

[3] Originally the KDP, the organization's name was usurped by Iraqi Kurds in the 1960s. In more recent years, the Iranian Kurd organization has been unofficially referred to as the KDPI. Though this name is not entirely accurate, and is anachronistic for its early years of existence, the name KDPI will be used throughout this text to avoid unnecessary confusion.

[4] "Iraqi Kurdistan's Misbegotten Mission,"in *Kurdish Life*, No. 8 (Fall, 1993), p. 6.

[5] Farouk-Sluglett, Marion and Peter Sluglett, *Iraq since 1958: From Revolution to Dictatorship* (London: KPI, 1987), p. 187.

[6] The word "Persian" is used here to designate an ethnic group. "Iranian" is employed as a term for a citizen of Iran, which includes Persians, Kurds and several other significant ethnic minorities.

[7] Marcus, Aliza, "Turkey's Kurds after the Gulf War: A Report from the Southeast," Chaliand, Gerard, ed., *A People Without a Country: The Kurds and Kurdistan* (New York: Olive Branch Press, 1993), p. 238.

[8] Other than tiny Jewish and Christian enclaves in the large cities, the religious minorities of Turkey are largely made up of an Islamic sect known as the Alawites. Approximately two-thirds of the country's population is Sunni and about one-third Alawite.

[9] al-Khalil, Samir (pseud.), *Republic of Fear: The Politics of Modern Iraq* (Berkeley: University of California Press, 1989).

[10] Reuters on-line wire service, C-reuters@clarinet.com, June 16, 1995.

[11] Iranian Kurds blame the government for Sharafkandi's assassination, but a number of outside observers suggest that Iraqi Kurd leaders may be behind it. See Chapter 6.

··

2

A HISTORY OF KURDISTAN

The male is born to be slaughtered.
          ——Kurdish adage

For 150 years the Kurdish movement was a fire,
sometimes stronger, sometimes weaker, but it was
never out completely. This fire is in the people.
          ——Kurdish human rights lawyer

TO WORLD WAR I

ANCIENT AND MEDIEVAL

The Kurds possess one of the oldest living cultures in the world today. The very beginnings of recorded history in the Middle East feature a prominent and strikingly familiar Kurdish presence: that of a mountain people struggling with emerging flatland states for political and economic control of the highlands around the fertile crescent. In the 4,000-year-old Sumerian *Epic of Gilgamesh*, the eponymous hero, representing lowland civilization, first defeats and then recruits the half-beast, half-man of the mountains, Enkidu. Not surprisingly, the Kurds' own origin myths tell a different story and are usually based upon escape from or triumph over lowland despots.

Still, despite such myths and a reputation for fierce independence, these early mountain peoples were already experiencing the Kurdish disadvantage vis-à-vis nearby lowland states. As Kurdish historian Mehrdad Izady points out, "The natural bounty of [Kurdish] land and ease of defending the mountainous landscape made unnecessary the expansion of the emergent bureaucracies and armies . . . [while] the defense of the exposed landscape [of the plains] necessitated a great deal of bureaucratic organization and a standing military force."[1]

Kurdish unity or, rather, Kurdish cultural homogenization came gradually, over a period of several thousand years, and as a result of long-term civilian migration rather than immediate military invasion. Weakened by frequent clashes with Mesopotamian states, the kingdoms and city-states of the Kurdish highlands offered little resistance to invaders and migrants from the Indo-Aryan-speaking north, the same nomadic peoples who were descending on Persia and India. For the last two millennia of the pre-Christian era, a variety of Indo-Aryan peoples brought their proto-

Persian/Kurdish language to the peoples of Kurdistan, even as they them-selves were absorbed and their Zoroastrian faith modified by the natives and their cult of the angels, an indigenous form of ancestor worship.

The most significant of these peoples, the Medes of the seventh century B.C., had such a profound impact on Kurdistan that historians often cite them as the first authentic expression of Kurdish culture and language.[2] But it was the Babylonian designation for this new mountain culture, the Qardu, that stuck. In the last years of the pre-Christian era, the Romans established a border between themselves and the Parthian Empire of the Iranian plateau that ran through Kurdistan and that has remained remarkably unchanged for 2,000 years, as a glance at a modern map of the Middle East suggests. At the same time, the *pax romana* in Anatolia encouraged a vast migration of Kurdish people towards the north and west, further homogenizing Kurdish culture and roughly establishing the outlines of present-day Kurdistan. With Rome's disen-gagement in the fourth century A.D., the last Kurdish/Median kingdom fell. Persian and nomadic invasions plunged Kurdistan into chaos for several centuries, until the coming of Islam ushered in an epoch of political power and cultural greatness often called Islam's "Kurdish age," or the Kurdish "golden age."

The Kurdish "golden age" was inextricably linked to Islamic power and influence. As Kurds gradually converted to Islam, the Muslim caliphate in Baghdad opened to them. Many became generals in Islamic armies; others acceded to power in subsidiary kingdoms of the plains and mountains of the Middle East; one changed the course of Western history. Salah ud-Din (Saladin), a Kurd of the Hadhabani tribe, reconquered Jerusalem and the Holy Land from the Christian Crusader Richard Lionheart. He also established the Ayyubid dynasty, which ruled much of the Middle East from 1169 to the end of the fifteenth century, when it was finally absorbed by the Ottoman Turks.

A high-water mark in Kurdish history had been reached. The reign of the Ottomans, a once-nomadic people of central Asia, now impressively organized within their new Anatolian home and aggressively expansionist without, coincided with the decline and virtual disappearance of a fully independent Kurdistan. Ironically, given Ottoman prowess of arms, the first blows to Kurdish independence had more to do with trade routes than military campaigns.

THE OTTOMAN ERA

As every schoolchild learns, European expansion into the Atlantic was triggered in large part by the Ottomans closing off overland trade routes to the east. Kurdish students of history, however, learn an additional aspect of that global reconfiguration of trade: it removed their homeland from the center of Eurasian trade to its periphery. The impact of that mercantile shift was immense. The revenue base of Kurdish kingdoms shrank with the loss of tolls and customs charged to the passing caravans. Whole classes of Kurdish men who had prospered as medieval-era teamsters were driven into poverty. Towns that hosted scores of craftsmen supplying both trade goods and the hardware of trade withered away.

To the decay of economic redundancy was added the devastation of imperial war. During the 1500s and early 1600s, the eastwardly expanding Ottoman Empire confronted the expansionist Safavid Empire of Persia. Numerous battles were fought by massive armies that survived by consuming what the land produced or denying its productivity to the enemy. The land, of course, was Kurdish, and the scorched-earth policies of two imperial armies ruined the Kurdish countryside and destroyed Kurdish urban life. Peace finally returned to Kurdistan in the mid-eighteenth century, but with a near-total cultural eclipse. Peace had indeed returned, notes Izady, but it was "the peace of wilderness."[3]

Still, a new equilibrium emerged in the region with the unofficial fixing of boundaries between the Persians and the Ottomans roughly where the Romans and Parthians had established them over a thousand years earlier, that is, through the heartland of Kurdistan. What emerged on the Ottoman side was a string of semi-independent emirates, or principalities. These merit some attention, for with the nineteenth-century demise of these principalities, agree most Kurdish historians, arose many of the problems plaguing the Kurdish nation today.

From the very beginning of their penetration into Kurdistan, the Ottoman sultans could not decide exactly what to do with their warlike and fiercely independent Kurdish subjects. On the one hand, the Kurds' prowess at highland warfare made them ideally suited to patrol the mountainous eastern marches of the empire. But that same prowess, in that same rugged and inaccessible land, made them potential rebels. This dual assessment by the Ottomans led to a dualistic administration of these provinces. Some areas were administered indirectly through local ruling houses in which rulers were chosen independently; in other areas Kurdish princely houses governed, but the sultan chose which member of the family would actually rule. In short, the independence and sovereignty of these Kurdish emirates or principalities often rested on a delicate balance of power between and among the Kurds and their formidable neighbors.

The system worked after a fashion. Where direct Ottoman rule was feasible, it was imposed. Where it was not, local emirs, or princes, were still made to understand the consequences of rebelliousness. If an emir challenged Ottoman authority, the sultan could send imperial troops, though diplomatic means were usually employed. In short, the relationship between the Kurdish emirates and the sultan's empire was a complex and occasionally volatile blend of independence and deference. Constantinople expected a steady stream of revenue and recruits. But this expectation was tempered with a realistic appraisal of several questions: Was the emirate accessible to the sultan's janissaries, or imperial forces? Secondly, how did relations stand with the Persian, and later Russian, empires? Powerful emirs frequently received exemptions from taxation and recruitment in exchange for patrolling the mountainous eastern marches of the empire. And thirdly, was the ruling emir obligated to the sultan or not?

Over time, however, the system grew increasingly exploitative. Misrule, court extravagance and an escalating imperial military budget led the government toward that favored standby of the Chinese Empire: tax-farming. Increasingly, Constantinople sold the right to collect revenues to private individuals, usually local landlords, who paid the government a fixed fee for the right to extract ruthlessly the maximum tax profit from their region.4

THE NINETEENTH CENTURY

The changes of the early nineteenth century had had a two-century-long gestation in the slow decay of Ottoman might and the increasing power and influence of the Christian states of Europe, most particularly Russia and Britain. The decline of Ottoman power encouraged separatist aspirations among the emirates, while the Russian victory over the Persians a decade earlier had brought a Russian presence to the area, and with it the introduction of nineteenth-century nationalism, bureaucracy and technology. Because of this decay and these defeats, reformist sultans began to hire European administrators to help modernize the decaying bureaucracy and army, and exerted greater control over the empire. Sultan Mahmud II (ruled 1808–1839) began the process by crushing overly independent Turkish governors and lords in the heart of Anatolia, and by the end of the 1820s was ready to move on Kurdistan. Although meeting with fierce resistance, Mahmud's successor, Abdulmejid (1839–1861), eventually destroyed the last of the emirates in 1847.

Historians' assessments of the emirates vary. Some argue that, compared with the subsequent century of local rule and central government ineffectiveness, the emirates represent, if not a golden age of Kurdish history, then at least a bronze one. For three hundred years the symbiotic relationship between emirs, tribal leaders and sultans imposed a modicum of social order. Their courts kept alive a vibrant cultural life. "These native institutions went back thousands of years," writes Izady,

> and were the most important source of development, promotion and dissemination of culture, new technology and new ideas in Kurdistan. The defunct princely houses tamed unruly tribal chiefs, checked the ambitions of fanatical religious leaders, and maintained economic contact with the outside world.5

Others disagree. The existence of the emirs prevented the evolution of pan-Kurdish institutions and, more debatably, a pan-Kurdish identity. Historian Nizzan Kendal writes, "the quarrels over supremacy and precedence endemic to feudalism set them against one another, and the pact with the Sublime Porte [Ottoman sultan] also prevented them from coming together and uniting."[6]

Nevertheless, for good or bad the emirates were gone, and the impact on the fragile Kurdish social structure was traumatic. The Turks had destroyed the princes, but failed to establish an effective administration for the Kurdish *vilayets*. Visitors to the region described an economy based on raiding and smuggling. "Brigandage is systematically established throughout Koordistan," wrote Frederick Millingen, a British traveler of the 1860s. "[There are] two processes: raids on caravans and a regular plan of forced contributions."[7] Historian Wadie Jwaideh concurs. "The suppression of the semi-independent Kurdish principalities was followed by lawlessness and disorder."[8]

With the emirates eliminated, a more chaotic tribal order emerged. Referring to the fall of one of the last Kurdish emirates, anthropologist Martin van Bruinessen writes, "in a few generations, tribal organization in Botan had shown a rapid devolution from complex, state-like to much simpler forms of social and political organization, as if it had taken a few steps back on the evolutionary ladder."[8a] The effects, says Izady, still haunt Kurdish politics. "The extinction of the native tradition of orderly government," he writes, "[has played a] decisive role in retarding the process of Kurdish social and political evolution."[8b] In places, the Ottoman state tried to replace the emirates with direct rule. The effectiveness varied, from virtually nonexistent administration to brutally exploitative taxation. Where the Turks could not impose administrative discipline, they ruled indirectly through the *aghas*. Visitors described how tribesmen "showed a far truer loyalty to their own leaders than to Turkish officialdom."

Yet despite the accelerating decay of the Ottoman Empire in the nineteenth century, several important economic reforms went forward. The 1859 Land Code reasserted government ownership of all Ottoman lands, but granted legal possession upon the filing of papers and the payment of a small fee. While the privatization of land was modeled on capitalist European statutes, its intent was specifically Ottoman: to break up the tribes and settle nomadic Kurds and others. The effects were predictable. The code inordinately benefited local elites who both understood the statutory reform and had the capital to take advantage of it. In Kurdistan, these were mainly *aghas*, merchants, government officials and *shaikhs*. Possession quickly turned into ownership; tribal communalism decayed, economic stratification increased, many became sharecroppers, and a new absentee landlord class emerged. Gradually, an alliance developed between wealthy urban landlords and those local *aghas* less able to acquire large landholdings. As the former established economic hegemony, the latter became their rural overseers.

Kurdish tribesmen and nontribesmen grew increasingly impoverished, and powerless as well. As Millingen observed in the early years of land reform, the chief was supreme. He could dispose of anyone's property, and usually shared extradition rights with other *aghas* in case a tenant absconded on his debts.[8c] William Hay, a British political officer in the mandate of Iraq, noted a similar local tyranny 50 years later. "The average tribal Kurd," he noted,

> regards the Government as some strange unknown deity, speaking an unintelligible language. Rather than appear before this monster he will allow his chief, whom at any rate he understands, to fleece him unmercifully, trusting in him to placate the aforesaid monster should occasion arise.[8d]

Kurdish rebelliousness against the state remained, for the causes of it, excessive taxation and brutal Ottoman justice, did not go away with the modernization of the empire. But with the disappearance of the emirates and the more expansive political orientation they offered, larger Kurdish aspirations for autonomy and self-rule languished. Out of that mid-nineteenth-century vacuum emerged a new leadership, pan-Kurdish in impact, protonationalist in ideology, and yet often reactionary and obscurantist in thinking.

The Kurdish *shaikhs*, like their Arab counterparts, were and are both secular and religious leaders, and their effectiveness in uniting Kurds was considerable. (For a fuller discussion of *shaikhs*, see Chapter 3.) "Even a cursory glance at Kurdish history," writes Jwaideh, "will suffice to reveal that *shaikh* leadership has been the most consistently successful type of leadership among the Kurds during the past one hundred years, especially since the disappearance of the last autonomous Kurdish principality."[9] The *shaikhs* were also, say some historians, the first quasi-nationalist Kurdish leaders of the modern age.

The first to lead a major rebellion was Shaikh Ubaydullah, an adroit and resourceful leader of the 1870s. Forced to flee Persia after he had united Kurds against the shah, Ubaydullah was aware of his vulnerability to state power, and in 1877 he established a closer alliance with the sultan by supporting him in his war with Russia. Meanwhile, the *shaikh* pursued a dual strategy: he appealed to the sultan and sought outside support from the British for a potential independence struggle. Early successes, including an invasion of Persian Kurdistan, could not be sustained, and the *shaikh*'s loose talk of an independent Kurdistan concerned the sultan enough for him to send troops. Caught between two imperial armies, Ubaydullah surrendered, but went unpunished by the sultan, who still hoped to use him as a bulwark against the shah.

The long-term significance of Shaikh Ubaydullah's rebellion has been contested by historians ever since. Some consider it the first true expression of Kurdish nationalism, citing Ubaydullah's modernist rhetoric. But, says Izady, Ubaydullah had no vision for an independent Kurdistan. Instead, he "had risen to power by opposing the progressive intrusion of the centralizing Ottoman government," not unlike other tribal leaders of the late nineteenth century, albeit with religious gloss.[10] Historian Nizzan Kendal offers, perhaps, the final word. Ubaydullah, he says, was simply the last in the tradition of emirate resistance to sultanate hegemony. With Ubaydullah's defeat, he writes, "the era of the great 19th-century Kurdish *feudal* revolts had come to an end" [emphasis added].[11]

WORLD WAR I

The short-term consequence of the rebellion was clear. Co-optation of the Kurds was substituted for coercion. Constantinople lavished titles and appointments on Kurdish leaders and created the Hamidiye, a new military force, in 1891. Consciously modeled after the Tsar's Cossack forces and organized on a tribal basis, the Hamidiye, named after its founder, Sultan Abdulhamid II, was created to patrol the Armenian regions of the Ottoman Empire and the Caucasus frontier with the Russian Empire.

The formation of the Hamidiye had another, unannounced, purpose, to maintain sultanate control of the Kurds. "In some cases the selection of tribes for the Hamidiye," Kendal wrote,

> was used to maintain the balance of power in the region, while in others it had the opposite effect. Weaker [Kurdish] tribes were usually chosen where possible because the better quality equipment and training available to them offset the greater strength of their traditional rivals.[11a]

The strategy both worked and backfired. For the government, there was a satisfying increase of intratribal feuding in the 1890s. Then things started to sort themselves out after a fashion. As van Bruinessen notes, "in any tribe the choice of one *agha* as the *hamidiye* commander, rather than any of his rivals, ended most disputes in his favor."[12] Protected by the military, the Hamidiye became a law unto themselves, extracting excessive tribute from townsmen and peasants, slighting civilian officials and constantly extending their rule. For a time, it did not matter to the government, which gave them free reign. Their intense loyalty to Sultan Abdulhamid, whom they called *Bave Kurdan*, "Father of the Kurds," satisfied Constantinople, until new and ominous events for the sultanate intervened.

In July of 1908, the Ottoman Empire was rocked by revolution and the government was taken under control by a group of liberal army officers and civilian officials known popularly as the Young Turks. Abdulhamid was deposed a year later. Some of the Hamidiye revolted, refusing to recognize the authority of the new government and declaring themselves independent, but not, significantly, for nationalist reasons; they wanted to provide a staging ground for the sultan's return to power. They were quickly put down. For their part, the Young Turks adhered to a pragmatic as well as an ideologically driven revolutionary agenda: a modern, more efficient, more democratic state. They deposed the reigning sultan, but not the sultanate. They got rid of the Hamidiye, then brought it back, albeit under tighter state control.

But the Young Turks had not solved the economic and strategic problems of the Ottoman Empire with their liberal and constitutional reforms. Now romantic nationalism was given a try. "The Turkish homeland is neither Turkey/nor Turkestan," penned the nationalist poet Zia Gokalp, "Our Homeland is an immense and/eternal country: Turan!"[13] Appealing to their Kurdish countrymen in the only way these secular nationalists could, with a rather two-faced defense of Islam and the caliphate, the Young Turks were largely successful in enlisting Hamidiye and general Kurdish support. As Kurdish historian and leader A. R. Ghassemlou notes, the Kurds got "entangled in the Turkish jihad against unbelievers," as Turkey itself was dragged into the maelstrom of World War I.[14]

Unfortunately for the people of eastern Anatolia, much of the Turkish part of the war was fought on their territory, as the Turkish and Russian armies, as well as their Kurdish and Armenian allies, swept back and forth across the region. Armenians suffered the worst casualties of the war, when Turkish and Kurdish forces engaged in a wholesale genocide of this Christian people, forcing them out of Anatolia. The Kurds endured, but lost nearly 700,000 people, and there were over a million Kurdish refugees. After Russia pulled out of the war following the October Revolution in 1917, the Turkish military reasserted its control in the east. But losses to Allied forces in the western part of the country forced the government to sign an armistice on October 31, 1918, and accept occupation by Allied troops, including the hated Greeks.

TURKEY

THE BIRTH OF THE TURKISH REPUBLIC (1918–1925)

"All nations have their great men: but I doubt whether anything quite resembles the cult of Ataturk in modern Turkey," wrote historian David Hotham. "He is the 'Eternal Leader.' Written references to him use the Turkish equivalent of He with a capital H, as though he were divine."[15] For the Turks after World War I, the worship of Ataturk may not be considered excessive. For Mustafa Kemal, dubbed *Kamal Ataturk*, "Father of the Turks," quite simply saved the Turkish nation.

As with Germany, the armistice terms the Allies offered to Turkey were humiliating. Under the secret Sykes-Picot agreement, the British and the French had agreed to seize the Ottomans' Arab territories and occupy the Bosporus. More insulting was the Greek occupation of Smyrna (now Izmir), where a substantial Hellenic population had lived for millennia. Unlike the Germans, however, the Turks had a dynamic nationalist leader who rallied them immediately after World War I and drove the infidels from the Turkish homeland in Anatolia.

Ataturk, a westernized career officer from Salonika (now Thessalonika, Greece), rallied the Turkish army in the early 1920s, driving the British, French and Greeks (including ethnic Greeks living in southwestern Anatolia) from the country by 1923. By the time the Allies sat down to hammer out the final treaty in Lausanne, Switzerland, in 1923, the Turks were no longer a defeated nation. With the exception of the *vilayet* of Mosul, Turkish sovereignty in eastern Anatolia was a *fait accompli*, implicitly acknowledged by the Allies. The final treaty of Lausanne failed even to mention the Kurds, who had sided with the victorious Turks, though the Allies included some vague assurances of cultural and linguistic minority rights. The Allied capitulation to Turkish strength also rested on assumptions of Kurdish political immaturity.

In fact, Kurdish politics and nationalism were in a fluid state. When Kurdish overtures to the Allies in Istanbul received a favorable hearing, the news stimulated political activism. In the countryside, a coalition of chieftains in the east demanded the withdrawal of non-Kurdish officers, the release of Kurdish political prisoners and a recognition of autonomy as a prelude to independence. The declaration was premature. Kurdistan was still torn by the rivalries of local leaders, and few backed the coalition. Their reticence allowed Turkish groups to suppress the rebellion quickly.

Moreover, allegiances were divided. Mustafa Kemal had established excellent contacts with a number of Kurdish chiefs. As one British officer observed, many Kurds had been deterred from nationalist declarations "owing to the Turks having won over two of the principal local notables [*shaikhs*] who are influential among surrounding tribes. . . ."[16] They also believed Kemal was the strongman best able to protect Kurdish interests. Urban Kurds, more attuned to the intensely Turkish nationalist atmosphere in Constantinople, remained wary, but rural leaders generally accepted at face value Kemal's early anti-imperialist, multiethnic vision of Turkey's future.

These differing perceptions did not last long, as the realization of the true nature of Turkish nationalism began to penetrate the countryside. In 1922, Kemal abolished the sultanate. Kurdish attitudes towards the sultanate had always been ambivalent but, like the tsar of Russia, the sultan represented an ideal of empire in which loyalty to the sultan transcended all nationalisms. Another blow to Kurdish ideas of an egalitarian union with the Turks followed in early 1924. By April, Kemal had abolished the caliphate, the Ministry of Religious Affairs, and religious courts and schools. Turkey was now a fully secular state. The destruction of the caliphate not only severed the last bond between Kurds and Turks, it deeply offended Kurdish Muslims.

The domination of Turkish nationalism was brought home to more secular Kurds by another proclamation in that same year, whereby the government prohibited all Kurdish schools, organizations, publications and religious fraternities. The victory of Kemal's agenda made things extremely uncomfortable for Kurdish nationalists in the capital. Those who had been too closely allied with Britain and France went into exile in the French-controlled mandate of Syria; others returned to Kurdistan.

KURDISH INTERWAR REBELLIONS (1925–1939)

A few Kurdish nationalists, mostly former officers of the Hamidiye, founded a secret organization known as Azadi, or Freedom. Headquartered in the northern Kurdish city of Erzurum, the officers traveled the countryside seeking support for their Kurdish agenda and came in touch with Shaikh Said, an influential political and religious leader with ambitious plans. While many of the commanders were cautious, Shaikh Said was an open supporter of an immediate declaration of Kurdish independence. His charismatic leadership did not impress the largely secular officer corps, but his broad support among the peasantry did.

The abolition of the caliphate convinced Said that Turkish nationalism was a real threat to the Kurds. But there were other grievances that spoke to the Azadi leadership as well: to a man, senior government officials in Kurdistan were Turkish; the government was continually pitting tribes against one another; Turkish soldiers requisitioned Kurdish property at gunpoint; and the government was encroaching on Kurdish land rights by opening up the region to German mining companies. The government was aware that these policies were stirring Kurdish unrest, but their harsh response only fueled it further.

By the end of 1924, Said and the officers had drawn up a well-coordinated plan for an uprising in May, 1925, but several unrelated incidents forced the date forward. Thus the rebellion, when it began in February, lacked a coherent chain of command. Nevertheless, by the end of March, Said's forces had overrun one-third of Turkish Kurdistan. The Turks declared martial law at the end of February, and sent 35,000 elite troops and the air force to suppress the rebellion, forming an iron ring around Said's headquarters by mid-April. While several rebel leaders formed small bands and escaped to the mountains, where they carried on small-scale guerrilla warfare into the 1930s, Said and his entourage were captured.

The reprisals were, as one historian puts it, "extremely brutal,"[17] establishing a pattern of Turkish response to Kurdish rebelliousness that continues to this day. Hundreds of villages were destroyed, thousands of civilians murdered, whole districts depopulated. Martial courts executed dozens of influential Kurds, including Said, who was hanged with 47 others at Diyarbakir in September. And because of the *shaikh*'s role in the uprising, the government closed all monasteries, *shaikhs*' tombs, and other pilgrimage sites.

Assessments of Said's revolt divide Kurdish scholars: Was it primarily a religious or a nationalist movement? A model for later rebellions or a replay of Ubaydullah's revolt in the 1880s? Izady argues the latter, citing minority Alevi (or Alawite) Kurd fears to depict the rebellion as primarily a religious affair and not a nationalist one. But historians Robert Olson and W. F. Tucker place it in the former category. They disagree with Turkish scholars who characterize the rebellion as "religious . . . instigated by reactionaries, who happened to be Kurds, against the secularizing reforms of the Kemalist government. . . ." In fact, they say, "the Sheikh Said rebellion was the first large-scale nationalist rebellion by the Kurds." And they go on to say that "Sheikh Said was an ardent nationalist."[18] Van Bruinessen discerns different motivations between leadership and their followers. "The *primary* aim of both Shaikh Said and the Azadi leaders," he argues,

> was the establishment of an independent Kurdistan. The motivation of the rank-and-file was . . . mixed . . . for them the religious factor may have predominated. The planners and leaders of the revolt, at any rate, thought that the religious agitation would be more effective in gaining mass support than nationalist propaganda alone. Partly for this reason, shaikhs were chosen as figureheads for the revolt [emphasis in original].[19]

The Mount Ararat uprising of 1929–1932 represented a further departure from the religious and tribal nature of rebellions past for several reasons. First, the sheer magnitude of Turkish repression could not help but minimize the differences among tribes. Second, the rebellion was planned and fomented by Khoyboun, or Independence, an organization founded in 1927 by émigré Kurds. As historian David McDowall writes of the Mount Ararat uprising, "it was the first time a nationalist organization, rather than a *shaikh* or *agha*, had taken so central a role."[20] Moreover, it actively cooperated with the Armenian independence organization, Dashnak. Another herald of things to come was the Kurds' alliance with the shah of Iran, who allowed his country to become a supply base for rebel troops. This alliance demonstrated another factor: Iranian treachery.

The Armenian-Kurdish intrigue clearly worried the Turks, who began negotiations with the Kurdish general and leader, Ihsan Noury. But in 1929, Noury began extending his control across eastern Turkey, delaying the talks as long as possible. By May of 1930, the Turks had seen through the ruse, and on June 11 they launched a major offensive. Their military strategy failed. The Kurds quickly captured nearly 2,000 prisoners, seized automatic weapons and artillery and shot down 12 planes. Istanbul's diplomatic efforts, however, succeeded. An agreement between the Turks and Tehran allowed the military to surround and crush the rebels.

Turkish Kurdistan's last interwar rebellion, indeed, the last sustained armed rebellion there until the 1980s, is a little-known affair in 1937 and 1938. Set in the isolated Dersim highlands of northern Kurdistan, which have been closed to foreigners until recently, the uprising involved two Kurdish minorities: Zaza-Kurd speakers and Kurdish Shiites. The government claimed to have achieved a quick and painless suppression of the revolt, which, they said, was sparked by reactionary religious leaders opposed to Turkish road-building in the area. But W. G. Elphinston, a British historian who was there in the 1930s and wrote about the war later, reported that approximately 40,000 Kurds were killed and 3,000 families deported. Moreover, he says, the war's causes were similar to those of other rebellions: forced assimilation and cultural proscription by the government.[21]

In conclusion, the tortured and bloody interwar history of Turkish Kurdistan can be explained in several ways that shed light on the post–World War II era: first, Kurdish national aspirations had been raised by the promise of democracy immediately following World War I; second, the leadership of the rebellions grew increasingly secular and nationalist in orientation; third, the cycle of rebellion and repression fed on itself; finally, and most important, Turkish nationalism was both aggressive and uncompromising, forcing Kurds to choose between outright rebellion and cultural suicide. That many chose the former should not seem surprising, given the history, tribal order and warrior ethos of the people.

THE POST–WORLD WAR II ERA (1945–1984)

From the end of World War II until 1984, when the Kurdish Workers' Party (PKK) launched its first attack against a Turkish military outpost, sustained armed rebellion ceased in Turkish Kurdistan. Three forces were at work during the long post–World War II years of Kurdish acquiescence to Turkish rule. First, of course, there was the continuing suppression of Kurdish culture and language. Second, the economic transformation of the Kurdish countryside was accelerated by government development projects, which created a system of access roads into the region designed for internal security and economic exploitation. And finally, there was a halting, gradual and uneven Kurdish participation in Turkish party politics, a process often held hostage to the bitter divisions and infighting between left and right within the Turkish political system.

Turkey's democratic tradition is not particularly strong. Ataturk wanted to Europeanize his country, and until his death in 1938 he approached the task with a blend of militarism and eugenics perfectly suited to the European fascism of the interwar years. His goals were embraced by his successors. But with the revival of European democracy in 1945, and the subsequent rise of American power in the region, postwar leaders focused their efforts on establishing at least the appearance of Turkish democracy. In 1945, President Ismet Inonu claimed to have transformed Turkey "overnight" from a dictatorship to a democracy. There were, however, several sticking points: religion, the military and, later, Kurdish unrest.

From the 1950s to the 1970s, Turkey seesawed between civilian and military governments as a familiar cycle began: civilian rule, usually but not always by conservative administrations, would gradually give way to political polarization, governmental paralysis and, in the late 1960s and 1970s, street-fighting between rightists and leftists. Three times in Turkey's post-war history, in 1960, 1970 and 1980, the military stepped in, as it claimed, to put an end to the political divisiveness and restore order. After each coup, leftist political organizations were temporarily forced underground and their leaders executed, jailed or forced into exile. Ironically, it was the military's own activities, including the sponsorship of right-wing death squads, which led to the chaos and violence in the first place.

The political disorder of the postwar era had a powerful impact on Kurdish politics and life, just as the military machine needed to maintain order in Kurdistan provided a launching pad for coup-making. In general, repression grew under military regimes and eased slightly during the civilian interludes. After the 1960 coup, for instance, over 500 Kurdish leaders were interned in military prisons. When a general amnesty was proclaimed the following year, the Kurds alone were exempted. Expressions of Kurdish nationalism, on the rise since the 1958 revolution in neighboring Iraq had given Kurds unprecedented access to power there, were particularly suspect. "If the mountain Turks do not keep quiet," junta leader Cemal Cursel declared, "the army will not hesitate to bomb their towns and villages into the ground. There will be such a blood bath that they and their country will be washed away."[22]

In 1961, a new constitution included liberal reforms, but retained restrictions on Kurdish nationalism. Protection of the rights to freedom of thought, the press and assembly, and against illegal search and seizure included both Kurds and Turks, as did court decisions recognizing the right to strike and to bargain collectively. But bans on regionalist associations remained in force, as did the prohibition on the Kurdish language. Nevertheless, Kurds took advantage of the liberalization and began to write about the 1961 Kurdish uprising in Iraq. In fact, the nationalist rhetoric of the Iraqi Kurds inspired many of the Turkish Kurds, who would later supply many of the shock troops of the Turkish left during the unrest of the late 1960s, unrest that led to the second military coup of the post–World War II era.

With the 1970 coup, a new crackdown against Kurdish leftists and nationalists ensued. Thousands were arrested and tortured in a massive counterinsurgency campaign officially directed at communist infiltration. While Kurdish workers, students and intellectuals were rounded up, 75 percent of the detainees were from the countryside, accused of belonging to Kurdish political parties, including the Turkish wing of Iraq's Kurdistan Democratic Party (KDP). The trials lasted two years: 15 detainees were sentenced to terms in excess of 10 years; the rest got six months to 10 years.

Kurdish nationalism was only part of the problem. The intense poverty and unequal distribution of wealth plaguing the Kurdish region during these years fueled much of the political protest. In many poor regions of the world, these problems led to land riots and even revolution in the 1950s. But in Kurdistan, there were significant internalized restrictions. "Blood ties, religious factors, and the patriarchal tribal relations," writes Kendal, "all help[ed] to camouflage these contradictions."23

Things, however, began to change in the 1960s, as old loyalties withered in the face of far-reaching economic transformation in the region that included much of Kurdistan. As *aghas* and *shaikhs* grew richer by turning themselves into commercial farmers and exploiting their leadership of Kurdish labor and control over Kurdish territory, the old tribal concept of *noblesse oblige* decayed, leading to increasing disenchantment among the peasantry. In addition, many Kurds began to flee the region for opportunities in western Turkish cities.

The same poverty and urbanization were also radically changing Kurdish politics. Freed from the hold of traditional leaders, increasingly disgusted with the inadequacy of middle-class Kurdish parliamentarians and exposed to the revolutionary rhetoric of urban unions, universities and coffeehouses, a new generation of Kurds formulated a radical nationalist and socialist agenda. Led by an Ankara university student named Abdullah Ocalan, they began to rally to a new banner and a new party in the late 1970s and early 1980s. They called it the Workers' Party of Kurdistan. Scrawled on walls across Turkey, it was more popularly known by its Kurdish acronym, the PKK.

THE KURDISH WORKERS' PARTY (PKK) (1978–1991)

On August 15, 1984, the tense peace in Turkish Kurdistan came to an abrupt end. A PKK attack on the towns of Eruh and Shemdinli killed 24 soldiers and nine civilians. Or perhaps it is more accurate to say not that violence reemerged, but that a one-sided war, the Turkish army against the Kurdish population, had a new dimension. For the first time in 45 years, Kurdish rebels were shooting back. Not just a new battle in a century-old conflict between the government and Kurdish tribes, the attack on the army garrison was the opening salvo in a new kind of war, involving a new kind of rebel movement, led by neither traditional *aghas* nor *shaikhs*, but by an organization and leadership presenting itself as a vanguard revolutionary party.

The advent of this new movement was a response not only to the economic and political changes in postwar Kurdistan, but to the volatile political situation in Ankara, the coup of 1980 and the subsequent crackdown on political dissidents across Turkey. Over 33,000 Kurds were arrested and 122 death sentences were passed against members of the PKK. Many fled to Europe, Syria and Lebanon. The failure of Turkish democracy led the PKK to emphasize the forcible national separation of Kurdistan from Turkey or, as Ankara put it, "ethnic exceptionalism," over a popular-front-type approach to the radicalization of Turkish politics. In March 1981, in a nationwide television program, the military regime admitted for the first time the existence of a clandestine Kurdish organization. The broadcast was designed to boost support for its mass trial of 447 PKK members and sympathizers, who were accused of murdering 243 people, including 30 members of the security forces, since 1978.

With parliament unable and unwilling to intervene, the PKK leadership had become convinced that party politics offered no potential for political self-determination, cultural freedom or even economic betterment of the Kurdish people. According to the PKK's Washington liaison Kani Xulum, history offered all the proof PKK leaders needed. In the thirty years since the first democratic elections, Turkish political parties, even those on the left like the pro-Kurdish Socialist Party, had not only failed to deliver the goods but had not even been able to stop recurrent coups and the ongoing assault on Kurds under both military and civilian regimes.

Rather than encouraging PKK participation in the Turkish political process, the return to civilian rule and the military-organized election of moderate Prime Minister Turgut Ozal's Motherland Party in 1983 confirmed PKK suspicions. Ozal lifted the general martial law for the country in 1983, but not in Kurdistan. Moreover, Ozal presided over a massive military buildup in Kurdistan in the mid-1980s and a ruthless counterinsurgency campaign. Harsh as the civilian government's measures were, the PKK's real fears concerned the military, which, they believed, continued to hold the real power in Turkey.

Regardless of who ran things in Ankara, the war between the PKK and the military was clearly expanding with each passing spring, when winter snows melted and fighting renewed. According to London's *Financial Times*, the real turning point in the war came in 1985, when a planned popular uprising failed and the "disappointment hardened into fierce [PKK] determination towards establishing a separate state."[24] Within a year, the government had turned up the heat. Recognizing that PKK forces were operating out of bases in Iran, Iraq and Syria, a number of villages along the various border were "cleared," reported the *Washington Post*, "and fences and floodlights set up to form a no man's land," approximately twenty kilometers deep.[25]

Because of the Turkish government's penchant for secrecy about its Kurdish problem, little is known about the war prior to 1987, when the Western press seems to have first discovered it. One thing, however, is clear. The Turkish government had taken the fight to neighboring Iraq, which was caught up in its own war with Iran. After Kurdish rebels ambushed a military patrol in August, 1986, Turkish jets struck an alleged PKK base in northern Iraq, killing an estimated 200 people. By the summer of 1987, however, the government was forced to admit that Kurdish guerrillas were also operating from within Turkey.

The situation worsened. By May 1987, the *New York Times* reported over 700 dead: 200 Turkish government personnel, including soldiers, local police and internal security forces, as well as 200 insurgents and over 400 civilians.[26] According to the government, these figures had increased 50 percent by September, 1988, when a flood of refugees fleeing Saddam Hussein's brutal anti-Kurdish campaign after the Iran-Iraq War dramatically altered the political and military situation in Turkish Kurdistan. In 1987 and 1988, the government reported over 700 "events" in the Kurdish war, a figure that increased by 20 and 30 percent in 1989 and 1990 respectively. By the end of the 1980s, the *Christian Science Monitor* reported over 2,500 dead in the six-year-old guerrilla war, a figure widely considered to be conservative.[27]

Until the end of the 1980s, the government's strategy to end the Kurdish conflict was simple: overwhelming force or, as one Kurdish writer put it, "all stick and no carrot."[28] It included the appointment of an emergency administration in Kurdistan known euphemistically as the "Extraordinary Circumstances Regional Governorship"; the forced evacuation and destruction of Kurdish villages in PKK-controlled territory; the conscription of a Kurdish militia; the use of both conventional and counterinsurgency warfare; spoken and unspoken agreements with Iraq and Syria allowing "hot pursuit" of Kurdish guerrillas in their territory; the recruitment of Kurdish religious leaders; subsidies of arms and money to conservative and progovernment tribal leaders; a propaganda campaign designed to portray the PKK as a Marxist and terrorist threat to Kurdish civilians and foreign journalists; the clandestine employment of death squads; and the mass arrest, imprisonment and torture of suspected PKK guerrillas and their sympathizers. Of the thousands of Kurds jailed for political activities in the 1980s, according to the estimates of the Human Rights Foundation of Turkey, over 300 have died, including some "due to illnesses because of torture" and 12 from hunger strikes conducted to protest conditions in Turkish prisons.[29]

As early as 1986, *The Middle East* described the Turkish army's presence in Kurdistan as "formidable," with over 45,000 troops stationed in the region. By mid-1990, the government admitted that 100,000 troops were patrolling the Kurdish provinces in eastern Anatolia, though this figure did not include local or national police. By including these forces, the PKK estimated the total security personnel in Kurdistan at triple the government's figures, or some two-thirds of the Turkish army.

In addition, Kurdish civilians were subjected to forced evacuation. In its efforts to isolate PKK guerrillas from the general population, over 30,000 villagers were removed from their villages and placed in strategic hamlet-type settlements in 1989 alone. In other Kurdish settlements, over 24,000 men had been conscripted into the village guard. Refusals to join were dealt with harshly, with collective punishment. Meanwhile the government and international human rights organizations accused PKK rebels of forcibly recruiting guerrillas, assassinating Kurdish government officials and their families and receiving arms from radical Middle Eastern states.

In the late 1980s and early 1990s, two related events, one outside Turkey and the other within, looked as though they might have ended the military stalemate for good. First, there was the massive influx of refugees following the Iran-Iraq War in 1988 and the Gulf War in 1991 that drew international attention to the Kurds, in Turkey as well as in Iraq. This attention and the resourceful leadership of President Ozal led to the overturning of the 60-year-old ban on the Kurdish language in 1991. This, of course, implied an admission by Turkey that it did indeed have a Kurdish problem, an admission that required the government to admit that it had Kurdish citizens at all.

While the measure caused an uproar among hardliners in the Turkish parliament—there were reports of delegates physically assaulting one another—it was actually a rather cautious reversal, in that only private speech was permitted. On the one hand, this was little more than a recognition of the facts of Kurdish life; most rural Kurds and many urban Kurds spoke their own language amongst themselves. On the other, it was a godsend to the many rural Kurds who, ignorant of Turkish, had been unable to conduct business in public, seek medical help or even speak to imprisoned loved ones during visiting hours, without incurring hefty fines. Still, the law maintained the ban on Kurdish publications and broadcasts. Whether this limited opening would be the first step toward ending government repression of Kurdish culture and finding a way out of the military quagmire was a test for the Turkish government as it entered the brave new post–Cold War world.

IRAQ

THE BRITISH MANDATE (1918–1930)

Iraqi, or southern, Kurdistan was a different kind of place from Turkish, or northern, Kurdistan when the British seized it during World War I, ending nearly four centuries of Ottoman rule. It was more accessible, since much of it was situated on the northern Mesopotamian plain and in the foothills of the Zagros Mountains. Thus, a different social and political order had emerged there. While much of Turkish Kurdistan was still tribal and pastoral at the end of World War I, Iraqi Kurdistan had been significantly altered by the Ottoman economic and administrative reforms of the late nineteenth century. "Much of the tribal system in Iraq had been rendered," to use historian Wadie Jwaideh's term, "moribund."[30] And according to British mandate administrator, Sir E. Dowson,

> Many of the villages appear to be . . . the personal possessions of local notables, without any consideration of the immemorial rights of those who had regularly occupied and tilled the land or pastured their flocks thereon. The pinch in these cases seems to have been mainly felt when the lands were pledged, and forfeited, to town-dwelling merchants for debt. The personal touch and interdependence that existed between even the most arbitrary local chieftain and the village cultivators appears not infrequently then to have been replaced by more mechanical efforts to exploit the land from outside and by obstruction to such efforts from within.[31]

The decline of Ottoman power in the early part of the century had encouraged Kurdish aspirations to self-rule. Writing of the impact of the Young Turks, British traveler Ely Soane noted, "Kurds regarded the new regime as a partial revival of their [the Kurds'] importance and a return, in a degree, to some of their independence. . . ." But when the new government tried to revive old taxes and conscription, the Kurds "rebelled against *Majlis* [the new parliament] and Sultan alike."[32]

This restlessness was exacerbated by events during and immediately after World War I. Despite the horrors on the battlefield in Kurdistan, the real action that would determine the Kurds' place in the postwar order was being determined in London and Paris. In 1916, the British and French governments signed the secret Sykes-Picot treaty (named after their representatives), dividing up Ottoman domains in the Middle East amongst themselves.[33] Sykes-Picot would become the basis of the openly arrived-at 1920 Treaty of Sèvres, which did indeed divide up these lands, but labeled them "mandates," with the explicit promise of granting them independence when the European powers deemed the peoples there ready for it. The Sèvres Treaty included among its provisions the distinct possibility of a Kurdish state:

> If, after one year has elapsed since the implementation of the present treaty, the Kurdish populations of the areas designated in Article 62 [east of the Euphrates, south of Armenia, and north of Mesopotamia] call on the Council of the League of Nations and demonstrates that a majority of the population in these areas wishes to become independent of Turkey, and if the Council then estimates that the population in question is capable of such independence and recommends that it be granted, then Turkey agrees, as of now,

to comply with this recommendation and to renounce all rights and titles to the area.[34]

Some Kurds have called the treaty their "Balfour Declaration," after similar British promises of a homeland in Palestine for the Jews. A problematic comparison, since the Jews in Palestine were a minority, but in any case, it was not to be. "The Treaty of Sèvres," notes one historian, "was . . . out of date before it was signed." The Turks had reasserted their control over northern Kurdistan, while southern Kurdistan became the subject of British imperial interests.[35]

To administer their new subjects, the British exploited Iraq's ethnic and religious differences. The Arabs were placed under direct administration, the Kurds were offered indirect rule and the Christian Assyrians, a numerically small upland people, were employed as levies, or conscripted troops, to keep the peace throughout the mandate. In this larger imperial scheme of things, the Kurds were a secondary problem. The Arabs, who had fought effectively with the British against the Ottomans during World War I, hoped that their military assistance would be rewarded with independence, as the British, including T. E. Lawrence (Lawrence of Arabia), had seemed to promise. The Sèvres Treaty, ratified by the League of Nations, spoke of a delayed independence, after perhaps 20 years, and allowed for British occupation and administration. This announcement fueled Arab rioting in 1920. To placate the Arabs, the British selected the Arabian Emir Faisal as the future king of Iraq. While Faisal claimed direct descent from the Prophet, he had never been to Iraq before, which offended nationalists, and, as a Sunni Muslim, he was doubly resented by the Shiite Arab majority of Iraq.

Nor did he please the Kurds, who recognized something even more insidious in these British actions: Kurdish subjection to Arab rule. For all the assurances of the Treaty of Sèvres, the British secretly had no intention of granting self-rule to the Kurds. "Most of the British officials in the Baghdad ministries and departments," noted British administrator C. J. Edmonds, "were as fanatical as any nationalist Arab in their refusal to admit that these Kurds . . . had any right whatever to their assistance" in achieving independence.[36] "As a race," another British administrator wrote in 1921, "[the Kurds] are not a political entity," and are incapable of self-rule.[37]

As yet unaware of their intentions, the Kurds enthusiastically welcomed the British at first. At a spring 1918 meeting in Sulimaniye, Kurdish notables decided "to offer the rule of their country to the British." Having already decided to follow Ottoman precedent and administer Iraqi Kurdistan indirectly, the British began looking for a "paramount leader" with whom they could work. "British policy at that time [1918]," wrote Edmonds, "was to avoid commitments in the hills by setting up one or several semi-autonomous Kurdish provinces to be loosely attached to whatever regular administration might ultimately be established in the plains."[38] In other words, the British intended to resurrect the "moribund" tribal system, establishing a new pro-British confederation under a supposedly tractable leader named Shaikh Mahmud.

As a minor and little-known *shaikh* of the illustrious Barzan confederation, Mahmud had big ambitions, which the British encouraged by telling him to recruit other tribes. The plan was a mix of British racism and the *shaikh*'s own venality. The British saw Kurds as primitive tribesmen, and saw their retribalization policies as the best way "to meet the national aspirations and preserve the characteristics of Kurdistan." At the same time, Mahmud viewed the revitalized tribal structure as a way to "rapidly attain the absolute power which was his aim."[39] Secretly, Mahmud imagined an independent Kurdistan with himself as a British-appointed king, a counterpart to Emir Faisal of the Arabs, whom the British seemed to be grooming to be king of Iraq.

It quickly became apparent, however, that Mahmud had overestimated his popularity. His ambitions, the British quickly concluded, were upsetting other Kurdish leaders. When the British restricted his bailiwick to Sulimaniye, Mahmud "lost no time organizing a revolt." But Mahmud remained unpopular among urban and lowland Kurds, who saw him as a "representative of the old order" and a major cause of the "Kurdish predicament," that is, growing tribal divisions and a lack of respect from the British. Still, Mahmud's plans, excepting the part about his kingship, were popular in the countryside. According to Wilson, "four out of five people support Sheikh Mahmoud's plans for independent Kurdistan."[40]

While all this was going on in Sulimaniye, a more serious challenge was emerging in the heart of Barzani territory along the mountainous Turkish border. The Barzani confederation was the most powerful political entity in Iraqi Kurdistan. By the turn of the century, the Barzani tribe included 750 families but had been expanding because many other tribes looked to the Barzani *shaikh* as their religious leader. In 1927, Shaikh Ahmed, angry at seeing revenues from Kurdish oil fields being siphoned off by the British and Arab administrators in Baghdad, led an uprising against British and Arab forces as well as rival *shaikhs* armed and supported by the government in Baghdad. Gradually, with the help of RAF bombers, in the first recorded bombing of civilians in military history, Iraqi, Assyrian and British troops quelled the uprising.

As the British prepared to turn the mandate over to their handpicked Arab successor in 1930, the near-constant state of rebellion in Kurdistan forced them to take Kurdish grievances seriously, if only for the sake of assuring a peaceful exploitation of the oil reserves there. One of the first acts of the new Iraqi government, still very much dictated to by the British, was the Local Languages Act of 1931, guaranteeing the teaching of Kurdish in Mosul schools, as well as an 11th-hour amendment to the final Independence Treaty of 1932, requiring the election of local Kurdish officials.

THE KINGDOM OF IRAQ (1932–1958)

From the establishment of the Kingdom of Iraq in 1932 until its overthrow in a military coup in 1958, the Arab government largely ignored the Kurds and their grievances. Indeed, Baghdad so blatantly failed to live up to its agreements to promote the Kurdish language and appoint Kurdish officials that the Kurds went to the League of Nations, which implored Emir Faisal, now King Faisal, to show more sensitivity to Kurdish demands. The king half-heartedly acceded, making some effort to right these violations while, at the same time, complaining that the Kurds were using these demands as a wedge to pry autonomy and even full independence from the Baghdad government.

The king's reluctance was understandable, but his efforts to secure his government's weak hold on power by pitting minorities against one another did not improve matters. When the Christian Assyrians rose up in 1933, Faisal rallied the Kurds to the faith. They responded by massacring thousands of Assyrians in the north of Iraq, where the two peoples had cohabited for centuries. The bloodletting, however, did not answer Kurdish grievances, which concerned cultural affairs, political power and, above all, economic conditions. The worldwide depression and its impact on oil prices heightened Kurdish feelings of being shortchanged in the distribution of oil revenues.

Meanwhile, intra-Kurdish fighting intensified as well. British efforts to foster a new tribalism had had an unfortunate legacy in the resumption of banditry and blood feuds, exacerbated by a lack of central government authority resulting from political unrest in Baghdad. In 1936, the government was overthrown in the modern Arab world's first military coup. In addition, sporadic resistance to Baghdad by Ahmed's forces continued until the *shaikh* was captured in 1934. But then others, including his younger brother Mustafa, took up the struggle.

Things worsened during World War II as food shortages became endemic in the mountains. In 1943, Mustafa led a rebellion against the government and the British, who had reoccupied Iraq. Seeing negotiations as a prelude to separation, Prime Minister Said Nuri sent in the *jash*, or progovernment Kurdish militia, who finally drove Barzani into Iran in the fall of 1945. There, Barzani joined forces with Muhammed Muhammed, leader of the independent Kurdish Republic of Mahabad. When Mahabad fell a year later, Barzani and his *peshmerga* fought their way across hundreds of miles of hostile territory, eventually reaching refuge in the Soviet Union. "This 'retreat of the Five Hundred'," writes historian Ismet Sheriff Vanly, "has passed into the annals of the Kurdish national movement."[41] Granted asylum by Moscow, Barzani and his followers lived in the Soviet Union for the next 12 years.

Between the end of World War II and the Revolution of 1958, Iraqi Arabs and Kurds faced two problems: continuing economic exploitation, and entangling Cold War politics. Poverty in the oil-rich nation was largely caused by two factors. First, British and American companies, in league with the Iraqi military and monarchy, dominated the nation's industry, especially the oil business. Until 1952, the Iraqi government received just 10 percent of oil revenues; after that year, the percentage was upped to 60 percent, but the companies conspired to depress crude prices. Still, oil revenues were gravy; the real basis of Iraqi poverty was the inequitable distribution of land. In the late 1950s, over half the arable land in the country was owned by fewer than 2,500 landlords.

The economic problems bred discontent among both Arabs and Kurds, the latter participating in the political unrest for both reasons common to their Arab neighbors and reasons of their own. Kurds, too, were largely landless, and saw little of the revenue generated by the oil reserves under their territory. Restless as a minority and antipathetic to the Arab-dominated government, they were also suspicious of the West. Despite the brief uprising of Mustafa Barzani, Kurds had demonstrated more loyalty to the Allies than had the government in Baghdad, which had briefly flirted with the Nazis. This loyalty and Allied propaganda about self-determination had fueled Kurdish expectations of independence in the immediate postwar era. But the United Kingdom and the United States did not aid Kurdish ambitions for fear that it might drive the conservative Iraqi regime, under increasing pressure from Arab nationalists, into the hands of the Soviet Union.

THE QASIM YEARS (1958–1963)

By the late 1950s, the various contradictions in Iraqi society, both Arab and Kurdish, came to a head. In 1958, General Abd al-Karim Qasim and his left-wing Free Officers' Association ended the British-imposed monarchy when they seized power in a largely bloodless coup. Qasim's initial moves to remake Iraqi society and reorient Iraqi foreign policy were extremely popular. The Qasim regime instituted land reform and rent control and negotiated higher royalties from the foreign-controlled Iraqi Petroleum Company, among other things. Abroad, Qasim pulled Iraq out of the Baghdad pact, evacuated British bases, and established diplomatic and trade relations with the socialist bloc.

The Kurds, too, were refreshed by the new winds blowing from Baghdad. When Qasim invited Barzani and his supporters back from the Soviet Union, a new era in Arab-Kurdish relations seemed to be dawning. "The KDP," an organizational declaration proclaimed,

> hails as solid bases for the welfare, freedom, and equality of the Kurdish and Arab peoples, the important Arab liberation movement, its success in liberating Iraq, the establishment of the Republican regime and the withdrawal

from the Baghdad Pact, which was clearly detrimental to the Kurdish nation.[42]

As for Qasim and the Free Officers, say historians Marion Farouk-Sluglett and Peter Sluglett, "they had no special interest in or commitment to finding a solution to the Kurdish question, but their general attitude seemed friendly."[43] In short, while the new regime was not openly antagonistic to the Kurds, neither was it very sympathetic. Qasim's first cabinet included no Kurds and, as one officer revealed later, "there was no Kurdish problem on the political scene that needed study or settlement."[44]

Several problems confronted the new government almost immediately. Though initially supporting Qasim, pan-Arabists and communists were soon challenging the regime. Kurds, who traditionally feared talk of a pan-Arab republic, sided with Qasim, as they did when he ordered them to turn on his communist allies, which they did, in an impressive and brutal display of their military strength, in 1960. This action, however, focused Qasim's concerns on the Kurds and their autonomy demands, which Qasim, like Iraq leaders before him, believed were a prelude to separation. Having dispatched two dangerous allies—Qasim had already used the communists and Kurds to purge the pan-Arabists—the general felt ready to take on a third.

Using the time-honored tactics of pitting tribe against tribe, Qasim armed the leaders of the Zibari confederation, a rival to the Barzanis. The strategy failed disastrously. Barzani, alienated from Qasim and playing to the discontent with Qasim's reforms among conservative *aghas*, formed an alliance and defeated the Zibaris. Facing continued pan-Arab and communist opposition in the lowlands, Qasim now confronted another formidable opponent in Kurdistan, now armed, organized and led by the undisputed leader of northern Iraq, Mustafa Barzani. Thus began the longest war in modern Kurdish history, triggered, ironically, by the actions of perhaps the best friend the Kurds had ever and would ever have in Baghdad. From 1961 until 1975, Iraqi Kurdistan was almost continually at war against four separate regimes in Baghdad: Qasim's; the first Baath regime in 1963; the nationalist-military government of the Arif brothers; and the second Baath regime, headed by Saddam Hussein, after 1968.

The first year's fighting was among the toughest, as the two sides soon found themselves at a stalemate. Barzani's guerrilla forces were unable to deliver the kind of knockout blow that might have extracted significant concessions from Baghdad, while Baghdad was not capable of dislodging the *peshmerga* who, according to *New York Times* correspondent Dana Schmidt, were "completely at home in the mountains, and had overwhelming support from the people." As he hiked through Kurdistan in the early 1960s, Schmidt was told by his Kurdish guide:

to watch for a great oak tree with four huge branches, three of them dead, one flowering. "You see, the flowering branch is the Iraqi part of Kurdistan, flowering in revolt. The other three branches [Iran, Syria and Turkey] are dead."[45]

And soon so was Qasim. His approach to the Kurds, say the Slugletts, exposed his inability "to remain in good standing with . . . natural allies."[46] He had alienated his pan-Arabist, communist and now Kurdish friends, the latter turning to Baathist conspirators for support. The Kurds' overtures to Baath might seem paradoxical at first glance; Baath leaders had, after all, criticized Qasim for not being hard enough on the Kurds. But, like Qasim, the Kurds had painted themselves into a corner, having turned on their only real allies, the communists. As for Qasim, his regime fell to a Baathist coup in February 1963, during which he was murdered. There was no one to save him.

THE KURDS AND THE BAATH (1963–1988)

When the Baath took power, notes one historian, they were "totally unprepared" for it. Unsure of the army's loyalty, party leaders wasted no time unleashing a "reign of terror" against their real and putative enemies, including the Kurds. Within months, they began systematically removing Kurds from their homes around the crucial oil city of Kirkuk and replacing them with Arab families, a policy that was continued even more efficiently and ruthlessly after their return to power in 1968. In June, they launched a new offensive in the north, but, as it turned out, the war, which Baath leaders termed "a mere stroll," outlasted the regime. Having unleashed a bloodbath in Arab Iraq, and having led the army to defeat in the Kurdish mountains, the Baath party had alienated both the populace and the army of Iraq, and was overthrown in a military coup in November.[47]

Meanwhile, the internal machinations of Kurdish politics continued and intensified. By the early 1960s, Iraqi Kurdistan was divided between two increasingly aggressive bases of power. On the one side there was the Barzani confederation in the north and on the other, a confederation of tribes in the east under the leadership of Jalal Talabani and affiliated with the KDP.[48] The rift was made to order for the new military regime in Baghdad. While the Baath offensive had temporarily united the two forces, the new government pitted them against each other. The strategy did not work, as Barzani remained the unchallenged leader of northern Kurdistan. This fact, and growing public weariness with the war, forced the government to the negotiating table in late 1965. Six months later, dovish Prime Minister Abd al-Rahman al-Bazzaz and Kurdish leaders announced the most ambitious plan ever to assure Kurdish autonomy. Among other things, the treaty recognized "the existence of the Kurdish nation," mandated Kurdish administrators for the region and local government, guaranteed bilingualism in Kurdish regions, and encouraged Kurdish culture, letters and the arts through statutes and subsidies.

Al-Bazzaz, however, was in no position to implement it. Behind the trappings of the civilian administration, the military, angered and humiliated by its drubbing during the Baath reign, still called the shots. Shortly after the government-Kurd agreement was reached, al-Bazzaz was ousted from power. Fighting between the government and the Kurds continued sporadically up to and beyond the second and permanent Baath coup of July, 1968. Kurdish leaders, convinced by their victories over government forces in the early and mid-1960s and receiving arms from the shah, believed that time was on their side.

The strength of Kurdish resistance concerned the new Baath government, especially after a failed military coup exposed the latter's weakness. An expanded Kurdish war, Saddam Hussein and other party leaders believed, would only strengthen opposition to Baath within the military. Thus, they opted for a two-front strategy: appeasement of the Kurds and a purge of opposition forces in Baghdad. Though skeptical of government offers, Kurdish leaders took a wait-and-see attitude, even as government negotiators tried to convince them a new era had opened up in government-Kurd relations.

On March 11, 1970, the fruits of the Baath-Kurd dialogue were announced to the Iraqi public on national TV. Under the new peace agreement, a virtual carbon copy of al-Bazzaz's 1966 plan, war in Kurdistan came to a halt, at least temporarily. The costs so far had been terrible. According to a UN report, 40,000 houses in 700 villages had been destroyed; 300,000 people displaced; and there were some 60,000 dead and wounded on both sides. War-weariness among the Kurds and the growing perception that this might be the best agreement he could wrest from the Baath government convinced Barzani to go along. "At first," recounted Barzani,

> they [the Baath government] came to us and said, "We will grant you self-rule." I said this was a ruse. I knew it even before I signed the agreement. But [our] people asked me, "How can you refuse self-rule for the Kurdish people?"[49]

He had other considerations as well. In fact, Barzani saw himself in a no-lose situation. As journalist David McDowall notes, "[he] saw the opportunity to consolidate his own position within the Kurdish movement to the detriment of the Talabani . . . faction. If the government reneged, he could always take to the hills once more, as undisputed Kurdish leader."[50] The agreement worked for the Baath too. The two-year peace allowed them to effectively crush the communists and other opposition forces.

Still, there were flies in the ointment. The two sides argued over the inclusion of the oil-refining city of Kirkuk in the Kurd-dominated region and the pace of change to Kurdish administration and education. By 1973, the situation was rapidly deteriorating, and distrust grew as both sides began to replenish their arms supplies. In the spring of 1974 fighting recommenced, and by early 1975 discontent in the army, grumbling among the populace and renewed Kurdish offensives, backed by Iranian arms and advisors, were forcing an Iraqi retreat from the north.

In desperation, Saddam Hussein turned to Tehran, granting long-sought territorial concessions in exchange for Iran's withdrawal of support to the Kurds. On March 5, 1975, the two sides signed a treaty to that effect at the OPEC conference in Algiers. Caught between the forces of the shah and of Saddam Hussein, the *peshmerga* were soundly defeated. Barzani and his immediate followers escaped to Iran, including some 30,000 to 40,000 *peshmerga* and over 150,000 civilian refugees.[51] This latest round of warfare had cost 20,000 Kurdish and Iraqi lives. Historians have widely blamed Iraqi Kurd leadership for the debacle. "I can think of no other example of a popular war ending so lamentably following a leadership decision at a time when the people were still willing to fight and had the means to do so," writes Vanly:

> This is what happens when the fundamental choices in a party's program are accepted enthusiastically by the rank and file but remain intangible because, as far as the leadership is concerned, they are merely tactical considerations of no great importance.[52]

By the end of the 1970s, things looked bleak for the cause of Kurdish nationalism in Iraq, that is until events across the border altered the history of the Kurds and everyone else in the Middle East forever. The Iranian Revolution and the overthrow of the shah in 1979 shocked and frightened the leaders of the Muslim world, most especially Saddam Hussein.

THE ANFAL CAMPAIGN (1988–1990)

Saddam Hussein launched the eight-year-long Iran-Iraq War in September 1980 for several reasons: to prevent unrest among Iraqi Shiites, to establish himself as leader of the Arab world, to reverse the humiliating concessions of the Algiers accords, and because he thought revolutionary Iran would be easy to defeat.

The consequences of the war for the Kurds were positive in the short run but disastrous in the end. With the Iraqi military focused on the Iranian front to the south, Kurdish guerrilla leaders, both Talabani and Mustafa Barzani's son and successor, Massoud, established control over a large swath of Kurdistan, a "liberated" zone where Kurdish men could escape military conscription and Kurdish leaders reestablish their *peshmerga* armies. Complicated power struggles and alliances soon began to emerge among Kurdish forces and between the Kurds and Iran.

Fearful of Talabani's potential to create havoc in his territory along the Persian border, and recognizing that the leftist Talabani was of a similar mind about the dangers of Islamist politics, Saddam Hussein formed an alliance with the PUK and the leftist Kurdistan Democratic Party of Iran (KDPI) under A. R. Ghassemlou. Talabani, meanwhile, was conducting secret negotiations with the Speaker of the Iranian Parliament, Hashemi Rafsanjani. "[Saddam Hussein] promised to put a stop to the Arabization of Kirkuk and join me on television to declare a new charter for Kurdish autonomy," Talabani later rationalized.

> Then, however, it became clear that the Iraqi army could successfully defend Basra [Iraq's port on the Persian Gulf] and Saddam Hussein went back on his word.[53]

By the time Talabani had broken with Saddam Hussein and launched an attack on the Kirkuk oil refinery in the fall of 1986, Tehran had begun supporting Barzani. Now in alliance with Tehran, the two Kurdish forces were finally prepared to negotiate with each other in earnest. On May 7, 1987, the KDP, the PUK and four minor Kurdish parties announced the formation of the Kurdish National Front, aimed at unifying their anti-Baghdad war efforts and planning for an independent Kurdistan. While denying it was receiving Iranian support, the Front drew up a military plan clearly coordinated with Tehran's. "We have no friends among the Arabs," Talabani told *The Middle East*:

> Only Iran supports us. We understand each other. . . . We have also learnt the lesson of 1975 when the Shah of Iran and Saddam Hussein shook hands at the OPEC Conference in Algiers and the Iranians abandoned our cause. We will never become dependent on another state.[54]

But they had tied themselves to Iran.

In 1987, Iran and the Kurds launched their last offensive, a drive on Baghdad through the mountains of Kurdistan. Iraqi forces held firm. The following year Iraq launched its own final offensive against Iran, recapturing all its lost territory on the gulf, and threatening to push into Iran itself. Faced with a potential uprising in the Iranian military, and with casualties in excess of a million, Khomeini, who had vowed to pursue the war until Saddam Hussein was driven from power, announced he would "drink the cup of hemlock" and halt the war against Iraq. On August 20, 1988, Tehran formally accepted UN Resolution 598, which called for a cease-fire, negotiations and a reestablishment of the *status quo ante bellum*. Baghdad was now free to turn its attention to the Iraqi Kurds, whose leaders had placed their faith in the promises of the Iranian government. Saddam Hussein would now make them pay for this error.

Beginning in 1987, the Iraqis had been using chemical weapons against the Kurds in a campaign that culminated in an attack on the Kurdish city of Halabja in April 1988, resulting in over 6,000 deaths, mostly civilian. After the war, the Baath government decided to punish the Kurds for their treachery and prevent any future rebellions by launching the infamous *anfal*, or "spoils of war" campaign. In several months, thousands of Iraqi Kurd villages were destroyed, their wells capped with concrete and their fields poisoned. Thousands of Kurdish *peshmerga* were summarily executed and tens of thousands of Kurds placed in concentration camps. When they got out, they were warned not to return to Kurdistan and threatened with severe penalties if they did so. Many were resettled in Arab areas; others were placed in specially built apartment blocks, surrounded by armed guards and barbed wire. While many Kurds eventually made their way back to their devastated homeland, the Baath government had effectively elimi- nated the Kurdish threat, at least until the Gulf War opened up new possibilities for the Kurds.

IRAN

EARLY MODERN TO EARLY 20TH CENTURY

The eastern slopes of Iran's Zagros Mountains are where archaeologists say the Kurdish people originated in prehistoric times. Then for centuries, the Kurds of Iran were isolated from their brethren to the west by imperial boundaries established 2,000 years ago. At the beginning of the modern era, the Iranian Kurds were nominally ruled, in a fashion similar to that of the Ottoman Empire, by the Safavid dynasty that ruled Persia from 1502 to 1736.

In the nineteenth century, the growing dominance of European empires, especially neighboring Russia's, had several important effects on the history of the Iranian Kurds. First, the Russo-Persian wars of the early part of the century transferred large portions of northern Iran to the expanding Russian Empire. This change in sovereignty exposed leading Iranian Kurds to the nationalist ideas of nineteenth-century Europe. Sec- ond, the application of new European technologies and bureaucratic ideas inspired Persian leaders to extend more control over their far-flung Kurdish subjects. The remaining Kurdish principalities were forcefully dismantled, breaking Kurdish society into a more disjointed and tribal structure and rendering it far less able to respond to the nationalist ideas and forces sweeping the Arab and Persian worlds in the late nineteenth and early twentieth centuries. As Izady points out, " . . . common Kurds, who were then living at the tail end of several centuries of national and intellectual regression, were completely unfamiliar with [these] novel political ideas."

> At the end of the 19th century, those who were at the helms of the Kurdish political leadership, the tribal chiefs and religious *shaikhs*, were far closer to their plebeian subjects in their ideological awareness than to . . . modern intellectuals. The intellectuals were perceived as detached dreamers, alienated from the realities and common problems of the average Kurds . . . [not] even remotely capable of fathoming the requirements of the fast arriving new world.[55]

The tribal leadership's ambitions, says historian Wadie Jwaideh, were parochial: local power, wealth and privilege, obtained by any means, including cooperation with the state, and defended fiercely against all Kurdish rivals.

This retrograde social order produced, says Izady, leaders like the "truculent" Ismail Aqa (*aqa* is the local Kurdish word for chief), known to his followers by the Kurdish diminutive Simko, and by his enemies as "the cannibal." Simko, says Izady, had no capacity for imaginative leadership. Rather than seeking an alliance with local Christian Assyrian tribes during World War I to establish joint sovereignty over northwestern Iran, he had them lured into negotiations and then massacred. In this way, Simko became the unrivaled leader of the Iranian Kurds. He refused to pay tribute to the government and, after World War I, established a personal satrapy in northwestern Iran.

Simko was able to achieve this autonomy because of the weakness of Tehran, until a nationalist coup led by War Minister Reza Pahlavi in February 1921 deposed the old shah. The new government intended to reestablish administrative and military hegemony over the whole of Iran and, after several unsuccessful offensives, finally defeated Simko in 1925. But like the British, Pahlavi, now Reza Shah, decided to administer the Kurdish tribes indirectly, through a Kurdish strongman. Unlike the British, however, the new shah opted for a proven leader. He pardoned Simko and appointed him the paramount leader. This strategy proved no more effective than the British one. Simko rebelled again and was killed by government assassins posing as negotiators in 1930.

Between Tehran's firm military hand and a modest effort to develop Kurdistan economically, peace was maintained through the beginning of World War II. Still, the shah was determined to expunge Kurdish nationalism from Iran and, taking a cue from the Turks, banned the use of Kurdish language (though only in official matters) and outlawed almost all expressions of Kurdish ethnicity. It worked, after a fashion. Kurdish nationalism was forced underground, but remained ready to blossom when domestic and international opportunities presented themselves, as they did when Britain and the Soviet Union occupied Iran during World War II.

WORLD WAR II AND THE MAHABAD REPUBLIC (1941–1947)

On August 25, 1941, World War II came to Iran when the Soviets and the British occupied the country. Three weeks later, the shah, who had flirted with the Nazis, was forced to abdicate in favor of his son Mohammed Reza Pahlavi. Both the British and especially the Russians were in desperate military positions that summer. Thus, both forces occupied Iran with a mission and a method: to secure the oil fields and stable southern supply routes to the Soviet Union, and to insure social peace by treating the various ethnic groups that composed the polyglot Persian Empire "cordially."

To the Soviets fell the northern third of Iran as well as a strategic headache: rebellious Kurds and Azerbaijanis. They tried to placate both groups, but it was not easy. In the spring of 1943, urban riots forced Iranian authorities to abandon Kurdistan. More significantly, the Kurds were organizing politically and militarily. On August 16, a dozen small merchants and petty officials in the town of Mahabad founded the secretive *Komala-i-Zhian-i-Kurd*, Committee of Kurdish Youth, usually shortened to Komala. It quickly spread. Komala grew because it was something new: a self-consciously modern nationalist organization with a progressive economic and social agenda intended to challenge both the central government and conservative rural Kurdish leaders.

The Soviets supported Komala and began to meet with its members secretly. "From that time," writes American diplomat and historian, Archie Roosevelt, Jr., "although the party program called for appeals to each of the Big Three [Britain, the US and the USSR] impartially, the Komala moved inevitably into the Soviet orbit."[56] In April 1945, Qazi Muhammed, leader of one of the most important families in the region, whose title, Qazi, means judge, joined the organization. In taking leadership of Komala, Muhammed faced the old dilemma of urban Kurdish leadership: how to persuade the conservative tribal chiefs in the mountains—who commanded the bulk of potential Kurdish forces and were wary of the socialist manifesto of the Kurdish Democratic Party of Iran (KDPI), successor to Komala—to join the nationalist movement.

Fortunately, Muhammed found an alternative force in Barzani's Iraqi *peshmerga*, fleeing Iraq after their wartime rebellion had been defeated in 1945. Mustafa Barzani brought several thousand well-armed *peshmerga*. While Barzani was conservative in outlook, and thus not particularly sympathetic to the KDPI's social agenda, he was also flexible enough to put aside ideological differences in the hopes that his efforts in Iran might, in some yet unspecified way, help his cause in Iraq.

Thus, on December 15, 1945, the Soviet-backed Kurdish Republic of Mahabad was established. A month later, Muhammed was elected its first and only president and by the spring of 1946, the republic seemed to be off to a good but somewhat shaky start. The people went about their business, the harvest looked to be a good one, and, in historian William Eagleton's words, politics were freer than the citizens of Mahabad, used to government repression and the arbitrary authority of traditional Kurdish leaders, "had ever had any right to expect."[57]

But events outside Kurdistan were conspiring against the new republic. By 1946, the Soviets were preparing for the breakup of the wartime alliance with the US and Britain. They abandoned support for independent pro-Soviet republics in Kurdistan and Iranian Azerbaijan, opting instead to bolster pro-Soviet forces within Iran itself. When Azerbaijan succumbed without a struggle to Iranian forces on December 17, 1946, Mahabad officials were "stunned." Soviet withdrawal, tribal hostility and Barzani's withdrawal in the fall of 1946 doomed the republic.

Encountering little resistance, Iranian forces occupied Mahabad on December 14, 1946, one week short of the republic's first anniversary. On March 31, 1947, Muhammed and several other Kurdish leaders were hanged from a scaffold erected on the same square where, less than 15 months earlier, they had proclaimed independence. Despite his shortcomings, Ghassemlou says, Muhammed remains a hero to the Kurds, his grave a "site of homage."[57a] Meanwhile historians have differing assessments of the Mahabad "experiment." Roosevelt portrays Muhammed as a tragic figure helplessly trapped between the Soviets and his tribal rivals. Socialist A. R. Ghassemlou, Muhammed's successor as leader of the KDPI, is less forgiving. By failing to distribute land and thus win the peasants to the Mahabad cause, he says, Muhammed had doomed himself and the cause.[57b]

THE YEARS OF THE SHAH (1941–1979)

The history of Iran between the end of World War II in 1945 and the Islamic Revolution in 1979 divides itself into five distinct periods: the years 1946 to 1951, as the shah began to consolidate his power; the liberal Mossadegh interregnum; the establishment of an absolute dictatorship under the shah between 1953 and 1963; the launching of the 1963 "White Revolution," the shah's plan to modernize the Iranian economy and westernize its society; and the rising tide of popular discontent from the mid-1970s on. During these years, the economy of Kurdistan experienced the same jarring changes that struck the rest of Iranian society, even as its political response to those changes took a characteristically Kurdish turn.

It began with the aftermath of the Mahabad Republic. For once in Kurdish history, someone else took the brunt of punishment meted out in the wake of rebellion by a vengeful and determined central government. "Thousands of Azerbaijan democrats were massacred by armed irregulars," says Ghassemlou, "while the Shah's generals turned a blind eye."[57c] In Kurdistan, however, the military was more circumspect. There were no massacres, no mass imprisonment and no mass executions other than

Muhammed and his immediate followers. According to Iranian officer Hassan Arfa, the reason for the clemency was simple:

> The tribes returned, not with bitter and humiliated feelings of a vanquished nation which had lost its dearly-won but short-lived independence, but only with the knowledge that this venture, like many others before, had not come off and that for the time being they had better sit quietly and show themselves good citizens.[58]

The "time being" was not long. By the early 1950s, Iran was torn by strikes and demonstrations, pitting supporters of the left-wing nationalist Mohammed Mossadegh against the conservative forces of the shah and the military. When elections brought Mossadegh to power in 1951, the KDPI took advantage of the politically fluid situation to press for an autonomous Kurdistan within an Iranian confederation. The overthrow of Mossadegh in 1953 ended such efforts. The shah, having quickly eliminated his leftist Iranian opponents with the help of the United States, went after the Kurds, banning their political organizations, including the KDPI. In addition, Kurdish-language radio broadcasts were limited to music and short progovernment newscasts intended to offset anti-Iranian broadcasts from Egypt. The policy worked, after a fashion. In 1963, a weak and fractured KDPI abandoned its progressive social and economic agenda. And owing to "difficult conditions and the choking atmosphere prevailing in Iranian Kurdistan . . . at this time," a 1987 KDPI communiqué recalled, party leaders were forced to settle in Iraq.[59]

That "choking atmosphere" was not, however, confined to Kurdistan. By the early 1960s, the shah's policies had so overheated the economy that the nation was on the verge of bankruptcy. Popular demonstrations pressed the shah's hand, but the "free elections" promised for January 1961, were, says Amjad, "as fraudulent as . . . previous ones."[60] Faced with nationwide unrest, the shah launched the "White Revolution:" land reform, rapid industrialization and cultural westernization.

The nationwide political repression and destabilizing economic forces unleashed by the shah triggered unrest first in Kurdistan. In 1967, a minor rebellion broke out in northwestern Iran over grievances familiar to Kurdish provinces elsewhere. Local religious and tribal leaders had taken advantage of the shah's programs to consolidate their exploitative grip on the Kurdish countryside. Led by urban groups, the rebellion failed to penetrate the countryside and, with the rest of Iran at peace, the shah could concentrate his forces there; he quashed the uprising within a year. When Iranian Kurds fled to Iraq, they were returned to the shah by Iraqi Kurds eager to maintain good relations with Tehran in order to sustain their own war against Baghdad. The only positive thing to come out of this event, says Ghassemlou, was the awakening to Iraqi Kurd treachery. From the early 1970s on, he says, the KDPI detached itself from the "feudal" Iraqi leadership, and returned to its progressive social and economic roots.

Meanwhile, by the early 1970s, Iran was entering a crisis period much like that of the late 1950s, made worse by the gross discrepancies in the distribution of the petrodollars flooding into the country. The result was a revolution very different from that launched by the shah almost two decades earlier.

THE ISLAMIC REVOLUTION (1970s)

By the middle of the 1970s, Iran's political and economic crisis had made its people especially amenable to the message of Islamist politics, though the Kurds came to the revolution for reasons of their own. Clearly there was no love lost between the shah and the Kurds. The many Kurds who had moved to the cities in the 1960s and 1970s joined the mass demonstrations and strikes; the attitude in the countryside was largely, if more passively, in support of any movement that would oust the shah's government. "They built nice roads here," one rural Kurd told the *New York Times*, "so people would drive right through and not stop to see how we live."[61]

But there was also ambivalence about the theocratic nature of the revolution. The vast majority of Kurds are Sunni, and while most are devoutly Muslim, their dominant allegiance is nationalist rather than religious. A popular adage about the Kurds in Iran and Iraq goes: "Compared to an infidel, the Kurd is a Muslim." But that is not entirely fair. As far as the Kurds are concerned, their oppression has always come at the hands of fellow Muslims. And underlying this ambivalence was traditional Kurdish skepticism about the intentions of the Islamist revolutionaries. "Five boys from our village were killed in the revolution," the man added, "but I don't think it's going to make any difference for us because no one cares about our cause."[62]

In fact, it did make a difference. The breakdown and ouster of the shah's government in February, 1979, created a power vacuum in the Kurdish highlands, while the revolution's radical rhetoric produced rising expectations. "We supported the revolution and we want to be treated fairly," a Kurdish truck driver said:

> We want freedom to speak our own language and teach it to our children in the schools, freedom to dress according to our own customs and to hear our own music on radio and television.[63]

On March 28, a delegation of Kurdish leaders traveled to Qom to meet with Khomeini, but were told their demands for autonomy were "unacceptable." Both religious and nationalist reasons lay behind Khomeini's refusal. First, Kurdish demands upset the idea of a unified Islamic community, or *umma*. Equally important, the Khomeini government was as much nationalist as it was religious and, on the subject of Kurdish autonomy, says journalist Gerard Chaliand, it was as "Persian and imperial in its implicit organization" as the shah's.[64]

But the Kurds were armed and willing to defend their rights, especially as they sensed a weakness in their opponent. While Khomeini insisted the Kurds need not fear the Islamic government, the Kurds remained unconvinced. In April, the KDPI denied government charges that they sought separatism but by then fighting between the Pasdaran, or Revolutionary Guards, and Kurds had already begun. At first, the fighting was desultory; Kurds clandestinely received arms from Iraq and Turkey and fought guerrilla-style in the mountains. The government's response led to civilian casualties. After a massacre in the village of Gharna, the Kurds stepped up their resistance. "I talked to members of several families who had lost a member of their family," one Kurd said. "I think they are more anxious to fight the regime now than ever before."[65]

In August, Khomeini took direct command of the military, and demanded results. The army moved in and made showy gains. Twice the front page of the *New York Times* featured pictures of mass executions of Kurdish guerrillas. But the dynamics had not changed: Kurds controlled the countryside and the night; the government occupied the towns and cities. It was an increasingly untenable position for the government, however, as discontent began to spread through the army's ranks. There were still many officers from the old regime, and recruits just wanted to go home. By autumn, the government was in full retreat and the Kurds in nearly complete control of Kurdistan. "Of course, we may be short of food and other necessities," a KDPI spokesman said,

> but we have our own councils, language, schools, roads, a kind of medical service in some areas and the freedom of expressing ourselves and choosing our own organizations. All these mean a new quality in our lives and it means *autonomy*.[66]

In fact it meant more than that. In the countryside, Kurdish peasants were seizing land and redistributing it among themselves; in towns, a lively political culture emerged, with much discussion about an independent and socialist Kurdish republic. A national referendum on the new Islamic government, held in early December, was boycotted by almost 90 percent of Kurdish voters. In mid-December, Tehran was forced to introduce its 14-point program on minority ethnic groups, including the Kurds. It unambiguously supported the right to cultural freedom, but stopped well short of autonomy and a federal Iran, the central demand of the KDPI.

But by the spring of 1980, leftist elements around Prime Minister Abolhassan Bani-Sadr, always more moderate on the Kurdish question, had become politically isolated. Building on the momentum following the seizure of the US embassy in November 1979, radical Islamists virtually controlled the government. Meanwhile, in parliamentary elections in March 1980, the KDPI won over 80 percent of the Kurdish vote, with Ghassemlou leading. Ghassemlou, wisely, had no intention of actually going to Tehran. When Khomeini heard the news, he was disappointed. "It's too bad," he was reported to have said, "we could have had him arrested and shot."[67] Both sides, it seems, were preparing for the inevitable confrontation when, in September 1980, Saddam Hussein attacked Iran.

THE IRAN-IRAQ WAR (1980–1988)

As in Iraq, the war seemed a godsend to the Iranian Kurds in the short run, but was disastrous in the long term. At first, the Kurds of Iran found themselves rid of Iranian authority, as the army pulled out of the region to defend the revolution against Iraqi aggression. But by 1982 Tehran's defenses were stiffening and the military felt confident enough to launch a major offensive against the Kurds. Yet even as Ghassemlou pleaded for outside support, he was defiantly spurning government pardons to insurgents who would lay down their arms.

The Kurds were not only isolated from the outside world, they were also isolated from Iraqi Kurds, armed by Khomeini in return for keeping KDPI bases out of Iraq, and from opposition forces in Iran. "I think it is the feeling of the people in Kurdistan that they are on their own," Ghassemlou said.

> They were expecting something to happen in Tehran, but, I think there is a change now. They are thinking more and more in terms of resisting by themselves for years to come and no longer have high hopes that Khomeini will soon be toppled in the central areas.[68]

Eventually, however, the KDPI joined the National Council of Resistance, an umbrella organization of the various opposition parties, including the new National Front, various ethnic parties and the left-wing Islamic Mujahideen, the only non-Kurdish organization actively fighting the government.

Nevertheless, this coalition could do little for the Kurds when the Iranians launched a huge new offensive against them in 1984. The blow was devastating—a 2,000-square-kilometer area was cleared and over 70 villages and towns were captured—but not decisive. With aid from Iraq, over 15,000 Iranian Kurdish *peshmerga* continued to resist over 250,000 Iranian soldiers. They even managed to maintain a semblance of governance. The KDPI ran a military school, hosted two French-run medical clinics, published journals and maintained a prison for Iranian prisoners of war.

By 1987, the war between Iraq and Iran was reaching a climax, with both sides preparing make-or-break offensives. Iran attacked first. With the help of Iraqi Kurdish forces, it drove deep into central Iraq, but was repulsed by the Iraqi army and air force, deploying chemical weapons. In 1988, Iraq launched a massive offensive, recaptured all the lost territory in the south and threatened to push into Iran itself. On July 18, 1988, Khomeini announced he would accept UN Resolution 598, which called for a cease-fire beginning August 20. Saddam Hussein's *anfal* campaign against Iraqi Kurds shortly after the war sent over 100,000 refugees flooding into Iran. But unlike Iraq, which ended the war in a position of strength, the government in Iran was in no position to launch an Iranian *anfal* against its own Kurds, nor did it need to, since the Kurds were in no position to offer anything but the most limited resistance to Tehran's authority.

NOTES

[1] Izady, Mehrdad, *The Kurds: A Concise Handbook* (Washington, D.C.: Taylor and Francis, 1992), p. 25.

[2] In fact, says Izady, ancient Kurdish culture was an amalgam of indigenous customs and the influences of a variety of Aryan peoples.

[3] *Ibid.*, p. 25.

[4] It should be noted that the gradual deterioration in the Sultan's administration and the increasing exploitation of his subjects was not confined exclusively to the Kurdish regions of the empire. Peasantry from every corner of the Ottoman domains found the yoke of taxation ever more burdensome, especially in the nineteenth century.

[5] *Ibid.*, pp. 56–57.

[6] Kendal, Nizzan, "The Kurds under the Ottoman Empire" in Chaliand, Gerard, ed., *A People Without a Country: The Kurds and Kurdistan* (New York: Olive Branch Press, 1993), p. 15.

[7] Millingen, Frederick, *Wild Life among the Kurds* (London: Hurst and Blackett, 1870), p. 241.

[8] Jwaideh, Wadie, "The Kurdish Nationalist Movement: Its Origins and Development," unpublished dissertation, (Syracuse, N.Y.: 1960), p. 212.

[8a] van Bruinessen, p. 181.

[8b] Izady, p. 56–7.

[8c] Millingen, Frederick, *Wild Life among The Koords*, London: Hurst and Blackett, 1870, p. 284.

[8d] Hay, William, *Two Years in Kurdistan; experiences of a political officer, 1918–1920*, London: Sidgwick & Jackson, Ltd., 1921, p. 67.

[9] *Ibid.*, p. 127.

[10] Izady, *op.cit.*, p. 57.

[11] Kendal, *op.cit.*, p. 24.

[11a] Kendal, "Kurds Under Ottoman Empire", p. 14.

[12] van Bruinessen, Martin, *Agha, Shaikh and State: The Social and Political Structures of Kurdistan* (London: Zed Books, 1992), p. 186.

[13] Kendal, *op.cit.*, p. 29.

[14] Ghassemlou, A. R., *Kurdistan and the Kurds* (London: Collet's Publishers, 1965), p. 44.

[15] Hotham, David, *The Turks* (London: John Murray, 1972), p. 21.

[16] van Bruinessen, *op.cit.*, p. 279.

[17] McDowall, David, *The Kurds: A Nation Divided* (London: Minority Rights Publications, 1992), p. 37.

[18] Olson, Robert and W. F. Tucker, "The Shaikh Said Rebellion in Turkey (1925)," in *Die Welt des Islams*, vol. 18 (1978), pp. 195–211.

[19] van Bruinessen, *op.cit.*, p. 298.

[20] McDowall, *op.cit.*, p. 37.

[21] Cited in Kendal, Nizzan, "Kurdistan in Turkey," in Chaliand, Gerard, ed., p. 58.

[22] *Ibid.*, p. 65.

[23] *Ibid.*, p. 74.

[24] *Financial Times* (August 16, 1989), p. 7.

[25] *Washington Post* (August 12, 1986), p. A22.

[26] *New York Times* (May 17, 1987), p. 1.

[27] *Christian Science Monitor* (August 13, 1991), p. 4.

[28] Izady, Mehrdad, "Persian Carrot and Turkish Stick," in *Kurdish Times*, vol. III, No. 2 (Fall 1980), pp. 31–47.

[29] Human Rights Foundation of Turkey, "File of Torture: Death in Detention Places or Prisons," (Ankara: Human Rights Foundations Publications, September 1994), p. 55.

[30] Jwaideh, *op.cit.*, p. 499.

[31] van Bruinessen, *op.cit.*, p. 182.

[32] Soane, Ely Bannister, *To Mesopotamia and Kurdistan in Disguise (1907–1909)* (Holland, New York: Armorica Book Co., 1979) (reprint of 1912), p. 10.

[33] The Russians were also represented, but the Bolshevik government refused to honor the treaty and revealed its existence. The Americans, who did not participate in the talks, were offered a sphere of influence in Kurdistan and Armenia, but declined.

[34] Izady, *Concise Handbook*, pp. 59–60.

[35] McDowall, *op.cit.*, p. 36.

[36] Edmonds, Cecil J., *Kurds, Turks and Arabs: Politics and Research in North-Eastern Iraq, 1919–1925* (London: Oxford University Press, 1957), p. 123.

[37] Hay, William R., *Two Years in Kurdistan; Experiences of a Political Officer, 1918–1920* (London: Sidgwick & Jackson, Ltd., 1921), p. 35.

[38] Edmonds, *op.cit.*, p. 29.

[39] *Ibid.*, pp. 29–30.

[40] Wilson, Arnold, *Loyalties in Mesopotamia, 1914–1917* (London: Oxford University Press, 1930), p. 41. Ironically, Mahmoud's struggle with the British ultimately consolidated the latter's hold over Mosul. In 1923, the Turks, fresh from their victories in Anatolia and eyeing the unrest in northern Iraq, marched into Mosul. Their "brutal" actions in Mosul and their harsh suppression of Shaikh Said's rebellion in northern Kurdistan led the League of Nations in 1926 to assign Mosul to the British.

[41] Vanly, Ismet Sheriff, "Kurdistan in Iraq," in Chaliand, Gerard, ed., p. 149.

[42] Hazleton, Fran, "Iraq to 1963," in CARDRI (Committee against Repression and for Democratic Rights in Iraq), *Saddam's Iraq: Revolution or Reaction?* (London: Zed Books, 1986), p. 22.

[43] Farouk-Sluglett, Marion, and Peter Sluglett, *Iraq Since 1958: From Revolution to Dictatorship* (London: KPI, 1987), p. 79.

[44] Hazleton, Fran, *op.cit.*, p. 22.

[45] Schmidt, Dana Adams, *Journey Among Brave Men* (Boston: Little, Brown and Company, 1964), pp. 68, 185.

[46] Farouk-Sluglett and Sluglett, *op.cit.*, p. 84.

[47] Zaher, U., "Political Developments in Iraq, 1963–1980" in CARDRI (Committee against Repression and for Democratic Rights in Iraq), *Saddam's Iraq: Revolution or Reaction?* (London: Zed Books, 1986), pp. 30–32.

[48] The KDP remained under the control of Talabani until after 1975, when its name was appropriated by Barzani forces. Talabani then organized the Patriotic Union of Kurdistan (PUK).

[49] Ghareeb, Edmund, *The Kurdish Question in Iraq* (Syracuse N.Y.: Syracuse University Press, 1981), p. 89.

[50] McDowall, *op.cit.*, p. 92.

[51] Barzani eventually sought asylum in the US, where he died of natural causes in 1979.

[52] Vanly, *op.cit.*, p. 177.

[53] "Interview with Mr. J. Talabani," unpublished manuscript (Brooklyn: Kurdish Cultural Institute, September 1985), pp. 10–11.

[54] "Now is the Time to Strike," in *The Middle East* (April, 1988), p. 22.

[55] Izady, *Concise Handbook*, p. 56.

[56] Roosevelt, Archie Jr., "The Kurdish Republic of Mahabad," in Chaliand, Gerard, ed., p. 125.

[57] Eagleton, William, *The Kurdish Republic of 1946* (London: Oxford University Press, 1963), p. 101.

[57a] Ghassemlou, A. R., "Kurdistan in Iran" in Chaliand, p. 110.

[57b] *Ibid.*

[57c] *Ibid.*

[58] Arfa, Hassan, *The Kurds, An Historical and Political Study* (New York: Oxford University Press, 1966), p. 105.

[59] KDPI, no title, unpublished manuscript (Brooklyn: Kurdish Cultural Institute, 1987), no pagination.

[60] Amjad, Mohammed, *Iran: From Royal Dictatorship to Theocracy* (New York: Greenwood Press, 1989), p. 71.

[61] *New York Times* (March 4, 1979), Sect. 1, p. 3.

[62] *Ibid.*

[63] *Ibid.*

[64] Chaliand, Gerard, "Iranian Kurds under Ayatollah Khomeini," in Chaliand, Gerard, ed., p. 212.

[65] *New York Times* (December 4, 1979), p. 3.

[66] *New York Times*, (March 22, 1979), p. 3.

[67] McDowall, *op.cit.*, p. 73.

[68] "KDP's Qassemlu: 'The Clergy Have Confiscated the Revolution'," in *MERIP Reports* (July/August 1981), p. 18.

3

KURDISTAN AND THE KURDS

If it is justice, I have a right;
If it is force, I have force.

My friend's friend is my friend;
My enemy's enemy is my friend.
———Kurdish proverbs

TOPOGRAPHY AND CLIMATE

Kurdistan is a land of extremes: rugged and bone-dry in parts, lush and well-watered in others. Kurdistan also knows a climate of extremes: harsh snowy winters, pleasant flowery springs and scorching hot summers. Mean annual temperatures range from subarctic levels in the high mountains to subtropical in the foothills. Unlike much of the Middle East, precipitation in the form of snow and rain is bountiful in much of Kurdistan. Precipitation averages 50 to 80 inches per year in the high mountains and 20 to 40 inches in the foothills and plains, though there is very little rainfall in summer.

For all the variations of land and weather, one constant unifies the Kurdish landscape and, by implication, the Kurdish people as well: the mountains. The Kurds have a saying: "we have no friends but the mountains."[1] A nineteenth-century American traveler noted that the Kurds always established their villages on the slopes of mountains, even if that inconveniently removed them from streams and made house construction difficult. "We don't like to stray far from our mother," a Kurd told him.[2] Indeed, when Stalin forcibly moved the small Kurdish population of the Soviet Union to Kazakhstan during World War II, it is said, they found the one small set of hills in the vast Central Asian plains and settled there.

Establishing the limits of Kurdish territory is a tricky business. Not only are population figures and settlement patterns hard to come by, but the very geographic parameters of Kurdistan are subject to intense debate. Do not look to your atlas. Kurdistan has been virtually wiped from the map in the twentieth century. Only in Iran is a single, truncated province labeled Kordistan. This cartographic obliteration has its origins in politics. No country, with the partial exception of the old Soviet Union, has been keen on promoting Kurdish identity.

But if we define Kurdistan by where Kurds predominate, then the parameters might look something like the map on page 2. They are not official borders, nor even generally agreed-upon ones. Nor are they all equally valid. While the southern and eastern borders of Kurdistan are easier to demarcate, as the Zagros Mountains give way sharply to the plains, and many Kurds live on the plains as well, the northern and western limits are less distinct. There the Taurus Mountains, including Kurdistan's highest peak, 16,680-foot Mount Ararat, continue beyond the Kurdish region, and there is a large overlap with other peoples, like the Black Sea Turks and the Armenians. Perhaps it is best to think of these boundaries as an unhappy medium: Kurds would find these borders too narrow, others in the Middle East too broad.

There are good reasons for these disputes. Kurdistan is extraordinarily rich in resources. Turkish Kurdistan contains large deposits of coal as well as the headwaters of the Tigris/Euphrates river system, with all its hydro-electric and irrigation potential; Iraqi and Iranian Kurdistan contain major oil reserves, with actively exploited fields and refinery complexes. Iraqi Kurdistan, in particular, has been one of the breadbaskets of the Middle East for thousands of years.

DEMOGRAPHY

Politically, the Kurds live in the territories of at least six nation-states (not counting the European countries to which many have emigrated). From most populous to least, they are Turkey, Iran, Iraq, Syria, Azerbaijan and Armenia, with the vast majority in the first three. But establishing population figures is even trickier than demarcating geographic boundaries. None of the countries likes to count Kurds separately. The Persians call the Kurds their "Aryan brothers" while the Turkish government officially refers to them as "mountain Turks who have forgotten their language." All official population statistics on the Kurds should be taken with a grain of salt since national governments have an interest in minimizing the count.

There are roughly 25 to 30 million Kurds living in the Middle East and Europe today. They are the fourth largest population group in the Middle East, after the Arabs, the Turks and the Persians. Approximately half live in Turkey, where they constitute about 25 percent of that nation's population, or 15 million. Another 6.5 million live in Iran and about 4 million in Iraq, where they make up about 12 and 20 percent of the population respectively. The remaining Kurds are situated in Syria (about 1.25 million), the former republics of the Soviet Union (about 330,000) and Europe (approximately 500,000). Moreover, Kurdish population growth is explosive. Historian Mehrdad Izady predicts that the Kurdish population will double in the next 25 years and, if current trends continue, will outnumber the slower-growing Turkish population by the middle of the next century.

Despite archaeological evidence that Kurdistan is home to some of the world's oldest urban centers, Kurdistan today is a largely rural region. In Turkey and Iran, Kurds are far less urbanized than their fellow Turks and Persians. In Iran, for example, only about one-third of all Kurds live in towns and cities, while almost two-thirds of Persians do. In Iraq, however, the urban-rural ratio among Kurds is only slightly lower than that for Arabs. In all of Kurdistan, there is only one city with a population in excess of a million, and that is the mixed Persian-Kurdish city of Khorramshahr, in Iran. On the other hand, approximately one-third of metropolitan Istanbul's 10 million people are of Kurdish origin, making it, in effect, the largest Kurdish city in the world.

Predictably, Kurdistan's relative poverty vis-à-vis the dominant population is reflected in social indices such as infant mortality, life span and literacy. In Turkish Kurdistan, doctors are rare in the towns and virtually nonexistent in the countryside, despite modest governmental incentives to get doctors to work in underdeveloped parts of the country. In 1970, there were approximately 4.3 doctors to 10,000 inhabitants in Turkey as whole, but less than one per 10,000 in Kurdistan. And according to historian Nizzan Kendal, the discrepancy is growing, with many doctors now afraid to serve in the war-torn region.

Statistics for Iranian Kurdistan in the mid-1960s are slightly better, about two doctors per 10,000, though again large areas of the Kurdish countryside have no medical care at all. Despite the beneficial effects of their mountain homes—especially the plentiful supply of fast-moving streams as a source of drinking water and waste disposal—malaria, tuberculosis and trachoma remain prevalent. On average, Kurds live about 10 years less than their national compatriots in Turkey and Iran, about the same as the Arabs of Iraq (though infant mortality and premature deaths have skyrocketed since the imposition of sanctions after the Gulf War). As late as the 1960s, Kurdistan's overall infant mortality rate stood at an appalling 30 percent—that is, almost one out of three babies born in Kurdistan did not live to celebrate a first birthday.

Literacy rates in Kurdistan lag behind the national averages as well. While approximately 60 percent of Turks are literate, less than 30 percent of Kurds over the age of six can read or write. "Illiteracy," says Kendal, "continues to be the major curse in Turkish Kurdistan."[3] A lack of resources and governmental negligence no doubt explain the gross discrepancy, but other factors should be considered as well. According to many Kurds, schools in their region have different pedagogical emphases from those in other parts of the country. While Turkish nationalistic indoctrination is an important part of the curriculum in schools throughout the country, schools in Kurdistan emphasize both the power of the Turkish state and, by its conspicuous omission, the worthlessness of Kurdish culture.

KURDISHNESS

Before examining Kurdish society and politics, it might help to define the people themselves: their Kurdishness, so to speak. The Kurds identify themselves as a people apart, especially in relation to the Turks, Arabs and Christian minorities (Armenians, Assyrians and so on) and to a lesser extent their linguistic and ethnic cousins, the Persians. Clear and objective differences abound. The Kurds speak a different tongue from any of their neighbors (albeit a mix of dialects mutually incomprehensible from one end of Kurdistan to the other); wear different clothes; dance distinctively to their own music; and practice different social customs. One of the most apparent manifestations of this latter difference is the interaction between men and women. Gender walls in Kurdish society are not as impenetrable as in other nearby Muslim societies.

But observable cultural and social differences are not sufficient to explain the ongoing struggle between the Kurds and the governments of the various states in which they live. To get a fuller understanding of this, the reader must look up and back: to the mountain landscape and its impact on Kurdish social organization, and to the Kurds' millennia-long struggle with lowland states. Kurdish origin myths, witty and tragic in equal measure, are a good place to start. These myths involve trickery, an old standby of a logistically weaker and oppressed people, and a retreat to the highlands, as in the myth of two children earmarked for sacrifice, who find substitutes for themselves and flee to the Zagros Mountains.

To outsiders, Kurdishness has traditionally been synonymous with brigandage, and not without good reason. Often poverty-stricken, usually isolated in their mountain valleys and almost always resentful of their powerful neighbors, many Kurds viewed highway robbery and its corollary, the exaction of tribute, as a legitimate economic endeavor. European visitors to Kurdistan in the nineteenth and early twentieth centuries were at once enchanted and repelled by the seeming violence and lawlessness of the Kurdish people. Nineteenth-century romantic sensibility, no doubt particularly acute in those intrepid enough to travel to Kurdistan, led them to identify Kurds as noble savages, both tragically succumbing to and heroically resisting the very forces of modernity represented by these travelers. Ely Soane, an English traveler to Kurdistan in the early twentieth century, offers an example:

> Shedders of blood, raisers of strife, seekers after turmoil and uproar, robbers and brigands; a people all malignant and evil-doers of depraved habits, ignorant of all mercy, devoid of all humanity, scorning the garment of wisdom; but a brave race

and fearless, of a hospitality grateful to the soul, in truth and in honour unequaled . . . boasting all the goods of beauty and grace.[4]

Kurds then and now would no doubt take exception to such a pejorative description, but only to its hyperbole. The Kurds remain proud of their warrior tradition and their independence. They scoff at the idea that the numerically superior forces of whatever country they are at war with can possibly subdue their *peshmerga*. Typically, as inheritors of a pastoral tradition of nomadism, they define themselves in opposition to their agriculturalist neighbors: freer, more proud, more alive. One Kurd expressed his people's distinctiveness to this author in a handshake. "You can always tell a Kurd by the way he shakes your hand," he said. "A Turk shakes your hand like this (he shook formally, with a single outthrust palm) and a Kurd shakes it like this (he looked me directly in the eye, grabbed with both hands, and shook vigorously.)"[5]

Sentiment, history and topography have shaped Kurdish distinctiveness, but they do not explain Kurdish rebelliousness nor the forms it has historically taken. To address these critical questions, we must examine Kurdish tribalism, even today the dominant political and social organization throughout Kurdistan.

TRIBES AND TRIBAL CONFEDERATIONS

MEMBERSHIP

Kurdish secular life was once and, to a large extent, still is dominated by the tribe, though this varies from Turkey, where tribalism is largely fading, to Iraq, where it has gained a new lease on life in the safe haven. Kurdish tribes vary greatly in size, from several dozen households to great confederacies of individual tribes. Depending on their size, Kurdish tribes are divided into subunits of clan, lineage and household.

The glue that binds these social units also has several components, including lineage, geographic proximity and, in incipient form, political affiliation. These bonds sometimes compete with and sometimes complement each other. And they vary depending on the size of the social unit: lineage is most important for household and clan; lineage and geographic proximity for clans and tribes; and political affiliation for subtribes, tribes and tribal confederations. Lineages are usually based on blood and marriage ties amongst households. Clans often incorporate several related lineages, and may also include families who, while they have no actual blood ties, have nevertheless been accepted by the clans after several generations of such affiliation—so-called fictive relations. Households, lineages and clans are primarily social and economic units. Tribes and tribal confederations are more overtly political units.[6]

Kurdish tribalism is ancient, but not unchanging. While tribal histories stretch back almost as far as the origins of the Kurdish people, the configurations and structures of present-day Kurdish tribes have evolved in response to events in the region's modern history; that is, to the collapse of empires, economic transformation, state-sponsored nationalism and so forth. The evolution and survival of the tribal unit can be seen as an effective response to the cycles of political chaos, geopolitical maneuvering and state oppression that have plagued the region through much of the twentieth century. Tribalism has helped the Kurds to survive as individuals as well as to retain their sense of identity as a people.

It is important to avoid a teleological approach to the Kurdish tribe. It is neither a primitive ancestor nor the inevitable precursor of more modern polities. Tribes have their own historical trajectory and their own reasons for being. Compare, for example, the nineteenth- and twentieth-century history of Kurdish tribalism in Iraq and Turkey. In their more accessible terrain, Iraqi tribalism had been effectively eroded by the incursions of the world market and Ottoman administrative expansion and modernization. When the British took possession of Iraq following World War I, they endeavored to and succeeded in reviving the Iraqi Kurdish tribe as a way of maintaining imperial authority. Historian Wadie Jwaideh describes the process.

> The [British] political officer . . . devoted his energies to retribalising. Every man who could be labeled as a tribesman was placed under a tribal leader. . . . Petty village headmen were unearthed and discovered as leaders of long dead tribes. . . . Revenue was to be paid on the estimation of this chief. . . . Law was to be administered by this chief.

In short, says Jwaideh, the British "revival of the tribal system was . . . a retrograde movement."[7]

In Turkey, a different policy was undertaken by the new government after World War I. As both a cause and a result of the several Kurdish uprisings of the 1920s and 1930s, Ankara largely succeeded in extirpating the Kurdish tribe, except in the most remote reaches of the country. This was achieved through military means, by the execution or relocation of tribal populations and leaders. The detribalization of Turkish Kurdistan was also effected in part by state economic penetration and bureaucratic modernization. Not surprisingly, Iraqi Kurd politics are still largely tribal, whereas Turkish Kurd politics are largely electoral or revolutionary.

LEADERSHIP

Aghas (Chiefs)

Every tribe has its chief, or *agha*. He (or, very rarely, she) is virtually always a member of the most powerful and respected family in the tribe, whose name is eponymous, like the Barzanis. Traditionally, Kurdish *aghas* ruled through a combination of deference, custom and raw power. The source of deference was both personal and familial. *Aghas* with a reputation for wisdom or courage commanded their tribesmen with a sure hand. Depending on the principal economic activity of the tribe, this could mean such peaceful and administrative duties as maintaining terraces and irrigation systems, or running smuggling operations or conducting raids against other tribes, state forces, towns and trading caravans.

If the system worked effectively, it was because the *agha*'s authority was rarely challenged. Nineteenth- and twentieth-century visitors were struck by the absolute power of the *agha*. Frederick Millingen believed the *aghas* could arbitrarily order death sentences, expropriate property and torture tribesmen to exact confessions.[7a] This was true in some places, especially where central authorities backed up a loyal *agha* with imperial troops, and can be observed in remote areas of Turkey today, where certain *aghas* command the local anti-guerrilla village guards.

But in fact, the *agha*'s authority relies on custom as well. It is not an infrequent occurrence for an agha to be challenged, often from within his own family. Several things might lead to this kind of intratribal confrontation: incompetence, manipulation by state authorities seeking to undermine an overly ambitious chief or a chiefly violation of tribal custom. Historian Stephen Longrigg sums up the nature of tribal loyalty: "[N]o aspect of tribal life was, or is, more difficult to speak of precisely than that of the tribe's internal organization or solidarity, or lack of these," he writes.

> One authority is "under" another only by virtue of admired qualities, birth, age, consent; and such subjection is always unstable. The Western mind is for ever puzzled by the fragility of tribal authority, upon the skill and firmness of which everything in the tribe would seem to depend.[8]

Events of the last 50 years have had a paradoxical effect on the power and authority of the traditional Kurdish *agha*. The expansion of a bureaucratic administration and judiciary has obviously undermined that authority, as has the impact of the PKK in Turkey. In both cases, an alternative authority now exists in the Kurdish countryside to which an aggrieved tribesman can appeal his case. On the other hand, many *aghas* have adjusted to modern times. In all three countries, but especially Turkey, tribal leaders have remade themselves into politicians and administrators. "Tribal leaders are by no means reactionary or uneducated folks," notes Izady. "As the older generation passes, the new Kurdish chiefs boast as much education and worldliness as any national-level politician in a recognized state."[9]

However, generational change is not always a modernizing phenomenon. "A traditionalism in values, mentality and behavior has still not been replaced by an alternative conception of things," writes Chaliand.

Instead there has been merely a degree of adaptation to the codes of modernity; however the knowledge and use of this ritual modernity engenders no real change. The fundamental values are still those of yesterday: tactical cunning instead of political analysis, clientist maneuvering instead of political mobilization, and a few revolutionary slogans instead of a real practice.[10]

This has been especially true of Iraqi Kurdistan, where tribal leaders now command the resources of a state, including vast armies of *pesh-merga*, which they can use to maintain an extraordinary level of authority over their spheres of influence. On a visit to Iraqi Kurdistan in the summer of 1993, one Kurdish writer noted the trappings of a new dictatorship being laid over the old structures of tribal authority in both Talabani's and Barzani's zones.

Like Saddam's, life-size portraits of Barzani are everywhere in the area he controls, sometimes on the same billboards that once pictured Saddam. Like the newspapers of Saddam, Barzani's . . . carry his portrait on the front page daily. And some of the exact words used by the Iraqi media to glorify Saddam, the "great leader," the "respectful leader," the "leader with a vision," are used by Barzani's media to glorify him.[11]

This kind of power is associated with great confederations of tribes, like the Barzani or Talabani confederations of Iraq. The political leaders of these confederations, or paramount chiefs, are connected to the most powerful clans or families in Kurdistan, and these clans or families, in turn, gain their authority from their associations with powerful politicoreligious leaders, or *shaikhs*, who are usually members of the family or clans as well as descendants of the founders of these families or clans.

Shaikhs (Sheiks)

All Kurdish *shaikhs* were and are members of two Dervish orders: the more dynamic Naqshabandi or the more insular Qadiri. The dervishes are Islamic mystical, or Sufi, brotherhoods, with similarities to Catholic monastic orders and Hindu gurus. They are a relatively recent phenomenon, having emerged only in the fourteenth century. Like monks, the dervishes began as hermits, achieving mystical and ecstatic communion with God by segregating themselves from human society. As dervishes gained reputations for wisdom and holiness, they attracted disciples and followers. Gradually, some *shaikhs* began to take on charismatic powers. Claudius Rich quoted one *shaikh*'s follower:

[H]e understands everything by miracle. If you spoke to him in your own language he would understand you, though he never learnt it . . . nay, he knows even what passes in your mind; and when you have the intention of consulting him, he will answer you without your having spoke a word.[12]

The *shaikh* combines several traditional Islamic and Kurdish traits. He often claims the status of *sayyid*, or holy man, and descendent of the Prophet

Muhammed. The *shaikh* might also play the role of mullah, Islam's only cleric in the Christian sense of the word, conducting religious ceremonies and education. While in Islamic tradition most *sayyids* take vows of poverty and humility, some have become powerful regional leaders.

Shaikhs have established not only dynasties across time but networks across space. The *shaikh* often forms alliances with local chiefs or landlords, and plants his followers as *shaikhs* in other localities. The *shaikh*'s family is usually quite powerful and wealthy, although, as historian Wadie Jwaideh points out, the founding *shaikh* often maintains his vow of poverty while his descendants grow rich. That wealth then becomes both an indicator and means of power. The often extravagant lifestyle of the *shaikh*'s descendants demonstrates his power. And like Tammany politicians, the *shaikhs* offer help, in the form of land, food or jobs, to needy constituents in exchange for their support.

While several *shaikhs*, most prominently Ubaydullah, Said and Ahmed Barzani, have led mass rebellions against the state, others have allied themselves in pacts of mutual convenience with the regimes in power, delivering votes and revenues in exchange for local political authority and economic power. While *shaikhs* usually do not run for political office, other members of their families do. And in recent years, some *shaikhs* have positioned themselves as leaders of the still small, but growing, Islamist political movement in Kurdistan.

The power of the *shaikh* was demonstrated to anthropologist Martin van Bruinessen on a visit to an émigré Kurdish union meeting in Holland. Despite the fact that these were among the most leftist and class-conscious of Kurds, he says, they became extremely respectful of his opinions when they learned he was a friend of a *shaikh* from their part of Kurdistan. Still a powerful force in Kurdish society, *shaikhs* have received mixed opinions from historians and sociologists, who have contested the benevolence, honesty and even decency of the Kurdish *shaikhs*. Izady calls them "demagogic" and practitioners of "religious bigotry."[13] Van Bruinessen likens their family networks, not entirely in a pejorative sense, to the Sicilian *mafiosi*.[13a]

NONTRIBAL KURDS

It is important to remember that not all Kurds are tribesmen. Kurdish society was and is divided between those who are affiliated with ruling families and clans—usually tracing their heritage to horse-riding pastoralists or herdsmen—and the unaffiliated peasant families. Clan or tribal membership can be quite fluid. "Being tribal or non-tribal," says one anthropologist, "are not absolutes, but matters of degree, and there are continually shifts within and between these statuses."[14] Nevertheless, tribal Kurds traditionally lorded it over nontribal Kurds, exacting revenue and corvées (conscripted labor for public projects, usually roads) in exchange for protection. This was where the relative power of the *agha* came into play. If a chief commanded a large force of *peshmerga*, he could control larger territories and exact more revenue from nontribal peasant farmers and even urban merchants and craftsmen. It is not so different today, especially in Iraqi Kurdistan.

While attacks against and repression of non-Kurdish peoples, that is, Christian minorities, have attracted international attention, most of the victims of tribal depredations have been nontribal fellow Kurds. As Izady points out, "the settled Kurds suffered far more from the lack of security perpetrated by the elusive, highly mobile, and unpredictable nomads than ever did non-Kurds or travelers in transit."[15] Detribalization due to the administrative influence of government and the Kurdish diaspora in all three countries has tended to narrow the differences between Kurds and non-Kurds, as have new political affiliations and nationalist politics.

Still, the legacy of tribal hegemony over nontribal Kurds lives on in the safe haven. Many of those who have never been affiliated with tribes or have lost their affiliation live in urban areas, where they are more vulnerable to the poverty that has struck northern Iraq since UN sanctions were imposed. The tribal *peshmerga* who control the black market make sure their own are taken care of first, leaving unaffiliated Kurds to scrounge as best they can by selling household possessions.

NON-KURDISH MINORITIES

The Kurds have shared their territory for hundreds of years with several non-Muslim, non-Kurdish minorities, as well as members of the nationally dominant Turkish, Arab and Persian peoples. The non-Muslim minorities once included Jews, Armenians and Assyrians (sometimes referred to as Nestorians). Of these three groups, only the Assyrians remain in significant numbers. Most Jews of Iran and Iraq left for Israel in the 1950s, while many Turkish Jews have moved to western Turkish cities or to Israel over the past several decades. During World War I, Turkish and Kurdish forces massacred approximately 1.5 million Armenians in the first genocide of the twentieth century. Most of the rest fled to that part of Armenia within the borders of the Russian Empire (later the Armenian SSR and now the independent Republic of Armenia).

Relations between Armenians and Kurds have a long and tortured history. While the two coexisted for centuries in relative peace, Armenians were a repressed minority within Kurdistan. Essentially defenseless against armed Kurdish tribes, the Armenians were often forced to pay tribute in exchange for protection. Kurdish oppression of the Armenians was largely economic rather than religious. The Armenians, wrote Millingen, "always got the worst of it from the Koords, [though the Kurds] regard a church as sacred as a mosque. They will destroy a village, but always leave the church standing."[16] Nevertheless, much of this tribute was exacted routinely, as a form of taxation. But several forces in the nineteenth century ended this relatively peaceful, if exploitative, relationship.

Many Armenians were successful farmers, merchants and craftsmen. As land and agriculture became increasingly privatized and commercialized in the nineteenth century, Armenians were better situated to take advantage of the changes. Many became landlords, with Kurds as their tenants. This reversal of the traditional relationship bred resentment among the Kurds, exacerbated by fear. Beginning in the mid-nineteenth century, European and American Christian missionaries began to set up schools and organizations for Armenians and Assyrians. In addition, Russia, increasingly making its power felt in the region, openly expressed its solidarity with its Christian brethren in Kurdistan. Kurds became increasingly fearful that Russia, the missionaries and the local Christians would form an unholy alliance to establish an independent Christian Armenia in Kurdistan.

The Kurds were not alone in these fears. By the late nineteenth century, the sultan was sufficiently concerned to establish the Hamidiye, a Cossack-like force intended to defend the Ottoman frontier against Russia and Persia, but also aimed at preventing a breakaway Armenian Republic. During the 1890s, the Hamidiye, instigated by the sultan, massacred tens of thousands of Armenians. A generation later, during World War I, the Hamidiye and other Kurdish forces readily participated in the genocide of the Armenians, many out of a fear of a Russian-Armenian alliance, others for more venal reasons, such as seizing Armenian property. Today, in Armenia, the tables are turned, as Armenians have evicted thousands of Kurds from a strategic corridor connecting two Armenian population centers.

The main minority group in Iraqi Kurdistan has been the Assyrians. During the years of the mandate, the British used Assyrian levied troops to police the Kurds. This use of Assyrian forces created permanent antagonism between the two groups. As Longrigg writes, "[the Assyrians'] retention as British-administered imperial troops . . . and their repeated use against the Kurds were all, in retrospect, to be regretted."[17] Writing in 1953, Longrigg did not know how prophetic his words would be. Six years later, Iraqi leader Abd al-Karim Qasim, facing an uprising of Assyrians, turned the Kurds loose on them. Fueled by the Mandate-bred animosities, the Kurds committed atrocities against the Assyrians so great that Qasim later admitted they exceeded even those of the Jews against the Palestinians, a rather remarkable statement for an Arab nationalist. In recent years, divisions seem to have healed. Under the rules of the Kurdish provisional government, Assyrians were guaranteed at least five seats in the parliament, giving them representation far in excess of their actual numbers.

TRIBAL FUNCTIONS

Political

When examining the politics of Kurdish tribes, a general rule of thumb should be kept in mind: relationships between people, the very anchors of tribal life, are frequently more important than ideology. Tribal culture is intensely personal, and its cohesion is based on almost viscerally felt loyalties as much as on any perceived commonalty of real interests and certainly on more than shared ideology. To that end, the traditional tribal leader maintained an open court, or *diwan*, where administrative decisions were made and where justice was meted out face to face, between tribesmen and chief. Depending on the wealth and size of the tribe, the *diwan* could be housed in buildings ranging from an elaborate edifice to a rude hut.

The *agha*'s political and judicial authority, however, was not absolute. Feuding among tribesmen and between tribes was a frequent occurrence of Kurdish life, and a test of an *agha*'s authority and the political cohesion of the tribe. These feuds were sometimes endogamous—often involving sexual liaisons and elopements—or instigated by outside authorities. British engineer A. M. Hamilton, assigned during the mandate to build a road through the Rowanduz Gorge of Iraq, one of the most inaccessible regions of Kurdistan, writes of a feud set off by British favoritism toward one tribal family over another. It lasted over ten years, until satisfaction was reached with the bloody assassination of one of the *aghas*. In this particular case, nobody—not the *aghas*, the local *shaikh*, or the British—could resolve the conflict.[18]

The relevance of feuding can be seen in the recent history of northern Iraq, where politics are still largely tribal. During the final and intense stages of the 1961–1975 war between the Kurds and Baghdad, numerous *aghas* formed units of *jash* and supported the government, rather than let Barzani win control of Kurdistan. "The very fact that a certain chieftain participated in the nationalist [Barzani-led] movement," says van Bruinessen,

> was often sufficient reason for his rivals to oppose it, and most commoners followed their chieftains without question. . . . Whatever the ideology embraced, in tribal feuds they perceived the machinations of their ideological enemies.[19]

Moreover, loyalty to the *agha*, he noted, was strongest not among the most backward and oppressed Kurdish peasants but among the better-off farmers and shopkeepers who, more often than not, are direct members of the *agha*'s lineage. This is not mere traditionalism, but often reflects the continuing usefulness of the tribal political order. For example, many landowning tribesmen still register their lands in the *agha*'s name. While this is done for very practical reasons—to avoid taxes and military conscription—it points up how the *agha* makes himself useful as a bulwark against a hostile government. Not only does this maintain traditional loyalties, but it also fills the *agha*'s coffers, since the taxes not surrendered to the government are given to him. What van Bruinessen detected in the 1970s applies equally in the safe haven today, where a nascent attempt at democracy has crashed on the rocks of tribal loyalties. Democratic politics, ideological pronouncements and the trappings of modern life have altered or disguised the underlying tribal order, but they have not replaced it.

In Turkey and to a lesser extent Iran, recent tribal history has taken a different course. In both countries, the government's systematic destruction of tribal hierarchies and the vast out-migration of Kurds to urban centers have conspired to undermine the traditional authority of the *agha* and *shaikh*, and the political cohesion of the tribe itself. In Iran, this political vacuum was filled, in the aftermath of the Iranian Revolution, by radicalized students, workers and peasants, many returning from the revolutionary front in Iranian cities, who challenged the authority of the *aghas* and seized their land.

The near-total destruction of the tribal structure in much of Turkish Kurdistan occurred before World War II. By eliminating traditional structures of resistance, the government created a vacuum that inevitably would be filled, given ongoing Turkish repression and the deep historical roots of Kurdish resistance. Given the severe limitations placed on Kurdish parliamentary politicians, the PKK has become the preeminent organization for the expression of Kurdish resentment of and resistance to state authority. With its revolutionary discipline and nontribal structure, it is a far more effective threat to the state than the *aghas* ever were, regardless of how well-armed and recalcitrant they might have been.

In recent years, the Turkish government, as did the British long before, has been trying to revive a state-controlled facsimile of the older tribal structure as a counterforce to the PKK. But as van Bruinessen points out, sponsoring compliant tribal leaders is very different from fostering a compliant, state-supporting, tribal system. The tribal leaders' authority over tribesmen was and is based in part on their credibility as opponents of the state. The government and military may offer *aghas* power in return for compliance, but cannot give them tribal authority. Thus, old patterns reemerge in new forms. Traditionally, tribesmen might challenge the authority of the *agha* if he failed, because of fear, or more likely co-optation, to maintain the tribe's interests in the face of state power. In past centuries, tribesmen might turn to another member of the *agha*'s family, to a nearby tribe, or to a higher authority such as a *shaikh*. Today, the PKK disciplines *aghas*. "Some areas [in Turkey] are still tribal and controlled by chiefs," said a spokesperson for the PKK. "The PKK is asking chiefs to treat their people better or else face the consequences. There is a lot of soul-searching in every village."[20]

Economic

The traditional economy of Kurdistan, at least since the collapse of the trans-Asian trade routes in the fifteenth and sixteenth centuries, rested on three pillars: farming, herding and activities we might label brigandage: highway robbery, smuggling and imposition of excise fees on goods passing through Kurdistan. Farming, occupying the bulk of the population of Kurdistan, was the province of tribal and nontribal Kurdish peasants and non-Kurdish peasants, including Armenians and other Christian minorities, while herding was conducted by tribesmen. There were also small urban economies in Kurdistan's scattered towns and cities; most of the traders and merchants there were non-Kurdish minorities, largely Armenians and Jews.

The economic structure of Kurdistan's farming regions varied from place to place. In some areas, feudal relations dominated, particularly in the emirates. Peasant farmers worked land controlled by powerful lords. Sometimes these were urban merchants who had invested in land; sometimes they were rural *aghas*. In these areas, Kurds shared their labor in two ways with the lord: a portion of the crops, and a corvée on their labor. In other farming areas and pastoral regions, tribal relations dominated. Here, land was owned collectively by the community. The only authority, the *agha*, distributed tribal pasturage and fields, as well as allotments of water from irrigation systems. He also managed communal enterprises such as terrace maintenance and irrigation projects, though custom usually dictated the amount of labor each Kurd committed to collective projects.

Brigandage was entirely a tribal affair. Some engaged in it much of the time, others only occasionally. "The Koordish shepherd," wrote Millingen, "is a suspicious and dangerous individual, it being difficult to say whether he is more of a shepherd than a robber."[21] During the nineteenth century, as the Ottoman and Persian empires grew more chaotic and emirates were abolished, violence and lawlessness increased. "The Kurds' pastimes are not many in number," wrote a British administrator in 1921:

> First and foremost comes highway robbery. In Turkish times every young *agha* would maintain a body of "Khubzas" or armed retainers, who lived in his house and fed at his table. When he was not engaged in fighting his neighbour . . . he would send his men out to watch one of the main roads. They would pounce on the first respectable caravan that came along (poor people with only one or two donkeys were not usually molested) and carry off the spoil to their master, who would divide it up, keeping the lion's share for himself.[22]

The small volume of trade within and through Kurdistan, however, limited this activity that had done so much to brand the image of the wild and lawless Kurd into the Western mind. In fact, tribal booty was usually gathered more prosaically, if no less ruthlessly, by taxes and raids on local nontribal peasants, Kurd or non-Kurd. "Here [near Diyarbakir] the people are poor and oppressed, God only knows how we live," an Armenian peasant told Millingen.

> If we were to cultivate orchards and to plant trees, do you think that we should ever eat their fruits or enjoy their shade? No sooner do you plant a tree here than some Koord or other comes and cuts it down. It is already a hard task for our people to preserve their crops and to gather them in. The Koords are the curse of the country.[22a]

Kurdistan, of course, is not and probably never will be at the center of the world market. Indeed, the Middle East as a whole has not been so since at least the sixteenth century. Moreover, since much of Kurdistan has been and continues to be a kind of internal colony within Iran, Iraq and especially Turkey, its economic transformation has placed particularly harsh burdens on the inhabitants of the region. Not surprisingly, Kurdistan continues to lag behind other parts of the countries to which it belongs, and to a degree largely determined by the intensity of the internal colonialism it has experienced.

For the most part, Kurdistan did not develop an indigenous mercantile or industrial bourgeoisie or proletariat, in the classical Marxist sense, with a "historical mission" to destroy tribal and feudal economic structure—at least not until recently, and then only as an outgrowth of the main thrust of national economic development. But even this national development has not followed traditional Western patterns. In all three countries, economic transformation and development have been largely as a result of statist measures, with political as well as economic agendas. The Ottoman land privatization law of 1858 was enacted as much to extend administrative control as to develop the empire economically. That is to say, it was intended to break up the tribes of the empire, both Kurdish and non-Kurdish, by undermining their economic bases of communal land and by collecting taxes from individual landholders, thus bypassing the *aghas*.

The first part of the plan failed and the second part was jettisoned. The *aghas*, *shaikhs* and a new class of urban and usually non-Kurdish landholders, using impoverished rural *aghas* as their local overseers, had the capital and the business acumen to take advantage of this law and subsequent ones. The process could be both corrupt and brutal. Landlords used legal subterfuge and gangs of hired thugs, often former *peshmerga*, to throw small peasants off the land or to exact higher rents. By the early twentieth century, most Kurdish tribesmen, especially in the richer and more accessible foothills and plains, were either renting or sharecropping, often on land belonging to *aghas*.

Since World War II, the process has accelerated with the impact of agricultural mechanization and export crop production which, because they are affordable only by wealthier landholders, have reduced even more Kurdish farmers to sharecropping and rural proletarian status or forced them to move to the cities where they are transformed into an urban proletariat and underclass. In addition, the development of a transportation infrastructure has made food cheaper, making small peasant farming, based on a mix of subsistence crops and cash crops for taxes and consumer goods, untenable.

The impact on tribal cohesion and Kurdish society generally has been mixed. On the one hand, there is no doubt that the impact of economic transformation has been largely corrosive, for several reasons: a reduction of the communal features of the tribal economy; an increased economic stratification; and a new class of detached (geographically or by class) landlords, with the subsequent diminution of their ability, desire or need to lead their former followers.

Yet older patterns remain. "Agricultural land has become fully private property," van Bruinessen notes of Kurdistan in the 1980s, "but not just anyone can buy it. [For instance] grazing grounds around the village are considered communal property."[23] In addition, Kurdish tenants or share-croppers have often rebelled in recent decades against not just their government but their local landlords, even if they are traditional *aghas* or *shaikhs*. What often appear to be straightforward uprisings of Kurds against their government are often, in fact, multidimensional struggles. During the Kurdish-Iraqi War of the 1960s and 1970s, there were frequent cases where peasants sided with the government against Kurdish nationalist landlords. And, clearly, some of the PKK's popular support is based not on its nationalist agenda but on its program of land reform.

Indeed, the economic resilience of tribal structures is often demon-strated in quiet ways. "Capitalism is often said to be the most powerful agent in breaking up such ties of loyalty," notes van Bruinessen,

> but it certainly does not do so immediately. On the other hand, the existence of primordial loyalties and their apparent ubiquity do not preclude the functioning of other loyalties. Conversely, when new loyalties such as those of . . . class emerge, the primordial ones do not suddenly cease to function. It often happens that these different loyalties interact with and mutually modify each other. The concrete situation then defines which will be force-fully asserted.[24]

Social

Secular By nature, tribalism is socially conservative. According to anthro-pologist Thomas Bois, the traditional Kurdish tribesman lived in a small, inwardly oriented, outwardly defensive culture. Tribal life was rooted in traditional behavior, traditional relationships, traditional economic activity and traditional obligations between members. Its cohesion was maintained internally by these traditions and externally by a sense of superiority over other tribes and by a hostility to outside authority, especially state authority.

At the center of traditional Kurdish social life and the heart of political activity was the *diwan*. Most *diwans* included guest-houses, and it was the exclusive prerogative of the *agha* to entertain visitors to the region. In the pretelecommunications age, travelers were the main source of information, and this enhanced the *agha*'s role as the link to the outside world. As one anthropologist noted, "the *agha* thus monopolized social life in the village. Common villagers, for instance, were not allowed to lodge guests in their own houses, but had to bring them to the guest-house, so that the *agha* kept close control of what was going on."[25]

Several factors have diminished the social isolation and cohesion of the Kurdish tribe in recent decades: the spread of primary and secondary education, literacy, modern transport and telecommunications (including, in Turkey, the semi-underground market in Kurdish-language music cassettes), increasing urbanization and mass emigration to major domestic cities and Europe. Each of these factors has increasingly connected Kurds to both the national culture and the international marketplace of goods and ideas.

Sacred   For reasons fair and unfair, Kurds have earned a reputation in the pious Middle East as somehow less devoted to Islam. Kurds are devout Muslims in the same measure that other Sunni populations are. That is to say, the vast majority of Kurds are faithful to the principles of Islam, but there exists a minority of westernized, urban Kurds for whom Islam is an identity and a moral code, more than a way of life.

The Kurds' reputation for religious laxity, however, has some truth to it. Because of Kurdish customs that derive from their traditional nomadic way of life and its constraints, Kurds have been less able and hence less prone to follow all the niceties of the Islamic faith. Situated in remote areas, the Kurds have had less access to mosque life and the teachings of *imams* and *mullahs*. Kurds are often lax about circumcision (many Kurds are forcibly circumcised when conscripted into national armies) and the veil. In addition, many Kurds, perhaps as many as 20 percent, do not practice traditional Sunni Islam. They belong to Shiite-like sects that Muslims, both Kurdish and non-Kurdish, deem heretical. Because followers of Alevism, Yezidism and Yarsanism were historically persecuted, they developed secretive rituals that only heightened the suspicions of orthodox Muslims. Since many of these rituals involved mixed-sex gatherings, they have been widely considered orgiastic and satanic.[26]

These "heresies" and the Kurdish laxity in following Muslim ritual are, however, more symptoms than causes of Kurdish religious dissent and heterodoxy. History, rather than ritual, distinguishes the Kurds from their Islamic neighbors. Kurds, of course, have an ancient history of resistance to outside authority, and outside authority has usually been Islamic, whether imperial, military or theocratic. In short, the political content of Islam has often been modified to fit the requirements of tribal society, and is conceptualized in opposition to, rather than in support of, Islamic state power.

Even the secularist Kemal Ataturk, however, found it necessary to appeal to Islamic brotherhood to rally the Kurds to the cause of driving foreign forces from Anatolia after World War I (the occupying forces were Christians: the British and the Greeks). Ironically, Ataturk's separation of church and state in the early 1920s, when he ended the Ottoman caliphate, sparked protests and rebellions by Kurds who felt the caliphate was their guarantee of equality as Muslims within the Ottoman Empire. More recently, the post-Revolution uprising in Iranian Kurdistan in 1979 and 1980 was caused, in part, by the efforts of the ayatollah to impose a Shiite orthodoxy on the Sunni Kurd minority, fitting into the old pattern of autocracy in an Islamic guise. Not surprisingly, Kurds have asserted their distinctive (for Iran) Sunnism as a political vehicle for Kurdish nationalism. "We accept Khomeini, and we support him," a rural Kurd told the *New York Times*, "but we're worried because he always keeps referring to Iran as a Shiite nation, and never speaks about the Sunnis."[27]

NEW AFFILIATIONS/NEW IDENTITIES

ORGANIZATIONS/PARTIES

Like the old academic saw about the rise of the middle class (open any textbook on the history of the modern age and one can find a reference to it), detribalization has been an ongoing process in late nineteenth and twentieth century Kurdistan. There is, of course, no single moment when one can declare this region or that nation of Kurdistan officially detribalized. The resilience of tribalism is found not only in continuing village tradition, but in more modern political organizations as well.

Aghas or their university-educated sons have frequently run for office in all three countries under many party labels, thus continuing their leadership roles within the context of electoral politics, through the distribution of patronage. Sometimes an *agha* will actually run various candidates under different party labels in order to assure representation. *Shaikh*-led tribal confederations have also allied themselves with political parties or vice versa. In the 1960s in Turkey, for example, virtually every party, even the antireligious and antilandlord Republican Party sought alliances with *shaikhs* in order to gain votes.

Traditionally, however, Kurdish politics have not revolved around parties or political programs. The Kurds' primary political allegiance, of course, was to the tribe, and the rebellions of the nineteenth century were largely reactions to initiatives and encroachments of the central administrations. In the twentieth century, however, political parties have vied, usually ineffectively, with traditional social groupings for the allegiance of the Kurdish people.

Turkey

The history of twentieth-century Kurdish political organizations in Turkey, which promoted some form of self-determination, bears a remarkable resemblance to that of their Arab counterparts. Both were formed out of confrontations with Ottoman power and misrule, both emerged among the educated, urban and westernized elite, often the sons and heirs of tribal chiefs and *shaikhs*, and both focused initially on educational and literary expression. In April 1898, the first Kurdish publication, actually a bilingual Turkish/Kurdish journal, was published in Constantinople. Other organizations followed, such as the Kurdish Committee for Diffusion of Learning in 1908.

These organizations did not exist in a vacuum. Not only were the Arabs and the Kurds forming new political affiliations; the Turks were too. In 1908, the Young Turks, a nationalist organization of military men, intellectuals and others, seized power in Constantinople. Despite, or perhaps because of, the fact that the Young Turks and the Kurdish groups advocated the same modernizing, nationalist agenda, they almost immediately clashed. In command of the state, the Young Turks easily crushed the fledgling Kurdish student, worker and intellectual organizations. "Generally speaking," says Kendal, "this pre-1914 period was a short-lived political apprenticeship for an emerging Kurdish intelligentsia which was only just beginning to feel its way. This hard-won potential was to be largely dissipated by the outbreak of war."[28]

There is much truth to this observation, especially in the choice of the word "dissipated." While wartime exigencies allowed the Turkish government to destroy Kurdish political organizations, much of the disaster that befell Kurdish nationalism was of the Kurds' own making. Divisions between urban nationalists and traditional tribal leaders enfeebled the Kurds. In this regard, the story of the Kurdish Hamidiye is revealing. Banned and then resurrected by the Young Turks before World War I, the Hamidiye fought for the Turkish government during the war. But some Hamidiye leaders also continued their depredations against Armenians, rival Kurdish tribes, and nontribal Kurds. When the Hamidiye was dissolved by Ataturk in the 1920s, some of its more forward-looking officers formed the clandestine Azadi, or Freedom Party. Thus from the Hamidiye emerged the first modern Kurdish political party—which did not put an end to the continual intra- and interethnic rivalries that have plagued Kurdistan for centuries.

Kurdish envoys to the various post–World War I peace conferences, where the fate of the former Ottoman lands was being decided, came with mixed messages and even bickered amongst themselves, tribe against tribe and urban nationalist against rural traditionalist. Traditional tribal leaders maintained allegiance to the defeated government in Constantinople, while Kurdish nationalists pushed for a separate Kurdish homeland. The Allies listened to neither, splitting Ottoman Kurdistan down the middle, part to Turkey and part to the British mandate of Iraq.[29] Kurdish disunity, along with Allied double-dealing, certainly played a part. While Arabs, too, were disappointed at first, Iraqi Arabs achieved nominal sovereignty 12 years after the Sèvres Treaty of 1920.

Turkish hypernationalism and the crushing military defeats of Kurdish insurrections during the interwar period prevented the formation of explic- itly Kurdish political organizations until well after World War II. The volatile political climate in Turkey during the 1960s and 1970s provided both an opportunity for and a challenge to Kurdish political organizing. On the one hand, leftist political parties such as the Turkish Workers' Party, which the PKK considers one of its forebearers, advocated a militant resistance to Turkish authority in Kurdistan. It received widespread support in the Kurdish countryside and the emerging communities of the Kurdish diaspora in western Turkish cities, until it was outlawed and its leader, Deniz Gezmis, assassinated following the military coup of 1970.

On the other hand, according to Chaliand, democratic politics in Turkish Kurdistan has undergone a dramatic change since the 1970s. Appealing to petit bourgeois concerns of richer peasants, tribal politicians have tried to work within the system by seeking piecemeal reforms, almost all of which have come to naught given the reality of Turkish politics. Parliamentary reform has been almost nonexistent in terms of relieving political oppression and economic hardship in the Kurdish countryside. Not only are most Turkish parties opposed to serious reform, but the military often subverts the intent of reforms even while ostensibly carrying them out. By the 1980s, the vast majority of the Turkish Kurds, especially the most economically marginalized, had become alienated from the electoral process, either becoming apathetic or turning to the radical program and ideas of the PKK.

The PKK is something new under the Kurdish political sun. It was founded by Abdullah Ocalan in 1978 near the tail end of the violent left-right confrontations that had characterized the Turkish political envi- ronment for over two decades. Born to a peasant family in 1948, Ocalan, affectionately known to his followers by his Kurdish diminutive Apo, entered Ankara University and embarked on two related careers in the early 1970s: political science and political activism. Jailed and tortured for the latter, he was released after seven months in 1973, then left for Kurdistan in 1975. For three years, according to a PKK-authorized biography, Ocalan and his colleagues "traveled to every corner of Turkish occupied Kurdistan in an intense effort to inform and enlighten the Kurdish people."[30]

Reflecting the university background of its founders, the organization had an ambitious and revolutionary two-stage program: the establishment of an independent Kurdistan, and the building of a "democratic and socialist" society. Support for the revolutionary organization has clearly grown over the years. But what is the source of this support? Are the organization and its shifting agenda positively embraced by the Kurdish peasants and workers, as PKK communiqués insist? Or does it gain adherents through terror, as the government claims? Or, as much of the international press reports, does its support simply come from Kurds unfamiliar with or even opposed to its radical agenda, who see it as the only alternative to ineffective parliamentary politics and their only protection from Turkish military oppression?

A Kurdish general in the Turkish military told *Newsweek* in 1987 that "only a tiny minority of mountain Turks [it was forbidden by law to refer to them as Kurds] help the terrorists, maybe 2 or 3 percent."[31] The PKK naturally disagrees with this assessment. Increasingly, villagers view the organization, argue PKK press releases, as their only protection from the brutal campaign conducted against the civilian population by the military. The PKK's consistent line on popular support is that its guerrillas simply could not survive and conduct their escalating campaign against the massive military presence of the Turks without widespread civilian support.

Exiled Kurdish author Kamal Merawdli offers a useful perspective on trends in PKK support in the late 1980s. The authorities, he wrote, "say they are fighting just a small group of terrorists, but their plan is to suppress a whole people. The more there is oppression, the more there is national consciousness and hate." Xulum agrees. PKK members and supporters, he says, are "injured souls who are filled with vengeance and want a way to get even." The organization merely tries to "channel that anger" into effective resistance. Many, particularly those in the cities, he adds, are "uprooted and disoriented." The PKK offers them services and acts as a support group.[32] And in turn, he says, they support the PKK.

Moreover, the organization rejects forming alliances with traditional leaders, and openly states its goal of replacing them with a democratically constituted political system. PKK leaders say they will avoid the traditional trap of Kurdish politics, in which traditional leaders remake themselves as electoral politicians, through revolutionary education of the Kurdish people and the creation of a cadre of future leaders with no ties to the feudal past. Interestingly, however, PKK guerrillas interviewed by journalist Aliza Marcus demonstrate a very traditional allegiance to Ocalan. Compare a statement made by a Kurdish tribesman to the English trader Claudius Rich in the mid-nineteenth century (on page 82 above) with that made to Marcus in 1994:

Can you imagine? He [Ocalan] reads everything. He takes such an interest in all of us. All of us dream of meeting him. He is so brave. With our blood and souls, we are with you Apo [Ocalan].[33]

Finally, a little-studied and little-known political phenomenon has occurred in recent years in Turkish Kurdistan: the rise of Islamist politics. Like their Turkish neighbors, some of Kurdistan's poorest citizens have begun supporting the Islamist Welfare Party, which garnered twenty percent of the vote in the most recent parliamentary elections in Turkey. In addition, several *shaikhs* have arisen as leaders of this movement, capitalizing on their traditional religiopolitical leadership position.

Iraq

As subjects of the Ottoman Empire, Iraqi Kurds participated in the pre–World War I nationalist organizations. However, their distance from the Ottoman centers of power in western Anatolia and the presence of the British during the war affected their subsequent loyalties and ambitions. By maintaining constant wartime contacts with tribal leaders, the British gained the support of the Kurds against Constantinople. But the Kurds expected the *quid pro quo* of postwar sovereignty. Despite their assurances in the Treaty of Sèvres, the British had little intention of granting self-rule to the Kurds, especially since their territory contained critical oil reserves.

Instead, the successful British efforts in the mandate era to resurrect the tribal confederation as the governing political structure of Iraqi Kurdistan have helped to impede all subsequent efforts to achieve Kurdish national unity in the country. The tribal confederations, particularly that of the Barzani clan, have maintained their hold on the Kurdish population through traditional means of tribal loyalties and coercion, and by harnessing and directing the powerful nationalist sentiment of the Iraqi Kurdish people.

This political atavism has been strengthened since the 1960s by the oppressiveness of the Baath government. While the Kurds of Turkey found a degree of political breathing space in the turmoil of Turkish politics of the 1960s and 1970s, permitting the formation of parliamentary parties and later the turn to a revolutionary organization, the totalitarianism of the Baghdad regime allowed no such alternative to the tribal confederations. For the Iraqi Kurds, the tribal confederations remained the only means of political self-expression.

There are several reasons for this. Hierarchical and authoritarian as they may be, the confederations are not entirely undemocratic. In fact, they utilize older tribal forms of democracy, soliciting information from local tribal leaders and attempting to influence Kurdish public opinion through them. In the process of this give-and-take, the party is partially legitimized as it passes through this traditional leadership. "The modern leaders therefore must gain information and support from the traditional tribal leaders," notes Izady, "in order to survive and be able to speak for some portion of the common Kurdish citizenry."[34] This is true, he says, even of leftist parties that publicly denounce tribal leaders as "feudal" and "reactionary."

The process works, but at a tremendous cost. Traditional tribal politics, says Izady, encourage "conservatism, nepotism, sectarianism, and provincialism," though each of these aspects is more marked in one party or the other.[35] Worse still, as far as Kurdish nationalists are concerned, the leaders' behavior is often detrimental to their own cause. The blunders of PUK and KDP leaders, say critics, are too many and too profound to be attributable to mere incompetence, though by all accounts there has been plenty of that. The problem, they say, is not one of ability, but of mentality. As the history of the safe haven illustrates, both Barzani and Talabani want an independent state of Kurdistan, but they want it on their own terms. That is to say, they expect it to be built on traditional tribal structures and ruled paternalistically rather than democratically.

Iran

The single most important nontribal political organization in Iranian Kurdistan, and the oldest existing Kurdish political party, is the Kurdish Democratic Party of Iran (KDPI). Founded in 1945, it was the ruling party of the Kurdish Republic of Mahabad. The KDPI has frequently found itself forced into unwanted alliances with its younger but more powerful counterpart, the KDP of Iraq. These alliances have been due to internal and external factors. First, until the post-shah period in Iranian history, the KDPI faced serious opposition from tribal leaders within Iranian Kurdistan who remained opposed to its agenda of economic and political democratization. Second, in the government of the shah, the KDPI faced a determined, ruthless and extremely well-armed adversary, capable of preventing or overcoming the kind of armed resistance so prevalent in Iraq. Moreover, in Izady's estimation, Tehran's "carrot" approach, under both shah and ayatollah, has been more successful than Ankara's "stick" in avoiding the kind of alienation and oppressiveness that led to the formation of a revolutionary organization like the PKK.

Only twice, during the Mossadegh period of the early 1950s and the immediate postrevolutionary years of 1979 and 1980, both interregnums between powerful regimes, has the KDPI had the manuevering room to establish its leadership in Kurdistan. But the fall of Mossadegh in 1953 ruled out the possibility of Kurdish parliamentary politics and the subsequent crackdown on Kurdish nationalism forced the KDPI into an alliance with the KDP.

After the revolution, the KDPI leadership split on the question of supporting or opposing the new government in Tehran. Most sided with party leader Ghassemlou in his militant opposition to the Ayatollah. But subsequent Iranian military offensives during the early years of the Iran-Iraq War forced the KDPI again into an unwanted and subordinate relationship with Iraqi Kurds, this time Talabani's PUK. Distrust between the two was rife, support was not forthcoming from the PUK and the KDPI was effectively broken up by the Iranian military in 1984. While the KDPI numbered as many 12,000 during the revolutionary upheaval of 1979, its current membership is measured in the hundreds, and its dependence on the Iraqi Kurds almost total. Despite this continued dependence, the KDPI remains a different kind of party, more urbanized, more elitist and with weaker tribal affiliations.

Another organization, the Komala, or Organization of Revolutionary Toilers of Iranian Kurdistan (no relation to the Komala of the Mahabad era), was established clandestinely in 1969, but emerged after the revolution. It was largely the Komala, an organization of Marxist- and Maoist-oriented students and young workers, that organized the peasantry in 1979 against their Kurdish landlords. In 1983, the Komala joined with like-minded Iranian organizations to form the Communist Party of Iran. When Komala refused to stop calling the KDPI a "class enemy," the KDPI declared war on it, and throughout the late years of the Iran-Iraq War there were numerous armed clashes between the two groups.

REFUGEES

No aspect of the Kurdish struggle has gained more international attention than the massive flight of refugees to Turkey in the wake of the post–Gulf War Kurdish uprising in the spring of 1991. Despite the media play this event received—*Newsweek, Time, The Economist, Paris-Match* and other international news magazines featured the Kurds on their covers—the 400,000 refugees clinging to snowy mountainsides on the Turkish-Iraqi border were but the tip of the iceberg. Not only was that number dwarfed by the nearly one million who fled to Iran, but much of the media's coverage failed to note the long history of Kurdish refugeeism.

Excluding Ottoman and Persian efforts before World War I, including Shah Ismail's sixteenth-century removal of whole tribal confederations to Khurasan in northeastern Iran (which created the largest rural enclave of Kurds in the Middle East outside Kurdistan), large-scale forced relocation of Kurds goes back to the Turkish government's crushing of Kurdish uprisings in the interwar period. In fact, most Kurdish refugees have owed their status to state-sponsored and state-enforced relocation. In this, Turkey and Iraq have taken the lead.

Following the collapse of the Iraqi Kurdish rebellion in 1975, the Iraqi government relocated tens of thousands of Kurds, both from their rural enclaves in the Zagros Mountains and from around the strategic oil-refining city of Kirkuk. While the aims of the government's relocation program will be discussed more thoroughly in Chapter Four, the main intention was clearly to break the back of Kurdish resistance and prevent future uprisings. A *cordon sanitaire* was established along the Iranian border and around Kirkuk, and at least 200,000 Kurds were removed to settlements surrounded by barbed wire and armed guards. On the effects and conditions of the relocation programs of the 1970s, historians Marion Farouk-Sluglett and Peter Sluglett write:

> Apart from the fact that very few of the deportees would have spoken Arabic, they were often intimidated by the flat and desolate landscape of the Arab South, and disoriented by the destruction of their communities and the disruption of their traditional way of life. Thus, as the regime must have intended, the mere threat of deportation could be used as a powerful weapon of control in the Kurdish area.[36]

Eventually, many of these refugees filtered back to Kurdistan, especially during the Iran-Iraq War, when a combination of circumstances, including a renewed rebellion in Kurdistan and the government's preoccupation with the war, diverted its attention from the Kurds. But in the aftermath of the Iran-Iraq War, the Baath government renewed its relocation efforts, though this time with the use of chemical weapons, under the operational rubric, *anfal*. In contrast to the 1970s, approximately 100,000 Kurds escaped to Turkey and Iran, where they found themselves crowded into refugee camps.

In Iran, the government at first welcomed the refugees, but then, citing an early cold snap and logistical problems, closed its border in mid-October. In Turkey, things were more complicated. At first, the Iraqi soldiers pursued the refugees, warning Turkish Kurds and officials not to interfere. Within two days, however, the Turkish government asserted its sovereignty and demanded the Iraqis leave. Then the Turkish army stripped all able-bodied refugees of their arms and interrogated them to make sure there were no PKK among them. The Turkish government was caught in a dilemma. For the sake of public opinion among Turkey's allies in the West, Prime Minister Turgut Ozal wanted to appear the humanitarian. But he also feared the rebellious Iraqi Kurds might "infect" his own Kurdish population with the wrong ideas. Eventually, the government arrived at a compromise solution. The refugees would be kept in armed camps in isolated areas and "policed like POWs."

Journalists, human rights organizations and other obsevers were kept out. Fearful of drawing any international attention to the Kurds generally, the Turks tried to cover up evidence of chemical attacks, listing the symptoms under headings such as "pneumonia," "exhaustion" and "injuries due to sudden flight." Eventually, the refugees returned after the Iraqi government, convinced of *anfal*'s success, issued a general amnesty to Kurds on September 6, 1988. Refugees were given until October 9 to return to Iraq. After that, they would be arrested and dealt with in ways unmentioned by the government's decree. While they could return to Iraq, many areas of Kurdistan remained off-limits.

Less than three years later, another Baghdad-initiated war, this time against Kuwait and then a UN coalition of 27 nations led by the United States, set the stage for another Kurdish uprising and, in its defeat, another refugee crisis. In late March of 1991, hundreds of thousands of Kurds fled from a regrouped Iraqi military. "It is as though all of northern Iraq has gotten up and walked," one diplomat on the scene reported.[37] Not quite half of Iraqi Kurdistan, some 1.7 million people, found themselves on the mountainous borders of Iraq, over a million on the Iran side and about half that number in Turkey.

Iran permitted the refugees to move to warmer and better-equipped lowland camps, but the Turkish government, fearing infiltration by PKK guerrillas posing as refugees, kept the Kurds isolated on windswept mountainsides. Food, medicine and shelter were in short supply. Some 1,000 people were dying daily, mostly the very old, the very young and urban Kurds unable to stand the unfamiliar exposure to harsh cold. "I was in Nam," said an American medic on the scene, "but I never saw anything like this." Iraq made overtures to the Kurds, offering amnesty to all Kurds who had fled the country. Nevertheless, either because of suspicion of Saddam Hussein or because of their leaders' orders, the Kurds largely stayed put. And as television footage broadcast the suffering to the international community, both Turkey and the Coalition were forced to act, though only after days of tragic hesitation.[38]

The delay was due, in part, to Turkish politics. While the allies requested that Turkey open its borders and set up camps, Ozal's government insisted on international aid first, arguing that it did not have the resources to handle such a flood of refugees. This was a bit disingenuous. The government may not have had the resources, but the Turkish Kurds did, and, as in the 1988–1989 Iraqi refugee crisis, they were more than willing to help. According to the *New York Times,* Turkish Kurds indeed aided Iraqi Kurds on the border in the initial days of the flight. Turkey's reluctance to permit the establishment of refugee camps on its soil was more likely motivated by fears of PKK infiltration and the possible influence of rebellious Iraqi Kurds on the Turkish Kurd population. It was not a far-fetched concern. As Britain's *New Statesman* noted, "the fortunes of Iraqi Kurds are radicalising their Turkish compatriots."[39]

Turkey's fears were as great as its ambitions. A Turkish cabinet minister told *Milliyet* that "Turkey reserved the right to intervene militarily if the Iraqis continue to drive the Kurds to the border."[40] The Coalition, hoping to placate Turkey, then pushed a resolution through the UN Security Council condemning Iraq for its actions against its own population. But opponents of the resolution argued that it represented an "unprecedented interference in the internal affairs of a sovereign state."[41] Baghdad's UN representative argued that the Coalition was trying to partition Iraq. With the UN on his side and fearing a public relations disaster, especially after cultivating a new image vis-à-vis the Kurds, Ozal finally allowed permanent camps to be set up on Turkish soil, and US President Bush began to drop aid to the refugees in mid-April.

As for Turkish Kurds, they too have faced forced relocation. Since the 1980s and the war with the PKK, the Turkish government has evacuated villages and defoliated countryside in an effort to deny the guerrillas food, shelter and support. According to a 1987 report from Helsinki Watch, the predecessor of Human Rights Watch, the Turkish military usually gave villagers a stark choice: form a village guard and fight the PKK, or see their homes and orchards destroyed. In one documented case, 270 villagers fled after such an order, and the threatened destruction ensued. They were then told by various government ministries that "they could not claim any rights because they had left voluntarily."[42] They had been forced to leave behind their lands and animals, and received no compensation, no jobs and no housing from the government. "What else can we do?" said a member of the Turkish security forces. "[The guerrillas] will only be finished off when all the villages in the region have been burned and destroyed."[43]

It is estimated that over 30,000 rural Kurds were removed from their villages and placed in strategic hamlet-type settlements in 1989 alone. In the 1990s, the effort has expanded exponentially. Turkish human rights organizations estimate that nearly 1,900 villages in the southeast, some 16 percent of the area's settlements, have been forcibly evacuated and many torched since the beginning of the 1990s. The Turkish government says about 300,000 Kurds have left the region due to the war; the PKK says the figure is more like 1.5 to 2 million.

THE KURDISH DIASPORA

The definitional boundary between political refugees and economic emigrants is not easily drawn, as Americans have recently learned in Haiti. While those forcibly removed by the Turkish and Iraqi armies clearly belong in the former group, those who have fled the economic crisis that military occupation and war have wrought are not so easy to categorize. For the purposes of this study, however, those who have not been forced to leave at gunpoint will be referred to as diasporan Kurds. Their numbers, approximately one-third of both the Iraqi and the Turkish Kurd population, one to two million and six to eight million, respectively, thus dwarf the number of political refugees.

Kurds have emigrated to the metropolitan areas of their countries for several reasons. Education is one factor, especially among younger Kurds. Primary and secondary schools are inferior in the Kurdish parts of these countries and centers of higher education practically nonexistent. The fact that the Kurdish literacy rate is half that of the Turkish population is an indication of the gap. Kurdish students face two problems. First, Kurdish schools are underfinanced and understaffed. And second, schooling in Kurdistan is offensive to many Kurds because of its overt Turkish nationalist content, a content that has diminished in western Turkish schools. In Iran and Iraq, the nationalist content is less intensive and the funding more equal. Not surprisingly, Kurdish literacy rates are far closer to the national averages in these countries.

Still, as important as education is to many Kurds, the vast majority have moved to urban areas for work. Economic modernization in the countryside and the call of well-paid factory jobs have lured millions of Kurds to western Turkish cities since the 1950s, a flow accelerated in the 1980s by the economic dislocations caused by the war. Some found a modicum of prosperity, but most, like other Turkish economic refugees, were disappointed by the country's inadequate job base. Kurds swelled the slums of western Turkish cities, where they inhabit shantytowns of *gecek-ondu*, or "night-built houses," so called because, under Turkish law, if a house could be constructed between dusk and dawn, the authorities must accept it. By 1970, Istanbul was, in effect, the largest Kurdish city in the world.

Moreover, the Kurdish working poor face an additional burden in their national metropolis: ethnic prejudice. "Abusive stereotypes about the Kurds abound among Arabs and Turks"; writes Hilal Khashan, "accusations of brigandage, evil-doing, treachery and cruelty disclose some of the unfortunate slurs hurled at the Kurds."[44] While Turkey boasts with some justification that Kurds have long been integrally involved in government, business and especially culture since the birth of the republic, it ignores a troubling component of that integration. For Kurds to succeed in Turkey, they must give up their ethnic identity.

Meanwhile, the Kurdish diaspora has both encouraged and impeded the cause of Kurdish nationalism. With many Kurds having entered the most dynamic sectors of their national economies in recent years, both a Kurdish proletariat and Kurdish industrial capital have developed, but both are outside Kurdistan. This has its effects on Kurdish nationalism, as van Bruinessen notes:

> Kurdish workers in Istanbul, for instance, are more likely to unite with Turkish workers on a class based platform than rally to vague nationalist appeals.[45]

Moreover, as former Turkish Prime Minister Turgut Ozal pointed out in rebuttal to Kurdish demands for self-determination, "the main body of the Kurdish people is not in east Anatolia anymore. . . . It is integrated into this society [that is, in western Turkish cities]."[46]

In Turkey, where the impact of emigration to urban areas both within the country and in Western Europe is greatest, the resistance movement is stridently antifeudal in its rhetoric, program and strategy. In Iraq, where economic migration has been less marked, both the KDP and PUK are more traditionally structured and motivated. Rhetoric notwithstanding, the leadership of both organizations seems incapable of conceptualizing a Kurdish national state transcending tribal loyalties, as the current civil war between the PUK and KDP in the safe haven makes clear. As for Iran, the Kurdish national movement has been temporarily crushed. But in its most recent manifestation, the armed uprising after the revolution, the regions that came under Kurdish control witnessed an assault on feudal social and economic institutions of all kinds. While the KDPI has always evinced socialist inclinations, the radicalism of the uprising was no doubt due in part to the impact of Kurdish participation in the revolution against the shah, generally in the leftist secular wing of the revolutionary movement, and the return to Kurdistan of many of those revolutionaries.

Meanwhile, there is an international dimension to the Kurdish diaspora as well. Iraqi Kurds have emigrated to the oil-rich, labor-hungry kingdoms of the Persian Gulf, though many have returned in the wake of the Gulf War. A much smaller number of urban Iranian Kurds fled to Europe and the United States in the wake of the 1979 revolution. But the largest component of Kurds abroad come from Turkey. There are an estimated half million Kurds in Western Europe, especially Germany. As *gastarbeiten*, or "guest workers," they have been treated as second-class citizens and, more recently, subjected to attacks by the xenophobic, neo-Nazi right. Unlike their Turkish compatriots, however, the Kurdish workers in Germany do not have a friendly embassy staff to turn to. Given their experience in Turkey, most are distrustful of government officials and do not seek help at Turkish consulates.

NOTES

1 Bulloch, John, and Harvey Morris, *No Friends but the Mountains: The Tragic History of the Kurds* (New York: Oxford University Press, 1992), p. i.

2 Marsh, Dwight, *The Tennessean in Persia and Koordistan Being Scenes and Incidents in the Life of Samuel Audley Rhea* (Philadelphia: Presbytarian Publications Committee, 1869), p. 190.

3 Kendal, Nizzan, "Kurdistan in Turkey," in Chaliand, Gerard, ed., *A People Without a Country: The Kurds and Kurdistan* (New York: Olive Branch Press, 1993), p. 40.

4 Soane, Ely Bannister, *To Mesopotamia and Kurdistan in Disguise (1907–1909)*, (Holland, New York: Armorica Book Co., 1979) (reprint of 1912), p. 367.

5 Anonymous, interview with author, March 25, 1995.

6 Kurdish tribes differ from Turkish and Arab tribes in one important respect. The cohesion of the lowland tribal peoples is based almost exclu-

sively on lineage; Kurdish tribes depend as much on territorial proximity as they do on kinship or clan ties.

7 Jwaideh, Wadie, "The Kurdish Nationalist Movement: Its Origins and Development," unpublished dissertation, (Syracuse, N.Y.: Syracuse, 1960), p. 499.

7a Millingen, p. 284.

8 Longrigg, Stephen Hemsley, *Iraq, 1900 to 1950: A Political, Social, and Economic History* (New York: Oxford University Press, 1953), p. 23.

9 Izady, Mehrdad, *The Kurds: A Concise Handbook* (Washington D.C.: Taylor and Francis, 1992), p. 205.

10 Chaliand, Gerard, "Introduction," in Chaliand, Gerard, ed., p. 9.

11 Sulaiman, Azad (pseud.), "The Politics of Green and Yellow," in *Kurdish Life*, No. 11 (Summer 1994), p. 2.

12 Jwaideh, *op.cit.*, p. 141.

13 Izady, *op.cit.*, pp. 204–205.

13a van Bruinessen, p. 211.

14 van Bruinessen, Martin, *Agha, Shaikh and State: The Social and Political Structures of Kurdistan* (London: Zed Books, 1992), p. 122.

15 Izady, *op.cit.*, p. 230.

16 Millingen, Frederick, *Wild Life among the Kurds* (London: Hurst and Blackett, 1870), p. 263.

17 Longrigg, *op.cit.*, p. 198.

18 Hamilton, A.M., *Road through Kurdistan: The Narrative of an Engineer in Iraq* (London: Faber and Faber Limited, 1937), p. 274.

19 van Bruinessen, *op.cit.*, p. 7.

20 Xulum, interview, November 21, 1994.

21 Millingen, *op.cit.*, p. 119.

22 Hay, William, R., *Two Years in Kurdistan; Experiences of a Political Officer, 1918–1920* (London: Sidgwick & Jackson, Ltd., 1921), p. 61.

22a Millingen, p. 62.

23 van Bruinessen, p. 184.

24 *Ibid.*, pp. 6–7.

25 *Ibid.*, p. 82.

26 Kurds are not alone in practicing these so-called Cults of the Angels. Many Turks, Arabs and Iranians do so as well. The Arab President Hafez al-Assad of Syria, for example, is a member of the Alevi faith.

27 *New York Times* (March 4, 1979), p. 3.

28 Kendal, Nizzan, "Kurds under the Ottoman Empire," in Chaliand, Gerard, ed., p. 29.

29 Actually, it was split into three parts. A small portion of Kurdistan was given to the French mandate of Syria.

30 "Abdullah Ocalan: Biographical Notes," in Kurdistan Solidarity Committee, *The Workers' Party of Kurdistan* (London: Kurdistan Information Centre, 1992), p. 6.

31 "A Remote But Bitter War," in *Newsweek* (March 30, 1987), p. 45.

31a Cited in Marcus, Aliza, "Turkey's Kurds after the Gulf War: A Report from The Southeast" in Chaliand, p. 245.

32 Xulum, interview, November 21, 1994.

33 Marcus, Aliza, "In Kurdistan," in *Dissent* (July 1994), p. 39.

34 Izady, *op.cit.*, p. 205.

35 Izady, p. 58.

36 Farouk-Sluglett, Marion, and Peter Sluglett, *Iraq Since 1958: From Revolution to Dictatorship* (London: KPI, 1987), p. 188.

37 "The Gulf between Rhetoric and Reality," in *Kurdish Life*, No. 10 (Spring 1994), p. 6.

38 Whether it was because Iranian camps for Iraqi Kurd refugees did not provide the same dramatic footage of suffering as Turkey's, or because Iran was still viewed as a pariah state in the West, the media generally ignored the far larger refugee crisis there.

39 Pilger, John, "Who Killed the Kurds?" in *New Statesman* (April 12, 1991), p. 6.

40 "Rhetoric and Reality," p. 5.

41 *Ibid.*

42 "The Kurdish Minority," in *Kurdish Times*, vol. 2, No. 1 (December 1987), p. 35.

43 Reuters on-line wire service, C-reuters@clarinet.com (November 25, 1994).

44 Khashan, Hilal, "The Labyrinth of Kurdish Self-Determination," in *The International Journal of Kurdish Studies*, vol. 8, No. 1 & 2 (1995), p. 11.

45 van Bruinessen, *op.cit.*, p. 20.

46 *Asbarez* (English edition) (May 9, 1991), p. 24.

4
....

NATION-STATES

There is only one cure for Kurdish troubles.
  Exterminate them.
          ——Turkish saying

Compared to an infidel, the Kurd is a Muslim.
          ——Islamic saying

TURKEY

Population: 62,153,898 (July 1994 est.)
Area: 301,382 square miles
GNP: $312.4 billion (1993)

NATIONALISM

For all its bureaucratic inertia, economic backwardness and political repressiveness, the Ottoman Empire offered a home to the Kurds, as it did to the many other restless peoples of an empire that stretched, at the beginning of World War I, from Arabia to the Balkans. Like all long-lived imperial rulers, the Ottomans had discouraged nationalism, including Turkish nationalism, in favor of an allegiance to the empire and, if not the empire, then the divine authority of the sultan, who was considered the last caliph of all Muslims. This pan-Ottomanism, however, was overwhelmed by the growing force of Turkish nationalism, which culminated, at least as far as the pre-World War I period was concerned, in the 1908 coup organized by the Young Turks and completed after the war by Kamal Ataturk, who was determined to drag the Turkish nation into the twentieth century.

Not only was the caliphate abolished, but the Arabic alphabet was replaced by the Latin, and even the wearing of the traditional fez was outlawed. There were also more sinister components of Ataturk's program. Turkey's descent into authoritarianism has often been forgotten in studies of Europe's interwar fascism. That oversight has been due to several factors: Turkey's marginality in the European imagination; the West's prejudiced assumptions of Turkish brutality as a matter of course; other more spectacular examples of totalitarianism in Italy and Germany; and, finally, Turkish nationalism's lack of expansionist ambitions.

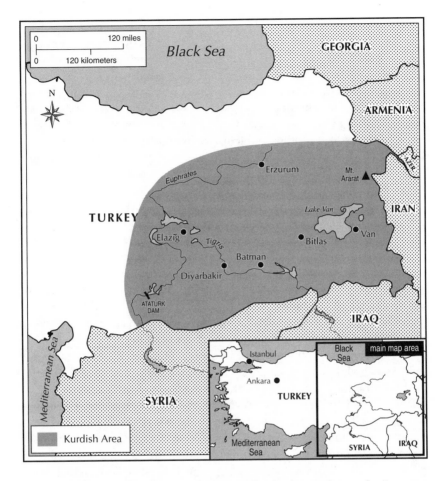

That Turkey was an increasingly authoritarian and even fascist state, however, is beyond doubt. A new national ethos emerged that sought not only to resurrect dubious Turkish claims to cultural and even linguistic superiority, but to rewrite history itself. Its source was a Turkish inferiority complex. Under the Ottomans, who saw any nationalism as a threat to imperial cohesion, the word "Turk" had become synonymous with "boor" and "peasant." Moreover, the idea that Europeans might think of Turks as an Asian "race" rather than a European one obsessed Ataturk, who made the rectification of this impression an important affair of state. To that end, the Turkish leader convened a Congress on Turkish History, which asserted that Turkish history went back much farther than the Ottomans and had always been based in Anatolia. This assertion had a double purpose: to deny the Turkish people's central Asian origins, and to situate them in one of the cradles of ancient civilization. Moreover, the congress declared that Turks had virtually invented civilization, including toolmaking, writing and urbanization, and then spread it to Mesopotamia, Egypt and the Aegean. As one Kurd noted, Ataturk would have prevented a lot of subsequent strife if he had called the new nation Anatolia, a neutral geographic expression, rather than Turkey, with all its nationalist associations.

Nevertheless, a certain ambivalence can be detected in the Turkish *Kulturkampf.* Ataturk not only substituted Roman letters for Arabic ones, he tried to purge from the Turkish language all foreign words and "impurities." This entailed another problem. Ataturk was also trying to modernize his country's economy rapidly, yet, like many languages, Turkish did not have readily available words for some of the products of twentieth-century technology. Eventually, the purification crusade was dropped in favor of a more elaborate linguistic theory. Known as the "sun theory of language," it asserted that Turks had invented language itself. Since all languages were therefore ultimately derived from Turkish, then *ipso facto*, all foreign words were not really foreign, but Turkish in origin. That this preposterous theory became required teaching at all Turkish schools and universities hints at the kind of society and state emerging in Turkey. And while these theories are no longer taught in public schools, as recently as the 1970s a leading Turkish intellectual, Ismail Besikçi, was prosecuted on charges of denying the validity of the sun language theory and Turkish history thesis.

Needless to say, the presence of a large minority of citizens who not only demurred from the nationalist ethos, but actively promoted their own, could not be tolerated. Indeed, the very existence of this minority was an ongoing challenge to Turkish nationalism. It is no wonder, then, that Kurdishness itself was prohibited in the 1930s, with bans on Kurdish dress, music, dance and other cultural expressions. Prohibitions on speaking Kurdish even in the privacy of the home were added to existing bans on public speech. The assertion of a separate Kurdish culture and history became a treasonous act, aimed, in the words of Turkish dissident Ismail Besikçi's judges, "at dividing and surrendering [the] nation to its enemies." Kurds were officially declared "mountain Turks who had forgotten their language."[1]

Moreover, the very crusade against the Kurds was turned to the advantage of the ruling party's ethos. It is worthwhile to quote Kurdish historian Nizzan Kendal at length.

What better "proof" of the superiority and glory of the "Great Turkish nation" could there have been than these "brilliant victories" over "those who are not of pure Turkish origin"? What better way to illustrate the idea that the "Turkish people is great, civilized and valiant" than to invent a palpable antithesis, the "savage and backward Kurds," the only large non-Turkish minority in Turkey? What better means could the Ankara government find to flatter its people than the military exploits of its expeditionary corps in Kurdistan? . . . Certainly not the economic situation, dominated as it was by a corrupt bourgeoisie and which condemned the mass of the Turkish people to vegetate in abject poverty under a growing burden of tithes, debts and taxes.[2]

The situation is familiar from the histories of other authoritarian states. To risk a hackneyed phrase, if the Kurds had not existed, the Turkish government would have had to invent them.

Ataturk's overpowering wish for European acceptance has been passed on to his political heirs, especially in the military. Much of the country's leadership, it might be said, still suffers from imperial hangover. While the acute distress of waking up after World War I with its empire lost and its homeland occupied by foreign troops has eased over the past 75 years, vestiges remain of the virulent nationalism that shock gave birth to. Turks and Kurds are no longer taught, as they were in the 1930s, that the Turks were the fount of all civilization and even human language itself. But students are still greeted with placards in classrooms proclaiming "one Turk is worth more than the universe." Moreover, the Turkish government regards any external criticism as an affront to its very identity and any internal ethnic protest of Turkish national precedence as a threat to its national integrity.

In the post–Cold War era, this ethnocentrism and nationalist paranoia have been supplemented by a revival of imperial ambitions, especially among the nation's military brass. The breakup of the Soviet Union and the establishment of independent republics in the ancient Turkic homeland in central Asia have inspired neocolonial ambitions of a Turkish sphere of influence stretching to the western border of China. Closer to home, say some Ankara watchers, Turkish support for the safe haven is inspired by ill-concealed hopes of reclaiming the oil-rich province of Mosul, once a *vilayet* of the Ottoman Empire, but lost to the British and then the Iraqis in the years following World War I.

Such hopes, however, are challenged by the reality of an armed uprising in the Turkish Anatolian homeland. Officially, the Turkish government downplays the seriousness of Kurdish national aspirations. A public relations officer at Turkey's Washington embassy told this author that the Turks "have no Kurdish problem. We have a problem with terrorists calling themselves Kurds."[3] The government also argues that Kurdish demands for autonomy threaten the unity of the Turkish state by encouraging other minorities to make similar demands.

This argument can be understood in part by examining the Ottoman imperial collapse. One of the principal justifications offered by the Allies for the dismemberment of the empire was the occurrence of various nationalist uprisings in the years preceding and following World War I. "It is therefore understandable," Izady argues, "that the young Turkish Republic [and arguably the more mature one of today] did not want to meet the same fate as the defunct Ottoman Empire in accommodating ethnic minorities."[4] The modern Turkish Republic however, is much more homogenous ethnically than the Ottoman Empire. More to the point, perhaps, Kurdish nationalism is an affront to Ataturk's (and his successors') program of inculcating Turkish pride and national feeling. Since Ataturk's time, Ankara has vigorously prosecuted and punished those sympathetic to Kurdish aspirations such as Ismail Besikçi.

POLITICS

Ataturk approached the problem of establishing a Turkish nationalist ideology through a blend of militarism and racial theory closely akin to the European fascism of the interwar years. But with the revival of European democracy and American influence after 1945, the more liberal elements of postwar Turkish leadership focused their efforts on establishing a new nationalism with a democratic face, a project openly despised and resisted by conservative elements in the Turkish government.

The elections of 1950 and the subsequent administration of President Adnan Menderes revealed the deep political fault lines in Turkish society. Menderes was that most peculiar brand of twentieth-century politician, the man of upper-class charm who developed a mystique among common people. He had big plans for Turkey and immediately embarked on an ambitious industrial, transportation and agricultural development program. This created a new class of industrial and commercial elites; Menderes's curious slogan was "a millionaire in every district." Despite a massive influx of American aid under the anticommunist Truman Doctrine, Turkey was quickly spending itself into bankruptcy. When protest emerged, the president pressured the judiciary and muzzled the press. The press law of 1950 restricted newspaper ownership, provided for prepublication censorship and held editors criminally and civilly liable for offenses against the law.

Much of the criticism came from the military. Not only was their conservative economic outlook offended by the deficits, but they were increasingly shut out of political power by the new bourgeoisie that Menderes turned to for advice. Moreover, the president was intentionally squeezing the military's budget. By the late 1950s, Turkish generals were forced to moonlight to support their families. Grumbling in the military led to open talk of a coup, but Menderes was still popular with the people. After escaping from an airplane crash in London, he returned to jubilant demonstrations of mass support in Turkey. To defend his flank against military plotters, he turned to the people in the time-honored Turkish tradition of appealing to their religious feelings. An army coup, he told them, would mean more forced secularism, a tactic designed to offend and, unsuccessfully as it turned out, isolate the secularist military brass.

The coup of 1960 brought to power the most reactionary elements in the Turkish army. Political activism and dissent were crushed during the early 1960s, until, by 1965, the generals felt secure enough to hold new elections. Turkish rulers were beginning to harbor ambitions to join the European Common Market (Turkey became a member of NATO in 1952). Suleyman Demirel's conservative administration was of necessity circumspect in its handling of the military. At a 1965 rally, Demirel received a note from an officer in the audience: "We hanged Menderes, and we shall hang you!"[5]

By the late 1960s, however, Turkey was caught up in the global trend of leftist upsurge and rightist reaction that struck democracies and would-be democracies from Prague to Mexico City. In Turkey, the clash led to political violence, spearheaded by right-wing death squads. In 1970, the military overthrew Demirel. Leftist parties—including the Turkish Workers' Party, the only Turkish party that consistently supported Kurdish autonomy—were outlawed and dozens of dissidents jailed, including writers who were sentenced to seven years for each banned publication. In 1973, national elections were scheduled by the military, though Kendal calls the mid-1970s the era of "parliamentary fascism."[6] Right-wing death squads continued their killings, while left-wing groups went underground and embarked on a series of terrorist attacks and kidnappings of prominent Turkish officials and industrialists. By the late 1970s, the military once again decided that parliamentary politicians could not be trusted to maintain civil order, and took power in a September 1980 coup.

Beginning with parliamentary elections in 1983, led by Motherland Party leader and prime minister Turgut Ozal, the Turkish political pendulum swung back to civilian rule, a trend that intensified with the election of Ozal as president in 1987. Ozal was an unusual leader, both a relative progressive on civil rights issues and a forceful politician capable of maintaining civilian control over the military. His adroit handling of the refugee crisis of 1991, his lifting of the ban on spoken Kurdish, and his antiterrorism law marked a shift in Turkish politics. Ozal was able to balance the military concern's over national security while attempting to find a new way out of the Kurdish quagmire.

But he had only begun the task when he died in 1993. According to journalist Aliza Marcus, writing in that same year, the military did as it pleased in southeastern Turkey with a minimum of civilian control. The army, she writes, continues to see itself "as the guarantor of the Turkish nation."[7] With Ozal's death, a weak civilian government under Prime Minister Tansu Çiller, the escalating war in Kurdistan, the ambitions of the former Soviet republics of central Asia, and their new role as the centerpiece of US strategy in the Middle East, the Turkish military is feeling a heightened sense of importance. In fact, says Middle East analyst Robert Kaplan, the Turkish military has organized a "quiet coup" in the country since Ozal's death, and its influence has been felt in all sectors of government and society, from parliament to the judiciary to the press. It was the military, some believe, that was behind the 1994 arrest and trial of six Kurdish parliamentarians.[8]

ECONOMICS

No state readily gives up sovereignty over a portion of its own territory. But for Turkey to relinquish claims to its Kurdish provinces would mean giving up control of water, a resource as valuable as oil in the arid Middle East. The Kurdish highlands of Turkey contain the watershed of the fertile crescent. Since the Menderes administration of the 1950s, Turkey has embarked on a massive effort to develop Kurdistan's water and other natural resources, under the general heading of "eastism." The centerpiece of this policy in recent years has been the Greater Anatolia Project (GAP), a series of hydroelectric and irrigation projects, most notably the massive Ataturk dam on the Euphrates River, completed with great fanfare in 1990. The importance of these dams to Turkey's economic health cannot be over-stated. Together, the 10 completed or projected dams in Kurdistan will irrigate over two million acres of farmland and generate almost 3,000 megawatts of electricity. The water itself is a marketable commodity and is sold to arid countries like Kuwait and Saudi Arabia, hundreds of miles to the south.

There are several reasons for Turkey's commitment to GAP. One is strictly pragmatic. When Ataturk embarked on Turkey's economic modernization in the 1930s, he pursued a statist approach on the Soviet model, emphasizing heavy industry in western Turkey, where rudimentary industrialization had been going on since the late 19th century. However he overlooked two important arenas of economic development; industrialization requires immense investments in electrical power generation, which was seen to be sadly lacking by the 1950s; and, again following the Soviet lead, agricultural investment was woefully inadequate. Though over 60 percent of the Turkish population worked in agriculture in 1985, only about 20 percent of the gross domestic product was generated in that sector. With the former figure nearer to 75 percent in the southeast, the relative poverty of the Kurdish countryside was even more pronounced. The GAP was dedicated to both modernizing the agricultural sector of Kurdistan and providing needed electricity for western Turkish industry.

Perhaps most important, however, the GAP is part of a 60-year-old government effort to open up Kurdistan to the larger Turkish economy and the international market. Beginning in the 1930s with railroads, and accelerating after the war with highway construction, the Turkish government had extended a transportation infrastructure to much of Kurdistan. Part of this has been for security reasons; troops could be delivered to trouble-spots that much faster. But the effect has also been to open up Kurdistan to outside capital and outside products. The influx of capital has driven up land prices, and mechanization has marginalized those farmers who cannot buy the equipment to farm competitively. Moreover, the new roads deliver cheap textiles that have driven craftsmen out of work and cheap tobacco that undersells the one commercial crop available to Kurdish farmers. "Kurdistan, in eastern Turkey," says historian Mordechai Nisan, "was a classic 'internal colony': Raw materials were extracted and exported, while rural poverty and underdevelopment persisted as government policy."[9]

IRAQ

Population: 19,889,666 (July 1994 est.)
Area: 168,754 square miles
GNP: $38 billion (1993 est.)

NATIONALISM AND POLITICS

The territory of Iraq, like that of most Middle East states, was initially carved rather arbitrarily by the victorious World War I Allies from the Arab provinces of the Ottoman Empire. Iraq comprises three: the largely Shiite Basra in the south, Sunni Baghdad in the center and the predominantly Kurdish province of Mosul in the north. While the majority of the population has always been Arabic-speaking, Kurds have constituted roughly 20 percent of the population since the republic's establishment in 1930, and the Arabs are divided between allegiance to Shiite and Sunni Islam, with a slight majority practicing the former. Nevertheless, the center of power in Iraq has always been the province of Baghdad, with its Sunni majority.[10]

The British took control of Iraq under a League of Nations mandate, ruling directly until the Anglo-Iraqi Treaty of June, 1930. From the beginning of their mandate, the British favored the Sunni Arabs of Baghdad, and made the city their administrative headquarters. To lend legitimacy to their rule, the British intended to establish a kind of interim protectorate with a British-imposed king. Their choice was the Emir Faisal of western Arabia (whose father, says American traveler E. Alexander Powell, "had made his fortune fleecing pilgrims to Mecca").[11] While Faisal claimed direct descent from the Prophet, he had never set foot in Iraq before and, as a Sunni, was doubly resented by the Shiite majority. The British strategy failed even before it went into effect. A mass uprising of Arab Iraqis in the summer of 1920, fed by rumors of the impending appointment of Faisal, took months to quell and cost hundreds of British and thousands of Arab lives.

The legitimacy of the king's rule was never established, even after full independence was granted. In Iraq, the British could and did create a state, but they could not fashion a people. According to historian Stephen Longrigg, there was "little sense" of an Iraqi national identity among the "poor and ignorant, let alone [among] minorities like the Kurds."[12] From

the beginning, the legitimacy of the state had been called into question, with some advocating a pan-Arab nation and others supporting the idea of an Iraqi state. The former maintained that Iraq was an artificial creation of European colonialists, while the latter, largely Shiites and Kurds, feared a pan-Arab nation would threaten these groups. In either case, says historian Edmund Ghareeb, the majority of Iraqis steadfastly supported a "secular [and] modern national state."[13]

Iraq remained, at least in name, a constitutional monarchy under a series of British-supported kings until a military coup in 1958 ousted the last Iraqi king. But continued disputes between Iraqi nationalist and pan-Arabist factions kept the nation in political turmoil, beginning with a military coup in 1936, the first in the Arab world. Over the next ten years, a nationalist movement began to grow, led by the military, and expressing itself in opposition to the British and the strongly pro-British civilian government. As the Slugletts note, "it is difficult to document the way in which the new national consciousness was diffused among the Iraqi population. . . ."

> [though] major indicators of the new awareness were the huge turn-outs and the militancy expressed in anti-British or anti-government demonstrations and activities, particularly in 1941 [the year Britain reoccupied Iraq to thwart pro-Axis sentiments] and after 1945.[14]

In 1948, the anti-British and antigovernment agitation came to a head. A series of strikes and demonstrations crippled the country and led to the downfall of the civilian government and the abrogation of the Anglo-Iraqi Treaty of 1930. Still, the hostility to the British and their American allies continued. The next ten years witnessed no fewer than 20 governments, all weak, all pro-Western and all unpopular, made more so by events outside Iraq, including the establishment of the state of Israel in Arab Palestine and the Suez Crisis, both blamed on the British.

If one can speak of an Iraqi nationalism, it came to power in the 1958 left-wing military coup under the leadership of General Abd al-Karim Qasim. The monarchy was ended, Iraq withdrew from the American-organized anticommunist Baghdad pact of 1955, and a series of economic reforms was initiated. "So great was the immediate popularity of the Revolution," writes journalist Fran Hazleton,

> with the Iraqi people giving their full support to Qasim and the Iraqi army, that, although US marines had just landed in Lebanon and the British moved Jordanian troops to the border with Iraq, direct Western military intervention was not attempted.[15]

Still, the major rift between pan-Arab and Iraqi nationalists continued, now aggravated by the 1958 creation of the United Arab Republic of Egypt and Syria (UAR). Using the pretext of a failed coup by the pan-Arabists, the pro-Iraqi nationalist government reluctantly formed an alliance with the Kurds and the single largest political force in Iraq, the communists. In a series of bloody purges, Qasim's alliance won the day. But in winning, the distrustful Qasim now feared the power of his political allies. He soon manipulated the Kurds to turn on the communists, while he supported one Kurdish faction against another.

Having turned on his allies and facing the growing popularity of the UAR's Gamel Abdel Nasser, Qasim and his Iraqi nationalists had become increasingly alienated from the majority of Iraqi citizens. Qasim's estrangement can be gauged by the fact that even the Kurds, who opposed pan-Arabism because it would render them an insignificant minority, supported his opponents. In 1963, Qasim was overthrown by the pan-Arabist Baath Party which itself was overthrown that same year, in part because of its continuation of Qasim's war against the Kurds. The Baathists

then returned to power, after a series of weak military and civilian governments, in a second coup in 1968.

The Baath Party was and is a unique force in Iraqi politics. Founded
in Damascus in 1940 by a Christian intellectual named Michel Aflaq, Baath,
which translated literally means "resurrection from the dead," conflated an
intense Arab nationalism, state economic planning and revolutionary fervor.
Likened to the Nazi Party by its worst enemies and hailed as the savior of
the Arab people by its supporters, the party offered a rather vague plan for
governing and an economic program filled with internal contradictions.
Take the following articles from the Party's Constitution:

> Article 26. The Party of the Arab Baath is a socialist party. It believes that the
> economic wealth of the fatherland belongs to the nation.
> Article 34. Property and inheritance are two natural rights. They are protected
> within the limits of the national interest.[16]

Nevertheless, the Baath Party had increased to 15,000 supporters by
February, 1963, when, "totally unprepared for power," it seized the state
in a lightning coup against Qasim and his eroded government. Not having
effective control of the military and unsure of their hold on power, Baath
leaders wasted no time unleashing a "reign of terror" against their real and
putative enemies, including the Kurds. A backlash led to the Baath's
overthrow in November, and for its leaders, including Saddam Hussein, it
was a powerful lesson learned.[17]

After returning to power in July of 1968 in the midst of a series of
antigovernment strikes and demonstrations, Baath leaders were determined
to avoid the mistakes they had made in 1963, that is, going too fast and
too far. They knew that support for democracy was strong among the Iraqi
people, they recognized the strength of the communists and they were
aware that memories of the 1963 bloodbath remained fresh in people's
minds. Instead of random attacks on their enemies, they slowly began
purging the military and other state institutions of opponents and replacing
them with party loyalists. They also began to set up the repressive super-
structure that Iraqi intellectual and Baath critic, Kanan Makiya, would come
to call "the republic of fear."[18] They offered popular programs and rhetoric,
but were secretly trying to divide and destroy opposition forces. By the end
of the war against Kurdistan in 1975, say the Slugletts, Saddam Hussein
and the Baath Party had effectively liquidated most of their internal enemies,
including the communists and noncommunist democratic opponents.[18a]

But in the process, the Baath Party had dropped its pan-Arabist
commitments, opting instead to build the revolution in Iraq. This decision
was no doubt promoted by Saddam Hussein, who had ambitions to lead
the post-Nasser Arab world and felt that a strong and united Iraq offered
his best base, as his ill-conceived invasion of, and eight-year war with, Iran
and his attempted annexation of Kuwait indicated. In effect, Baath ideology

did not and does not recognize a nationalism separate from the Baath revolution, the Baath Party and Baath's supreme leader Saddam Hussein. In short, opponents of the regime are, by definition, opponents of the Iraqi nation and the Iraqi people. Thus, Kurdish support for and acceptance of aid from the Iranians were viewed as betrayal of not only the regime but Iraqi nationhood. Only in this context can the postwar *anfal* campaign, with its wholesale imprisonment, displacement and murder of Kurdish guerrillas and civilians, be understood if not condoned. As one government doctor treating Kurds for burns sustained during the chemical warfare campaign remarked, "you deserve to be treated like this because you are traitors."[19]

Despite the defeat in Kuwait, including the massive destruction of Iraq's infrastructure, the quasi-partition of the country and crippling post-war sanctions which have devastated the Iraqi economy and immiserated its people, and despite the defection of two of Saddam Hussein's most important officials (and sons-in-law), the Baath Party appears to be in no danger of internal collapse or of defeat by uprising. A series of minor coups in the mid-1990s involving disgruntled army officers have been easily crushed by forces loyal to the government. Virtually every serious opponent of the regime has been murdered or imprisoned, or is in exile, including a weak democratic opposition coalition headquartered in London.

ECONOMICS

While the discovery of large petroleum reserves in the Ottoman province of Mosul (northern Iraq) just before World War I had enormous political ramifications for subsequent Iraqi history, including the establishment of the mandate and subsequent British hegemony, developments in a more traditional economic arena—agriculture—have had a more profound effect on the Iraqi people. As part of the Ottoman Empire, Iraq had been deeply affected by land privatization efforts that had been going on since the mid-nineteenth century and were accelerated by the British after they occupied the region in 1915. As in Anatolia, much of the land came under the ownership of well-connected families of tribal leaders and urban merchants, both in Arab and Kurdish areas, though the more inaccessible mountainous regions of the latter maintained their communal ownership over pasturage until well into the post–World War II period.

British-sponsored legislation during the mandate further enhanced the holdings of the very largest landholders. By 1958, approximately 1 percent of the landholders owned over 55 percent of the arable land in private hands. At the same time, nearly two-thirds of landholders owned less than four percent of all cultivated land, and another 600,000 rural heads of household (out of a total rural population of 3.8 million) were entirely landless. Moreover, due to the wasteful agricultural practices of many of the largest landholders, agricultural productivity declined steadily from about 800 pounds of grain per acre to about 500 between 1920 and 1960.

Moreover, during the mandate, the government of King Fahd had signed an oil concession with the British Anglo-Persian Oil Company "on terms," say the Slugletts, "most unfavourable to itself for the exploitation of Mosul oil."[20] Still, by the 1930s Iraq had become a major oil exporter, and by 1953 petroleum accounted for nearly half the nation's income. Only a small portion of the populace enjoyed the fruits of this revenue, which in fact accelerated land consolidation, as fortunes made in petroleum were plowed into real estate. Industrialization before the revolution and, indeed, before the 1970s explosion in oil prices was minuscule, representing a mere 10 percent of national income in 1960.

After the revolution of 1958, the economic picture, at least at the planning stage, began to change dramatically, though it took the increased oil revenues of the 1970s to turn these plans into reality. The Qasim regime, the various military and civilian administrations of the 1960s, and the post-1968 Baath regime were all committed to statist economic development, as were most third-world countries in those years, regardless of political doctrine. Qasim immediately passed a slew of reformist economic legislation, including price controls, legalization of unions, increased oil royalties and, most significantly, land reform, though this last law had by 1968 distributed less than 20 percent of the land mandated under it. Resistance by landholders, who signed land over to relatives and other willing front persons, and the turmoil of Iraqi politics were largely responsible for the failure.

It is important to keep in mind, then, that until the 1970s and the sudden influx of vast new revenues, the majority of Iraqi citizens remained either small landholding peasants, tenant farmers or landless rural peasantry. Iraq, like much of the Arab Middle East, was a desperately poor if well-fed region, with little modern infrastructure beyond a few British-financed railroads and a hydrocarbon industry that largely profited Western oil companies. The sudden rise in oil prices in 1973–1974 (Iraqi oil revenues jumped from $1.8 billion in 1973 to $5.7 billion in 1974) was preceded by a wave of oil industry nationalization that swept the Middle East, reaching Iraq during the summer of 1972.

While much of this wealth was controlled by a favored few businessmen with solid connections to the Baath regime, the vast expansion of social services, new economic opportunities in the growing industrial and service sectors, subsidized food and fuel prices, increases in wages and salaries and a burst of housing construction consolidated support for the Baath regime despite its heavy-handed political repression. During the 1970s, the development of heavy industry and import substitution became the goals of state economic planners. But as in other countries blessed with sudden riches, Iraq's economy suffered severe distortions, particularly in the agricultural sector, as hundreds of thousands of peasants, experiencing a growing gap between their standard of living and that of their urban fellow citizens, moved to the cities.

Despite a further increase in oil prices following the Iranian Revolution in 1979, Iraq's economy stagnated from the early 1980s, for several reasons, including the decline in oil prices from the mid-1980s on. Nevertheless, first and foremost, it was the long war with Iran that crippled Iraq's economic development. Projects were abandoned and existing infrastructure and industry deteriorated for lack of investment funds that were going to pay for Iraq's immense military machine. The wartime labor shortage, though partially compensated for by an increase of women in the workforce and a further influx of rural peoples, exacerbated the problem of lowered productivity. Equally debilitating was the huge foreign debt accumulated to pay for the war. In fact, it was this immense debt, along with the Persian Gulf oil producers' unwillingness to raise oil prices (an unwillingness that Saddam Hussein saw as an act of ingratitude for his efforts to halt the spread of Iranian-style Islamist politics), that led to the 1990 invasion of Kuwait.

The Gulf War was an unmitigated disaster for the Iraqi economy. The devastation of the Coalition air attack, which saw more bombs dropped on Iraq in several weeks than in the entire Vietnam War, laid waste to much of the industrial and social service infrastructure. "Once a highly technological society," writes Iraqi archaeologist Selma al-Radi, "Iraq today [March, 1995] is barely mechanized." Meanwhile, continuing international sanctions prevent Iraq from rebuilding. "Iraq's economy," al-Radi goes on to say, "is in free fall. Inflation is rampant. Even affluent middle-class families feel impoverished. Flea markets flourish, as people sell off whatever they can."[21] The dinar, once traded at par with the dollar, is now worth a fraction of a penny. With spare parts virtually unavailable, transport is unreliable and industrial production intermittent at best. And since the UN ban includes refining agents for petroleum, vehicles, utilities and industry must burn crude oil, producing a blanket of smog that envelops much of the Mesopotamian plain and reducing agricultural output by as much as half, a problem further exacerbated by the loss of trade with important agricultural regions now part of the safe haven.

Meanwhile, trade deals are being signed with Western European and Japanese firms to rebuild the economy, but all stipulate that funds will not be forthcoming until the UN embargo on Iraq is lifted. While some of the UN coalition is eager to see that happen, the US insists on maintaining the pressure, and pushed a continuation of the sanctions in the spring of 1995.

IRAN

Population: 65,615,474
Area: 636,293 square miles
GNP: $303 billion (1993 est.)

NATIONALISM AND POLITICS

Unlike Turkey, which had to build its national identity on the ruins of an empire, and Iraq, "an artifical creation of European colonialism,"[22] Iran emerged from the trauma of World War I relatively intact, its borders roughly corresponding to the ancient core of the Persian Empire. Of course, Iran had been partitioned into spheres of influence by Russia and Britain after the turn of the century and again during and immediately after World War II. All in all, however, the government formed by Reza Khan—a military officer who deposed the old shah in a 1921 military coup and declared himself Reza Shah Pahlavi in 1925—inherited a long tradition of ruling over a polyglot empire, where Persian-speakers barely make up a majority, if that. About 25 percent of the population is Turkic-speaking, primarily Azerbaijani, and another 10 percent is Kurdish, a figure that includes the Lurs-speaking population in the southwest of the country, a people whose Kurdish identity is a subject of dispute among scholars.

Because of his pro-Nazi sympathies, Reza Shah was deposed by the British in 1941 in favor of his pro-Allies son Mohammed Reza Shah. Following the war, the new shah faced a serious political challenge, not only from separatist Azerbaijanis and Kurds, but from a powerful coalition of left-wing students, workers and the Iranian Communist Party, or Tudeh. While the ethnic rebellions were put down with relative ease, once their Soviet patrons withdrew their support, the struggle between the conservative, pro-Western shah and the Soviet-leaning Tudeh plunged the country into turmoil until the early 1950s, culminating in the victory of Mohammed Mossadegh and his left-wing, nationalist coalition in 1951 in "the first honest elections since the Pahlavi dynasty came into power."[23]

The battle lines quickly became clear. On one side was a coalition of forces around the shah, mostly the comprador class of major industrialists, large rural landholders, heads of government agencies and, most important, the military. On the other were students and intellectuals, worker and peasant organizations, Kurdish and Azerbaijani nationalists and the petit bourgeoisie, or *bazaaris*. The issues were politically and economically contentious: breaking the shah's grip on government, and a series of economic reforms, including land reform and nationalization of the Anglo-Persian oil company. Mossadegh's attempt to enact these reforms led to his overthrow two years later in an Iranian military-led, CIA-sponsored coup.

The shah made it his first priority to crush his democratic, ethnic and communist opposition. Mossadegh was imprisoned and then put under

house arrest until his death in 1968. His National Front and the national trade union confederation were banned. Kurdish and Azeri parties were effectively banned as political organizations. Divided between support-ers of the Soviet Union and strict nationalists, the Tudeh Party was immobilized when support from the Soviet Union failed to materialize before and during the coup. The party, says historian Mohammed Amjad, "had failed to mount resistance against the coup [and] paid a heavy price." Many members went into exile; others were imprisoned, tortured and executed. In 1955, the underground military wing of

Tudeh was discovered and crushed, "putting an end to the *Tudeh* Party as a viable political organization."[24]

By 1955, the shah had consolidated his grip on power to such a degree that he felt comfortable dismissing General Fazlollah Zahedy, head of the army and mastermind of the coup, and sending him on a "permanent vacation" to Switzerland. "By removing Zahedy," says Amjad, "the shah intended to let the military know that he was in charge and would not tolerate any power base in the army."[25] Two years later, under the guidance of the CIA, the shah organized a new security and intelligence service, the Organization of Information and Security of Iran, known popularly by its Farsi acronym, SAVAK. The shah left no aspect of the new regime to chance. For appearances' sake, he established a bipartisan political system, then appointed personal friends to head both parties.

Internationally, the shah firmly aligned Iran behind the West. A year after the coup, he reached an agreement with a British, French, Dutch and American oil company consortium that split revenues with the government on a then-generous fifty-fifty basis. Iran was also becoming a strategic Cold War bulwark in the American anti-Soviet campaign. It became an original member of the anti-Soviet Baghdad pact (later the Central Treaty Organization after Iraq dropped out following Abdul Karim Qasim's coup) and was rewarded with over $1 billion dollars in US military and economic aid between 1954 and 1962.

Facing renewed political unrest due to economic collapse and widespread governmental corruption, the shah launched his "White Revolution" in 1962. The "revolution" had several key components: land reform, rapid industrialization and import substitution, cultural westernization and a more sophisticated form of political repression. Together these were the ingredients for a dramatic transformation of Iranian society and, as it turned out, an unsettling transformation. Politically, the program was intended to create a vast progovernment constituency. Poorly conceived, directed from above and overly ambitious, it had very different consequences. Instead of creating a thriving middle class in the countryside and a well-paid working class in the cities, it produced a bloated bureaucracy, a class of well-heeled and well-connected entrepreneurs, a volatile working class and an aggrieved religious community. And by stifling all democratic political opposition, the shah both fueled and legitimized violence and the politics of the street. When the contradictions inherent in economic modernization ignited large-scale protest, there was only one serious opposition force left in the country, the Shiite Islamic *imams* and their followers.

In the early 1960s, the Shiite spiritual leader, the Ayatollah Khomeini, based in the holy city of Qom, preached a traditionalist message of piety and personal morality. But beginning in the early 1970s, from exile in France, the ayatollah's message changed. In his writings and speeches, widely disseminated through the new technology of cassette tapes, the ayatollah began to offer a more activist and political message: the need for an Islamic republic, based on religious teachings of the Koran and other holy writings, as interpreted and administered by a religiously inspired leadership. In his charismatic way, Khomeini denounced the West, defended petty entrepreneurs and the poor, and attacked corruption; he offered dreams of a cultural and national renaissance and promises to raise the standard of living—all couched in comforting, familiar and yet energizing Islamic symbolism, imagery and rhetoric.

By the middle 1970s, Iran's deepening political and economic crisis made its people especially amenable to this message. To *bazaaris*, or the traditional petit bourgeoisie, the ayatollah promised both an end to their marginalization vis-à-vis the comprador class, and a new estimation of their worth to Islamic society; to the poor in the countryside and cities, the ayatollah's movement offered a vehicle for their frustrations. For students, workers and bureaucrats, all hit hard by the inflation of the mid-1970s, the left seemed more promising. But in the heat of the anti-shah struggle, the most unlikely coalitions were possible. Moreover, the political infrastructure of the left could not compare with the thousands of mosques controlled by the Islamists, and the left knew it. Not surprisingly, the shah's attacks on protesting workers, students and poor people—his police violently broke up religious meetings and the army bulldozed rebellious shanty-towns—only served to inflame the situation and broaden the coalition against him. By February of 1979, an escalating series of mass demonstrations and national strikes, each sparking and in turn sparked by government massacres of opponents, led to the overthrow of the shah and the return from exile of the ayatollah, who took the helm of the provisional revolutionary government.

Two months later, on April 1, a national referendum on the establishment of an Islamic Republic was overwhelmingly approved by the electorate, though the ballot was not secret and voters had but a single yea/nay option. Two political trends emerged in the first few months of the republic: a strong anti-Western sentiment, primarily anti-American, and a push to impose Islamic law, or *sharia*, on all matters of social behavior. A sporadic bombing attack against religious leaders and members of the government by left-wing Islamic militants, or *mujahideen*, led to a serious crackdown by the government against all opponents of the government, as well as the impeachment of the secular prime minister Abolhassan Bani-Sadr. This was just before Saddam Hussein launched his invasion in September 1980.

The Iran-Iraq war was one of the bloodiest in modern times and, to outsiders, one of the most senseless. Still, for the Islamic government in Iran, it was a fight for its life in a war against not only Saddam Hussein, but most of the Islamic and even the Western world. While Iran suffered substantial setbacks in the early years of the war, Iraq was unable to deliver a quick knockout blow. Rather than causing the collapse of the Islamist government, the Iraqi invasion had, in Amjad's opinion, "allowed the regime to stabilize itself . . . [keep] the army busy . . . and help to mobilize the masses against the Iraqi regime . . . [and] international atheism."[26]

Eventually, however, the long war of attrition with Iraq and the revelation that the government, with Khomeini's consent, had made a hostage-for-arms deal with the United States demoralized the populace, already hit with high unemployment, inflation, and war-related shortages. In the summer of 1988, after years of proclaiming that the war would not end until the Baath Party was driven from power in Iraq, the Khomeini government capitulated to Iranian public opinion and international pressure and agreed to a cease-fire with Iraq.

Despite these massive setbacks for the Islamic Republic, the transfer of power upon Khomeini's death in June 1989, was "surprisingly smooth, orderly, and quick."[27] The Council of Experts, a religious body, held an emergency meeting and chose a new ayatollah. That same year, Speaker of Parliament Hashemi Rafsanjani was elected president with 95 percent of the vote. He was reelected in 1993 with 63 percent of the vote.

Rafsanjani is widely considered a "pragmatist" and "moderate" both in Iran and the West. His administration has tried to rebuild the country through economic liberalization and cooperation with the West. He has also opened up the political arena. Over 75 political parties are now legally licensed by the government, though all armed opposition groups, including the KDPI and the *mujahideen,* have been forced either underground or out of the country. The Communist Party was largely destroyed during the early years of the revolution, though many members shifted their allegiance to the outlawed Society for the Defense of Freedom. In general, however, and in spite of the economic troubles confronting the country, support for the current administration and the current form of government appears to be strong.

Despite the dramatic changes in society, culture and politics instituted from Tehran since the Revolution, the Islamist government has accepted, as did the shah, that Iran is a multicultural nation, with Persians the dominant group. As for Kurdish or Azerbaijani autonomy, the Islamic government is as intensely nationalist as the shah's, though the grounds on which this policy is based have shifted.[28] While the shah cited a 2,500-year-old tradition of Persian rule, the theocratic government bases its sovereignty on the ideal of the diverse but united Islamic *umma,* or community of believers. According to Islamic tradition, challenges to the *umma* and its leadership are rarely justified, except in cases where that leadership or that *umma* are clearly violating Islamic law, custom or practice. Kurdish demands challenge the unity of the Iranian *umma,* on grounds wholly unacceptable to the Islamist leadership in Tehran: ethnic separatism.

ECONOMICS

Since the end of World War II, Iran's economy has been subject to huge swings in the business cycle, caused largely by national and international political events which, in turn, have set off further political crises. After returning to unchallenged power in the coup of 1953, the shah immediately undid the reforms of the Mossadegh years by shifting financial resources to the banks, large commercial estates, and shareholders and managers of foreign and domestic industries. With the increase in petroleum revenues negotiated with the Anglo-Persian Oil Company as part of the shah's return to power, Iran in the late 1950s was awash in foreign goods and imported staples, the latter undermining the economic well-being of many peasant farmers.

By the early 1960s, the shah's policies had so overheated the economy that the nation was on the verge of bankruptcy. The banks and the government had squandered their credit, the markets were saturated with luxury goods, businesses were going bankrupt in record numbers and unemployment had skyrocketed. Faced with nationwide unrest, the government had two options: military coup or genuine reform. Under the prodding of the Kennedy administration, Tehran took the latter route. The shah appointed a reformist prime minister, Ali Amini, intent on pushing land reform, busting corruption, downsizing the military and stabilizing the economy. But Amini's agenda interfered with too many vested interests—among them the military, well-connected industrialists and large landholders—and he was quickly dismissed. Again under pressure from Washington, the shah agreed to implement the reforms himself. At the end of 1962, the shah announced his ambitious plan to remake Iranian society, the grandiloquently titled "White Revolution."

The revolution focused mostly on industrialization and import substitution, with a corollary aim of reforming the nation's agriculture. The Iranian countryside in the 1950s was still largely shaped by feudal agricultural relations, with a small sector of large and small commercial farms near the cities. Peasants continued to pay excessive rents to local chiefs, as well as fees to pick fruit in orchards, collect wood in forests, pasture animals and even participate in religious ceremonies. The use of labor corvées was still widespread. After a few highly publicized instances of redistribution of the shah's own lands to the peasants who worked on them, land reform either ground to a halt or was manipulated by large landholders and richer peasants to their own benefit. In either case, the growing commercialization and mechanization of the nation's agricultural sector accelerated the impoverishment of small landed peasants and tenant farmers.

The peasantry was lured, as well as pushed, out of the countryside. The massive industrialization program undertaken by the shah, accelerated by the influx of vast new oil revenues in the mid-1970s, offered relatively high wages and did make Iran more self-sufficient, but at an unsustainably high price of subsidies and tax exemptions. It expanded both the class of state-dependent entrepreneurs who made vast amounts of money through their connections, and a volatile working class. The growth of the former class perpetuated the insatiable appetite for imported luxuries and further unbalanced Iran's import-export ratio. The expansion of the latter aggravated tensions over the basic economic injustice of the White Revolution, making the economy ever more vulnerable to trade union and left-wing activism.

By the early 1970s, the nation was approaching a crisis similar to, though far more acute than, that of a decade earlier, with one important difference. The sudden flood of petrodollars following OPEC's boycott of the West postponed the crisis, even as it aggravated its underlying causes. The ever-more-obvious gap between rich and poor widened through the rest of the decade. Corruption, defense spending and luxury imports increased dramatically, as did farm prices. As landholders in the countryside mechanized and expanded their holdings to take advantage of inflation, more landless peasants were pushed into urban slums, where that same inflation made their living conditions even more marginal. With dramatically higher oil prices, the government had reaped a windfall but sown a whirlwind.

For all their radicalism on social and cultural issues, the Islamists behind Ayatollah Khomeini continued in the statist tradition of the shah. Khomeini, for example, had once denounced the shah's land reform ideas as un-Islamic, since they pitted Muslim against Muslim, thereby disrupting the Islamic *umma*. In fact, the Islamists had little to say about economic reform during the revolution and after, other than their denunciations of the comprador class and the government corruption that enriched them. Pronouncements about creating a twentieth-century Islamic economy, presumably without traditional financial institutions since usury was forbidden by Islamic law, were left vague, either by intent or because few Islamist theorists had any idea about what such an economy would look like.

In any case, the international sanctions imposed on Iran following the seizure of the American embassy in November 1979 and the war with Iraq, which began less than 18 months after the establishment of the Islamic Republic, forced Tehran to put the nation on a war footing with an emphasis on military production and rationing of consumer goods, a move made even more necessary when the Iranian oil complexes around Abadan were heavily damaged by the Iraqi military. (Unlike Iran, which abstained from attacking civilian and commercial targets until late in the war, Baghdad fought a total war from the beginning.) Needless to say, the war and continued international isolation ravaged the Iranian economy. Large segments of the industrial base were destroyed, and what remained deteriorated in the face of labor shortages and a lack of spare parts. What foreign revenues still came in went toward weapons purchases. By the end of the war, Iran's estimated gross domestic product was around 50 percent of what it had been in 1978, the last full year of the shah's reign.

Following Khomeini's death in 1989, the Iranian government was torn between two economic factions. Those surrounding newly elected President Rafsanjani remained committed to the Khomeini regime's emphasis on a state-run and state-planned economy and restrictions on big capital. Conservative forces, including many of the main industrialists and landowners, opposed continued national control of industry and any attempts at major land reform. While Rafsanjani has attempted to hold back privatization and economic liberalization, there has been some reform; the rebuilding of the war-ravaged economy required renewed openness to foreign investment, though a 1994 CIA report says the economy remains largely under central planning with state ownership of oil and other large enterprises. In addition, many International Monetary Fund (IMF) suggestions, including dropping price subsidies on basic foodstuffs and energy, have not been taken up, at least not to the degree advocated by the international financial institutions, for fear of political unrest.

Nevertheless, the continued *fatwa* (doctrinal decision or judgment) and accompanying call for the killing by pious Muslims of British writer Salman Rushdie—a religious order over which the government claims it has no jurisdiction—as well as continued accusations by the United States that Tehran sponsors international terrorism, have kept the new regime in a state of economic isolation, though not as extreme as that imposed after the revolution and during the war with Iraq. Tehran's studied neutrality in the Gulf War encouraged European and Japanese firms to reinvest in Iranian industry. Still, Iran continues to face a severe financial crisis. By the mid-1980s, Iran's foreign debt stood at $30 billion, with several billion in arrears, and little hope of relief as long as international oil prices remain depressed.

MIDDLE EAST AND INTERNATIONAL

Sometimes the Kurdish struggle seems like modern tragedy, a drama from the theater of the absurd or the theater of cruelty, involving the Kurds in various shifting alliances which have ended up doing them more harm than good. The Kurds have the misfortune of occupying lands ruled by governments struggling to maintain their legitimacy at home and determined to project their power regionally. The Kurds struggle with another unfortunate legacy: they have no permanent allies in the region or the world. Britain, the Soviet Union and the United States have been the most important international players in the Middle East since World War I, and each has involved itself with the Kurds in turn, only to withdraw its assistance when international strategic requirements changed. The British first promoted, then used compliant tribes to maintain their rule over mandatory Iraq. When it came time to relinquish control to local authorities, the British sided with the Arabs, who were both more numerous and, in the British measure of things, more reliable.

The Soviets encouraged Kurdish nationalism in Iran after World War II. Looking to create a friendly state on their Caucasus flank, the Soviets armed and helped organize the short-lived Republic of Mahabad, short-lived in part because of subsequent Soviet actions. In one of the first eyeball-to-eyeball Cold War confrontations between the United States and the Soviet Union, the latter blinked in Kurdistan. Unwilling to risk conflict with the United States and having set out a new policy of supporting leftist movements from within a unified Iran, the Soviets unceremoniously dumped their Kurdish and Azerbaijani allies after less than a year, and left them to the mercy of the shah's military.

The United States has been involved in Kurdish politics on two occasions. In the early 1970s, the United States stood by its ally, the shah, as he used the Kurds to keep Baghdad off balance. When Tehran and Baghdad worked out a *modus vivendi* in 1975, the shah, with American acquiescence, abandoned his Kurdish allies. In 1991, after the expulsion of Iraqi forces from Kuwait, President Bush publicly encouraged internal opponents of Saddam Hussein to rise up and overthrow the regime. No explicit offers of aid were made, but the Kurds and other opponents of the regime, such as the Shiite Arabs of Basra, sensed an implicit promise: rise up against Saddam Hussein and the UN Coalition will support you. For strategic reasons—the United States and its Coalition allies favored a unified Iraq, however despotically governed, to the mutually hostile splinter states likely to emerge from such a conflict—Coalition support did not materialize.

The great tragedy in Kurdish relations with the West has been the Kurds' indefatigable faith in the Western powers, and those powers' repeated use of the Kurds to further their own ends, with subsequent abandonment of the Kurds to their enemies. As early as 1878, Shaikh Ubeydullah told a visiting American that, with European and American help, he could and would establish a pro-Western state in Kurdistan. Since this would have required the powers to, in effect, wage war against the Ottoman Empire, they did not take him up on this offer. Under the Sèvres treaty after World War I, however, the Kurds were all but promised a state of their own by the Allies. Instead they became part of the imperial powers' League of Nations mandates. Nearly 60 years later, Mustafa Barzani, leader of the Iraqi Kurdistan Democratic Party (KDP), floated the rather far-fetched but apparently sincere idea of exchanging Kurdish oil concessions for membership in the American union as a 51st state! Nothing, of course, came of this proposal either.

Regionally, the Kurds have had a history of alliances based on a combination of wishfulness, naiveté and ruthless power politics. But given the protean nature of the region's alliances and politics, these have necessarily been convoluted and temporary. Every regional power with a Kurdish minority—and even a few without, like Israel, Libya and Egypt—has tried to use the Kurds for its own ends, sometimes for the purposes of keeping rival states off-balance and sometimes, much to the chagrin of pan-Kurdish idealists, for the purposes of pitting one Kurdish national group against another.

Turkey, according to the British, financed Iraqi Kurds during the mandate. The Turks were trying to disrupt the establishment of a viable Iraqi state that incorporated Kurdish Mosul, the highly coveted northern province of Iraq. And again in the period of the safe haven, say some experts, the Turks continue to work with Iraqi Kurds in a *quid pro quo* arrangement: Turkish support for the safe haven in exchange for Iraqi Kurd support in flushing out PKK bases in northern Iraq. As one Kurdish expert who subscribes to this theory noted, "who better than a Kurd to fight the Kurds."[29]

Except, of course, that it is not that simple. Turkey has historically displayed more hostility than friendship toward Iraq's Kurds. As the most rebellious of the region's Kurds until the militancy of the PKK began in 1984, the Iraqi Kurds, in Ankara's thinking, have traditionally been a worrisome source of political infection of Turkey's Kurds. On more than one occasion during the Iran-Iraq War, the Turks conducted relatively high-profile invasions and numerous small-scale incursions into northern Iraq. Their stated mission was to flush out PKK guerrillas operating there. But journalistic accounts show that numerous Iraqi Kurds, both civilian and *peshmerga*, were attacked and killed in these assaults. Baghdad's official permission for Turkish incursions lends credence to the idea that Turkey had a secondary item on its agenda, the destruction of KDP bases, though Iraq's permission may have been simply a friendly gesture to a key ally (albeit technically neutral) during the war with Iran.

At the same time, Turkey, seeing the Islamic Republic of Iran as its main ideological and strategic rival for the loyalties of the new, post-Soviet, Muslim-dominated republics of central Asia, has secretly supported Iranian Kurds in their struggle with Tehran. This was so during the Iran-Iraq War and has continued under the safe haven. Some observers have noted that in the aftermath of recent Turkish incursions into the safe haven, incursions that have gone virtually unchallenged by the US and its coalition partners,[30] Iranian Kurds operating out of the safe haven have found themselves in possession of arms conveniently left behind by the Turkish military.

Syria has long financed anti-Turkish groups on its own soil and permitted the establishment of PKK guerrilla training bases in Lebanon's Bekaa Valley, which it has controlled since the early 1980s. Syria also broadcasts Kurdish-language radio and news programs into Turkish Kurdistan. In recent years, at least since the anti-Iraq Coalition established during

"Operation Desert Shield" in 1990, a coalition that included both Syria and Turkey, the former has cut back on Kurdish broadcasts and funding for the PKK, though PKK bases remain in Syria proper and in the Bekaa Valley.

The complexity of Turkey's alliances with Iraqi and Iranian Kurds, as well as Syria's relations with Turkish Kurds, pales by comparison to the relations between Tehran, Baghdad, and Iraqi and Iranian Kurds, a web of alliances and relations that are positively Byzantine. In the 1960s and 1970s under the shah and again in the 1980s during the Iran-Iraq War, Tehran actively supported Iraq's Kurdish rebels. In return, Iraqi Kurds did the shah's bidding. During the brief Iranian Kurd uprising in 1967–1968, for instance, the shah increased his aid to Barzani's forces with the stipulation that Barzani "collaborate with the Iranian authorities in restraining any political activity by the Kurds of Iran." Barzani then issued his infamous "thesis," calling on Iranian Kurds to "freeze" their activities against the shah. As Iranian Kurd leader A. R. Ghassemlou noted indignantly, "every serious Iranian KDP action against the shah's regime was considered as a hostile act toward the 'Kurdish revolution'."

> This, at a time when hundreds of Iranian Kurdish militants had joined the ranks of the [Iraqi Kurd] *peshmerga* to fight against the forces of the Baghdad government.[31]

Trapped between Barzani's forces and the Iranian military, the movement, poorly organized to begin with, collapsed rapidly in 1968, and the shah's support for Iraqi Kurds increased. Then in 1975, the shah abandoned his Iraqi Kurdish allies and signed the Algiers Agreement with Saddam Hussein in exchange for territorial concessions. This, in turn, paved the way for future troubles. According to historian Kamran Karadaghi, "Saddam Hussein made humiliating concessions to the shah in order to end his support for the Kurds; those concessions in 1975, of territory in the border areas and the strategic Shatt-al-Arab waterway to the Gulf, were the major cause of the outbreak of the Iran-Iraq War."[32] This may be an exaggeration, but the concessions were surely a significant factor in the decision.

During the Iran-Iraq War, things became even more complicated. When the war began, Iraq Kurdish leaders were at each other's throats. Baghdad used its solid relations with Ghassemlou's Kurdish Democratic Party of Iran (KDPI) to encourage the KDPI to persuade its Kurdish ally, Talabani's PUK, to stop its anti-Baghdad activities. Barzani's KDP forces saw betrayal and launched an offensive against the PUK. With arms pouring into the region from all sides—Iran, Israel, deserting Iraqi Kurd soldiers—the fighting escalated to a point that both Talabani and Barzani became alarmed. With the help of Libya and Syria, both nominal allies of Iran, the PUK, the KDP and other Iraqi forces in opposition to Saddam

Hussein formed the National Democratic Front (NDF) in the Libyan capital, Tripoli, in 1984.

Iran, of course, was delighted with these developments and was soon cooperating with the NDF, an alliance that culminated in the October 1986 raid on the Iraqi oil refinery at Kirkuk, where Kurdish troops and Iranian artillery virtually annihilated the facility. A last joint Iranian-Kurdish offensive near Sulimaniye in 1988 was stopped by Iraq, in part through the use of chemical weapons. In the wake of the war and Saddam Hussein's *anfal* campaign that followed, hundreds of thousands of Iraqi Kurdish refugees fled to Iran. They were welcomed until the government, alarmed at the dimensions of the flight, began turning them back. Since the Gulf War and the establishment of the safe haven, Iran's relations with Iraqi Kurds have been tense, especially since 1992, when Iranian Kurds established bases in the safe haven.

Baghdad, of course, has sought to do unto Tehran what Tehran has done unto it. In March 1979, Iran's Revolutionary Guards marched on Kurdistan to quell a growing autonomy movement. Khomeini claimed Iranian Kurds were receiving aid from Iraq, a claim vehemently denied by Ghassemlou. The evidence both for and against such charges remains circumstantial. On the one hand, Ghassemlou has enjoyed warm relations with the Baath government in Iraq. But on the other, the suddenness of events, from the shah's fall in February to the Kurdish uprising in March, caught Saddam Hussein off-guard, as it did most regional and world leaders.

During the Iran-Iraq War itself, the government frequently charged Iranian Kurds with treasonous acts of support for the Iraqis. But a major Iranian offensive into Kurdistan early in the war eliminated an independent base under Kurdish control, thus forcing the Iranian *peshmerga* to break up into small groups. This made it difficult for the Iraqi government to supply arms, though it continued to offer modest help to the KDPI until the cease-fire in August 1988.

Outmanned and outgunned by their governmental adversaries, the Kurds have been forced by necessity to seek foreign alliances for their separatist cause. Those alliances are usually with threatening enemies of the government in power. In the 1970s, the Iraqi Kurds' decision to accept military aid from Iran further justified the Iraqi government's charges of Kurdish treason and hardened Baghdad's commitment to eliminate that treason with force of arms. The situation was much the same in Iran. When asked in 1981 to respond to Tehran's charges that the KDPI was receiving arms from Baghdad, Ghassemlou replied, "These accusations about us working for a foreign power are nothing new; every time the Kurdish people have tried to raise demands they have been accused of being enemy agents."[33] But of course the KDPI *was* receiving Iraqi arms, and *was* thereby serving Iraqi purposes.

Unlike Iran and Iraq, Turkey perceives no immediate foreign threats from neighboring states, at least not in the Middle East. In the early years of the PKK's struggle with the Turkish military, the guerrillas occasionally launched raids on Turkish soil from bases in Syria and Iraq. Turkey retaliated against PKK bases in Iraq, but sought to negotiate with Syrian President Hafez al-Assad. Turkey, which remained officially neutral during the Iran-Iraq War, but clearly leaned toward Iraq, continued to accuse Iran of supporting the PKK. This was true, but the support did not amount to much in practice. Pro-Iranian forces in Lebanon trained with PKK forces, but direct Iranian support for the PKK was not possible given the strained circumstances of the war. When Turkish forces launched an attack, prearranged with Baghdad, against PKK bases in northern Iraq in 1987, Iran loudly protested, saying that the Turks were, in fact, killing Iraqi Kurds as well. Again, Turkey responded with claims that it attacked PKK forces alone, asserted its neutrality, and hinted that Iran's outrage was *prima facie* evidence of Tehran's support of the PKK.

Before the fall of the Soviet Union, the Turks also blamed the Russians and their Soviet Bloc allies of supporting the PKK. That accusation, of course, disappeared with the Soviet Union's demise. More important, the Turkish government began to admit in the late 1980s that the PKK was indeed operating from bases within Turkey, as the PKK had claimed all along. Turkey continues to call the PKK a terrorist organization, but admits that it is, at least in part, a homegrown one. Recently, however, Turkey has been making accusations that its longtime NATO rival, Greece, has been "openly" funding the PKK, a charge Athens denies, though it does have official contacts with the PKK.

NOTES

[1] "The Trial of Ismail Besikçi" in *Kurdish Times*, vol. 1, No. 2 (Fall 1986), pp. 16–17.

[2] Kendal, Nizzan, "Kurdistan in Turkey," in Chaliand, Gerard, ed., *A People without a Country: The Kurds and Kurdistan* (New York: Olive Branch Press, 1993), pp. 59–60.

[3] Anonymous, interview with author, November 21, 1994.

[4] Izady, Mehrdad, "Persian Carrot and Turkish Stick," in *Kurdish Times*, vol. 3, No. 2 (Fall 1980), p. 38.

[5] Hotham, David, The Turks (London: John Murray, 1972), p. 57.

[6] Kendal, *op.cit.*, p. 71.

[7] Marcus, Aliza, "Turkey's Kurds after the Gulf War: A Report from the Southeast," in Chaliand, Gerard, ed., pp. 239–240.

[8] Kaplan, Robert, "MacNeil/Lehrer Newshour," (March 21, 1995).

[9] Nisan, Mordechai, *Minorities in the Middle East: A History of Struggle and Self-Expression* (Jefferson, N.C.: McFarland and Company, 1991), p. 35.

[10] This is not the place to go into the differences between these two sects, products of an early Islamic schism; suffice it to say that Sunnis regard Shiites as somewhat heretical and Shiites regard Sunni authority as somehow illegitimate. Both views are based on rival lineages descended from the Prophet; the Sunni a continuous one through the last Ottoman caliphate in 1924, and the Shiite a broken one ending in 661 A.D.

[11] Powell, E. Alexander, *By Camel and Car to the Peacock Throne* (New York: The Century Company, 1923), p. 192.

[12] Longrigg, Stephen Hemsley, *Iraq, 1900 to 1950: A Political, Social, and Economic History* (New York: Oxford University Press, 1953), p. 222.

[13] Ghareeb, Edmund, *The Kurdish Question in Iraq* (Syracuse N.Y.: Syracuse University Press, 1981), pp. 192–193.

[14] Farouk-Sluglett, Marion, and Peter Sluglett, *Iraq Since 1958: From Revolution to Dictatorship* (London: KPI, 1987), p. 18.

[15] Hazleton, Fran, "Iraq to 1963," in CARDRI (Committee against Repression and for Democratic Rights in Iraq), *Saddam's Iraq: Revolution or Reaction?* (London: Zed Books, 1986), p. 23.

[16] Farouk–Sluglett and Sluglett, *op.cit.* p. 89.

[17] *Ibid.*, pp. 85, 92.

[18] al-Khalil, Samir (pseud.), *Republic of Fear: The Politics of Modern Iraq* (Berkeley: University of California Press, 1989).

[18a] Slugletts, p. 182.

[19] Middle East Watch, *Genocide in Iraq: The Anfal Campaign against the Kurds*, (New York: Human Rights Watch, 1993), p. 234.

[20] Farouk-Sluglett, and Sluglett, *op. cit.*, p. 8.

[21] al-Radi, Selma, "Punishing the People: Iraqi Sanctions—A Postwar Crime," in *The Nation*, vol. 260, No. 12, pp. 416–419.

[22] Vanly, Ismet Sheriff, "Kurdistan in Iraq," in Chaliand, Gerard, ed., p. 145.

[23] Amjad, Mohammed, *Iran: From Royal Dictatorship to Theocracy* (New York: Greenwood Press, 1989), p. 57.

[24] *Ibid.*, pp. 58–65.

[25] *Ibid.*, p. 75.

[26] *Ibid.*, p. 152.

[27] Central Intelligence Agency, *World Factbook* (CD-ROM), (Parsippany, N.J.: Bureau of Electronic Publishing, 1992), p. 10 ("Iran" entry).

[28] Chaliand, Gerard, "Iranian Kurds under Ayatollah Khomeini," in Chaliand, Gerard, ed., p. 212.

[29] Anonymous, interview with author, March 25, 1995.

[30] The accidental shooting down of an American helicopter by an American fighter pilot in 1994 may, in fact, have been the result of the fact that Turkey operates with relative impunity in the safe haven. The existence of a command structure independent of the Coalition may have contributed to the pilot's confusion.

[31] Ghassemlou, A. R., "Kurdistan in Iran," in Chaliand, Gerard, ed., p. 112.
[32] Karadaghi, Kamran, "The Two Gulf Wars: The Kurds on the World Stage, 1979–1992," in Chaliand, Gerard, ed., p. 215.
[33] "KDP's Qassemlu: 'The Clergy Have Confiscated the Revolution'," in *MERIP Reports* (July/August 1981), p. 18.

5

ISSUES, TACTICS
AND NEGOTIATIONS

Believe neither in the oppressor's laugh
nor the pleasantness of winter weather.

In his own home a man is free to say
he will break the sultan's neck.
                    —Kurdish proverbs

ISSUES

It is probably not exaggerating to say that, in their heart of hearts, the vast majority of Kurds would prefer an independent and sovereign Kurdistan, encompassing Kurds throughout the Middle East. Of course, most Kurds would also readily agree that this millenarian goal is precisely that, an exercise in wishful thinking. Moreover, while political self-determination, cultural autonomy and economic justice are important to Kurds in all three countries, they are not equally important in each. In Turkey, for example, cultural autonomy is a more pressing issue than in the Kurdish regions of Iraq and Iran. Similarly, self-determination is a more pressing goal in Iraq than in Iran.

The reason for these differences are many. They include demographics, degree of socioeconomic integration of the Kurds into the larger society, Kurdish identity, national history, as well as a host of other factors. But the most important determinant is a simple fact: the Kurds are a minority of not more than 20 percent in every country in which they dwell. Thus, the key factor in determining Kurdish political, cultural and economic priorities is the national regime and dominant ideology against which the Kurds in each country struggle to define themselves.

POLITICS AND NATIONALISM

There is no denying the powerful sense of national identity most Kurds share. But what is it based on? As a minority without a state of its own, the Kurdish people defines itself through perceived differences with the dominant groups in each state. Yet Kurds are largely Muslim like their neighbors, and they are not remarkably different in any obvious way.

What, then, makes the Kurds a single people? Kurdish identity, like other's, can be understood as the product of a shared language, culture and history, of which the most influential elements have been the mountainous topography of the Kurds' homeland, the hostility of powerful states, and the development of nationalist ideology among neighboring peoples, particularly those who controlled the machinery of the states in which the Kurds have lived in the twentieth century.

PRE–WORLD WAR I

Kurdish national aspirations are at least 400 years old. According to scholar Mehrdad Izady, the very first written history of Kurdistan evokes national feeling. In the late-sixteenth-century *Sharafnama*, written by Prince Sharaf al-Din, Mir of Bitlis, the author laments the absence of a pan-Kurdish king and blames all the troubles besetting Kurdistan in an age of Ottoman and Persian imperial ambition on that regrettable fact. The prince's sentiments were echoed a century later by Kurdish poet Ahmad Khani, author of the Kurdish epic *Mem o Zin*. "Behold! From Arabia to Georgia is the Kurdish home," he wrote in 1695. "But when the Persian ocean and the Turkish seas get rough, only the Kurdish country is spattered with blood." Khani, too, believed a unified Kurdistan, under universally respected leaders, was the only way for Kurds to defend their cultural heritage and assert their political and economic nationhood. Rife with patriotic themes, Khani's epic and Sharaf's history, says Izady, are the first "concrete expression[s] of a pan-Kurdish awareness, if not of nationalism in the modern sense."[1]

Equally notable, he says, are the two authors' thoughts on Islam. In an age when the principle, if not the practice, of Islamic unity, or *umma*, was paramount in the Middle East, Prince Sharaf and Ahmad Khani asserted a higher secular allegiance: Kurdishness above Islamism. Moreover, both works established a theme that has resonated through subsequent Kurdish history: Islamism as the enemy of Kurdishness or, more precisely, the ambitions of Islamic emperors, who invoked the ideal of the *umma* as an obstacle to Kurdish freedom. Oppression has always arrived in Kurdistan riding an Islamic steed, hence the Kurds' traditional resistance to the concept and practice of Islamic unity, one of the key principles of the faith laid down by the Prophet Muhammed.

The rule of the Kurdish emirs, or princely vassals, of the Ottoman sultan and the Persian emperor, simultaneously challenged and reinforced the ideal of Kurdish unity from the sixteenth to nineteenth centuries. While the patronage of the emirs sustained Kurdish cultural achievement and a degree of political and economic autonomy, it also promulgated an allegiance to the individual prince rather than to the ideal of a pan-Kurdish kingdom. This allegiance, of course, was frequently exploited by the imperial governments in Constantinople and Tehran who, when necessary and when possible, pitted emir against emir, further undermining the possibility of Kurdish unity.

The destruction of the Kurdish principalities and the assertion of imperial authority in the early nineteenth century unmade and remade Kurdish national identity. That is to say, the fall of the emirates eliminated one level of state authority (and the only effective local government), loyalty to which had been encouraged by the Kurdish princes and their imperial benefactors. The collapse of princely authority thus plunged Kurdistan into social and political chaos. By the mid-nineteenth century, much of Kurdistan answered to either local tribal chiefs or imperial bureaucrats, none of whom were capable of or interested in fashioning a new Kurdish polity.

The chiefs jealously guarded the economic and political prerogatives that came from doing the bidding of the central governments in Constantinople and Tehran. Imperial administrators attempted to foster loyalty to or at least fear of the central governments; in general, imperial governments tried to foster a kind of antinationalism. Things Ottoman were praised rather than things Turkish or Kurdish. The designation "Turk," as historian David Hotham writes, became a synonym for "boor" and "peasant," and Kurds were always poor cousins of the Turks as far as the empire was concerned.

Yet even during the period of least Kurdish unity, the late nineteenth century, Kurdish identity as a "nation apart" was maintained and passed down from generation to generation. Travelers to the region often commented on this "inheritance." "The tales of all the raids and feuds and wars in these mountains," said Carleton Coon, a British writer of the late nineteenth century,

> deeds of daring, self-sacrifice, greed and treachery form the subject for Kurdish epic songs, which the young warrior hears as he lies awake in his cradle. One cannot fail to be impressed by the thorough indoctrination in the heroics of bloodletting that young Kurds . . . undergo.[2]

Two critical factors in the development of Kurdish nationalism emerged in the late nineteenth century, though they would not become significant until after World War I. First was the growth and expansion of the state. Both the Ottomans and the Persians, influenced by the European state model and the European advisors the courts employed, were determined to extend judicial and administrative control over their domains, including Kurdistan. But because of Kurdish resistance, including the new religious messianism of *shaikh*-led rebellions and the general ineffectiveness of the imperial bureaucracies, this process had barely begun by the time World War I demolished the old imperial order in the Middle East.

Second, Western ideas of nationalism began circulating among the Kurdish population in the early twentieth century. Not surprisingly the first converts to the new nationalist thinking were educated urban Kurds, who formed literary and educational societies in Constantinople, organizations that Americans today might call consciousness-raising groups. Composed mostly of urban intellectuals, these groups were isolated both geographically and ideologically from the mainstream of the Kurdish community. Despite their minimal impact, however, their mere existence was deemed enough of a threat by their rival nationalists, the Young Turks, to warrant their being disbanded.

Not so easily closed, however, was the back door through which modern ideas of nationalism entered Kurdish consciousness. The growing presence of the Russian Empire in the region in the nineteenth century, as well as the appearance of British and American missionaries, introduced Western nationalist ideas directly into the Kurdish countryside. By supporting and promoting such ideas among the Armenians and other Christians, the Russians, British and Americans inadvertently inspired a competing nationalism among the Kurds, who felt threatened by the assertiveness of their traditional rivals.

TURKEY

Politics and nationalism

During and after World War I, disunity continued to characterize Kurdish politics, except that now the problem played out on an international stage. As the victorious Allies dismantled the Ottoman Empire, the Kurds were unable to take advantage of the opportunity. The fluid political situation soon set, and the Kurds were left without a state, indeed without even basic guarantees of minority protection within the new states and mandates of the Middle East. The geopolitical considerations of the Allies worked against them, as did the sudden surge of Turkish nationalism; but the Kurdish leaders bore much responsibility for this outcome. Instead of uniting at the various postwar conferences, they bickered among themselves, tribe against tribe and urban progressive against rural traditionalist.

The interwar period provided further setbacks to Kurdish national aspirations. The hypernationalism of the Turks in this period both sparked Kurdish uprisings, then effectively crushed them. The first several decades of the post–World War II era were marked by a cessation of Kurdish armed rebellion, a continuing campaign against Kurdish and pro-Kurdish politicians and intellectuals (including imprisonment and torture), as well as a fitful participation in Turkish electoral politics. As one Kurdish scholar noted, "it was a generational thing. Those who experienced the terrible fighting before [World War II] just wanted to live in peace, and they taught their children to obey authorities and just go along with things. It took a second generation to challenge the government again. . . . It's an old pattern in Kurdish history."[3]

Recent history, especially since the rise of the PKK in the early 1980s, reveals another pattern. The harsh Turkish repression of Kurds and Kurdish organizations after the military coup of 1980, including the arrest of over 33,000 "leftist secessionist activists," sparked the growth of the PKK and its decision, in 1984, to launch guerrilla attacks on Turkish security forces. This was just one incident, albeit a catastrophic one, in a series of crackdowns that convinced PKK leaders that electoral politics would not bring effective change. Meanwhile, the government, rightly believing it had a Marxist-led secessionist movement on its hands, immediately counterattacked with overwhelming military force, as it had done in the interwar period.

Thus the war in Kurdistan has created its own issues and demands. The Kurds insist that Turkey cease its human rights violations, including the use of torture, military-connected death squad attacks on Kurdish political organizers and institutions, and the destruction of villages; end its emergency rule that allows for mass arrests for political crimes and a militarization of the countryside; and repeal the rebellion-inspired antiterrorist law of 1991 that permits governmental suppression, in the name of national indivisibility, of pro-Kurdish media and parties. For its part, the government claims that its effort to defeat the PKK militarily is both constitutional and legally mandated. Under both statute and constitutional provision, acts aimed at destroying the national unity of Turkey are proscribed. The government claims, not without reason, that the PKK's solution to the Kurdish issue is the partition of Turkish territory.

Clearly, despite the issues that have arisen out of the current 12-year war, the main point remains the two sides' differing ideas of the appropriate political relationship between the Kurds and the government in Ankara. Are these differing ideas mutually exclusive? That is to say, will the PKK settle for nothing less than an independent Kurdistan? Will the Turks continue to insist that not even a vestige of political autonomy and self-rule be granted to the Kurds? And what of the subsidiary, war-related issues? The Kurds insist that these have to be resolved before they can negotiate the sovereignty issue. The government says that it will never negotiate with the PKK because it is, by definition, a terrorist organization and a threat to national security. Besides its domestic mandate, Ankara also claims it has an international obligation to fight terrorist organizations.

The first point of contention between Kurds and Turks remains one of identity. Until the late 1980s, and even today on the Turkish right and in some circles of the military, the very fact of Kurdish existence has been denied. "In Turkey," a leader of the then-ruling Motherland Party noted in 1988,

> there is no such thing as [a] Kurdish question. There are mentalities in Turkey
> who think there is a Kurdish question and who want to divide our country

by saying there is a Kurdish question and thereby cause havoc. I myself am from the east. I know all the problems of the east. . . . [Kurdish] is a dialect. It is definitely not a language and those who are called Kurds do not belong to a separate nation. They are a branch of Turks who migrated from Central Asia.[4]

Since the late 1980s, Turkey's official position on Kurdish identity has been modified and liberalized to a degree. Kurds have been partially recognized as a distinct ethnic group, and in the 1991 semi-legalization of the use of the Kurdish language there was an implicit recognition that the Kurds are of different origin from the Turks. Today, the government's reticence to acknowledge Kurdish identity rests on three factors: the Kurds' Turkish citizenship, demographic change, and Kurdish political support for the government. In an unpublished letter to the *Washington Post*, Turkish ambassador to the US Nuzhet Kandemir wrote that "the Kurds in Turkey are not a 'minority,' but equal members of society by virtue of their status as equal Turkish citizens, serving throughout all levels of Government,"[5] while the late President Turgut Ozal told the *Los Angeles Times* in 1991 that there is no real Kurdistan anymore since "the main body of the Kurdish people is not in east Anatolia anymore. It is in Istanbul, Ankara, Izmir . . . they are part of the majority."[6] The Turkish government also points to election figures, pointing to a roughly 80-percent participation rate in the southeastern provinces.

Not so, say opponents of the regime and many outside observers. Elections figures, says a PKK spokesperson, are "cooked-up figures" with no real bearing on actual participation, while scenes of Kurdish people waiting in long lines in recent elections are propaganda photos.[6a] In general, insist Kurdish activists, the massive military presence in the southeast makes a mockery of the electoral process. As for equality of citizenship, that too is denied, as Kurds point to the fact that "emergency rule" remains in effect only in Kurdistan. As for Kurds in western cities, they are forced to assimilate and give up their Kurdishness if they expect to succeed. "In Turkey people must still deny their Kurdish origins if they wish to become successful," notes journalist Sheri Lazier.

> Kurds can own foreign cars, live in big homes and be seen in all the right restaurants like their Turkish equivalents if they upgrade their social class to that of "bourgeois Turk." For many, it is no sacrifice to deny their Kurdishness, for Kurdishness has been equated with social inferiority by the Turks. To get ahead, one must play the Turkish game. Such is the case of numerous Kurdish actors and singers who gain fame and wealth only within this framework.[7]

Finally, they say, Ozal's statement about the Kurdish diaspora over-estimates its size and ignores the fact that many Kurds live in western Turkey precisely because of Turkish oppression in the east, and that most would readily return if the situation there improved.

The issue of Kurdish sovereignty is, if anything, even more divisive than that of Kurdish identity. But as with the former, the terms and conditions of the debate have changed dramatically in recent years, at least on the Kurdish side of the issue. Part of the problem is deciphering what is meant by political terms such as "independence," "federation" and "autonomy" that get bandied about by both sides. When the PKK first took up arms, its manifesto proposed a pan-Kurdish state that spanned the borders of Turkey, Iran, Iraq and Syria. How much of this was posturing is difficult to say, and now somewhat academic, since the PKK claims it has dropped the idea of a separate Kurdish nation, even within Turkey, at least for the immediate future. The current position of the PKK includes a proposal for a "federal" Turkey, with an as-yet-unspecified but negotiable degree of self-determination, self-rule and, of course, full cultural freedom in an autonomous Kurdish republic. Implicit in these specific measures is an important prerequisite: the democratization of Turkey. "Lately," says journalist Aliza Marcus, after a 1994 trip to Kurdistan, "the PKK has been using the language of democracy."[8] Indeed, PKK leader Abdullah Ocalan insisted in a 1992 interview that "the oppression of Kurdistan also means the oppression of the Turkish people."[9]

The PKK's position on Kurdish self-determination is somewhat contradictory. At times Ocalan has spoken of the need for the "independence, democracy, and unity of Kurdistan," and at others, indeed in the very same communiqués, says "unquestionably a [federative solution] is what we seek."

> Our goal is not to divide Turkey, but to share it. I don't see it as either reasonable or necessary that [a Kurdish region should] be detached from the country as if cut by a knife. But the Kurds will determine their own fate.[10]

Exactly what that last line means is left unclear. Ocalan wrote in 1992 of a "parliament of national representatives . . . that will play the role of a control and leadership organ, [even] if it is not an actual government it will possess a government-like leading role."[11]

The recent emphasis on representative government and democracy in PKK's pronouncements is in part a shift in rhetoric, if not ideology. The PKK claims the shift from Leninist to democratic rhetoric reflects both the organization's increasing sophistication and the feedback it solicits from the Kurdish people. Skeptics say the change reflects a more subtle PKK appeal to potential supporters in the European and international community. On the other hand, the emphasis on democracy is nothing new. Ocalan has long made it clear that he believes the PKK represents a break from the Kurdish past, a past he says still lives in northern Iraq. There will, he says, be no deals that establish a false "autonomy" in which a few handpicked Kurdish leaders do the bidding of the government. "A fundamental lesson drawn from Kurdish history by the PKK," writes Ocalan,

> is that the demand for "autonomy" expresses the interests of the Kurdish feudal and bourgeois sectors seeking an alliance, on the best terms they can get, with one or other of the colonial ruling classes. . . . This is the lesson of the Barzani clan's long history of failed deals with the Shah of Iran, the Iranian fundamentalists, the Iraqi Baathists and now the Turkish government.[12]

Ocalan's increasingly nuanced position on Kurdish sovereignty, however, is often lost on his followers. Marcus found PKK guerrillas talking of setting up a "Marxist-Leninist state" and insisting that "there is only one thing, revolution" as recently as 1994.[13] Among the population, the strength of support for the various sovereignty options is equally hard to decipher, since no opinion polls are permitted and, with the ban on explicitly pro-Kurdish political parties, there can be no real test of electoral strength. A recent underground survey of Turkish Kurd public opinion, conducted in secret by the American-based Kurdish Cultural Institute, revealed 90-percent approval of an independent Kurdish state, though the tiny sample base makes it rather unreliable. Journalist Arnold Hottinger writes that "the prevalent tendency is to fight for Kurdish cultural rights and to see autonomy as a long-term goal."[14] While most Western journalistic accounts indicate that support for the PKK has grown dramatically in recent years, it is unclear if this has anything to do with the PKK's recent moderation of its stance on Kurdish independence.

For the Turkish government, the issue of PKK support among the Kurds and popular sentiment for an independent Kurdistan are clear. "The fact remains," says Kandemir, "that mainstream Turkish citizens of Kurdish origin [oppose] the PKK, its separatist goals, and its terrorist tactics."[15] The government has long maintained that vast majority of citizens in southeastern Turkey agrees with Ankara's position that advocacy of Kurdish self-determination represents a threat to the integrity of the Turkish state, which those same citizens support and to which they are loyal. "It should also be borne in mind," notes a report from the officially sanctioned Ankara Journalist Association:

> that the people living in the southeastern region of Anatolia are not all Kurds. . . . It is populated by just about all the different kinds of people of varied roots who make up the Turkish nation as defined by the Constitution. . . . If a name is to be give to the problem, this should never be named as the "Kurdish" problem. It is the "Southeast Anatolian Problem."[16]

Economics

The poverty in southeastern Turkey is palpable. "The peasants work tiny plots of land, with a few sheep or cattle, or are completely landless and work for a pittance on the vast estates of the . . . local Kurdish landlords who rule over the countryside with an iron hand," reported journalist Sam Corbin on a visit to the region in 1985. "Considerable mineral wealth . . . is extracted by Kurdish workers for the benefit of Turkish or multinational corporations, which contribute nothing to the region's development."[17] The poverty is exacerbated by the region's explosive population growth and an unemployment rate estimated at over 30 percent. As one villager related his experience, "For six years I studied in a technical college to be an electrical engineer. Today there are no jobs. . . . My family lives in this area, so all I can do is repair our water pump or mend my brother's motorcycle."[18] According to one government report, the Kurdish economy, like that of Turkey, as a whole, depends heavily on the more than $1 billion repatriated every year by Turkish citizens working abroad.

As virtually every journalist who has visited the region points out, Kurdistan suffers from an underdeveloped infrastructure. "The Kurdish villages of eastern Turkey lack modern amenities," writes Corbin. "There are virtually no schools or hospitals, and no electricity for homes."[18a] It is not so much that Kurdistan lacks an infrastructure as that it lacks one designed to serve the people of the region. Electric power lines crisscross the region, several large gas and oil pipelines run through Kurdistan and a major highway links Turkey and Iraq via Kurdistan. Except for the last, which has created employment for Kurdish truck drivers, none of these projects benefits or employs significant numbers of Kurds.

Critics of the government who say that the continuing poverty and lack of development in Kurdistan are major factors in the PKK's appeal are, surprisingly enough, joined by the government, which admits that Kurdish poverty is a serious issue. Differences between the two viewpoints emerge over what and how much the government is doing to address the problem. "Turkey," says Kandemir, "has long recognized that the best tool against the PKK terror is economic and social reforms."[19] To that end the government claims that it spends 13 times as much in investments in Kurdistan as it collects in tax revenues and that in fiscal 1993, for example, per-capita investment in the southeast was 1.6 times greater than in western regions. In 1994, it announced an initiative to spend almost $200 million on developing Kurdish agriculture, and claimed it has begun a mass housing project in both rural and urban areas of Kurdistan, though it earmarked funds that year for just 2,200 houses and apartments.

The centerpiece of the government's efforts to revitalize the Kurdish economy is the Greater Anatolia Project (GAP), a massive hydroelectric and irrigation project involving over a dozen separate dams, as well as roads and other infrastructure connected to them. The project is immense: the Ataturk Dam alone, the fifth largest in the world, completed in 1992, generates over 2.4 billion watts of electricity, while the Lower Euphrates irrigation project, currently under construction, will water over 1.7 million acres of farmland.

There is a dispute between the government and its Kurdish critics about the effect of the GAP on Kurdistan. Critics say it is simply a project in Kurdistan, like previous infrastructure projects and investments, but not for Kurdistan. Others go farther and say it will set back Kurdish development by flooding productive valleys and displacing even more people. As a Kurdish shopkeeper in Bitlis noted, after the hydroelectric project near his town was finished, high unemployment returned, because there was less land to work. "Even fewer men are employed," he said, "and now all the electricity goes to the west."[20] The shopkeeper's own electricity, like that in most of Bitlis, came from diesel generators.

The government disagrees with this assessment, saying GAP will solve the economic problems of the southeastern provinces better than will the socialist agenda of the PKK. And, indeed, the PKK has reiterated many times that its economic agenda is socialist, though it has modified some of its economic ideas in recent years. While Ocalan has frequently claimed that the Kurdish landholders and bourgeoisie are as big an obstacle to the development of the Kurdish economy as the government itself, he has lately talked of the need for local capitalists to help participate in the building of a free and prosperous Kurdistan. The PKK has also altered its position on foreign investment. Where once it charged that Western corporations were "bleeding" Kurdistan, it now sees a constructive role for them in the future. And the idea of state-run farms has given way to calls for land redistribution, with compensation to the owners.

All of this, says the government, is a ploy to create "useful dupes" in the West. The PKK, it insists, remains Marxist in its economic orientation, an assessment seemingly confirmed by the PKK guerrillas Marcus interviewed in 1994. "Socialism is our target, we will never give it up," one of them told her. Among the populace, however, there appears to be less interest in the PKK's socialist agenda than in its nationalist one. "Socialism? What does that mean?" a villager asked. "All I know is that the PKK is fighting for our rights."[21] To this the government responds that it is the PKK itself which is to blame for the continued economic stagnation of Kurdistan. "Anything constructive in the region," says Kandemir, "becomes a target for the violence of the PKK, which understands that ongoing successful reforms would eradicate its very existence."[22] But as *Kurdish Life* editor Vera Beaudin Saeedpour notes, "if the PKK wanted to blow up the [GAP] dams, they could do it in a minute. But they've told me: why should we? They're going to be ours soon."[23]

In either case, the war itself is clearly hampering the development of Kurdistan's economy. According to one recent visitor, the only substantial economic activity in many parts of Kurdistan is military-related. "Until recently, Hakkari was little more than a village," noted *The Middle East*.

Now 10-story apartment blocks are being built by the army and civil service to house their personnel. The tall concrete buildings are in stark contrast to older mud-and-straw houses nearby. But in Diyarbakir, which is of little strategic value, there has been no real development.[24]

Culture and society

Until 1991, when Turkish President Turgut Ozal[25] legalized the use of spoken Kurdish for nonofficial purposes (the ban remains on the use of Kurdish in court, government and the media), the law on Kurdish cultural expression was simple: prohibition. It was illegal to wear Kurdish costume, sing Kurdish songs, write Kurdish poetry, study Kurdish history, or speak Kurdish in the home or in public. The very mention of the word Kurdistan was illegal. Kurdish names for towns, villages and features of geography were officially changed to Turkish ones and all references to Kurdistan were expunged from maps printed in the country. Members of the print and broadcast media were fined and imprisoned for violating the ban, which applied to Turks and Kurds alike. Turkish writer Ismail Besikçi spent 12 years in jail for advocating the Kurdish cause in books and essays. In 1979, an ex-minister of public works was charged with "weakening national feelings" and sentenced by a military tribunal to two years hard labor for, among other offenses, uttering the words, "in Turkey there are Kurds. I too am a Kurd."[26]

With all business and government dealings in Turkish only, rural Kurds, many of whom spoke little or no Turkish, were at a disadvantage both in the marketplace and government offices. Human Rights Watch noted, in its 1987 report on Turkish human rights abuses, that Kurdish families were not permitted to speak to their imprisoned loved ones in Kurdish, making communication for many impossible. The report also cites the use of fines and jail sentences for parents who insist on registering Kurdish names for their children. One former Kurdish political prisoner talked of being beaten for refusing to answer to his legal Turkish name, insisting his jailers use his Kurdish one. Nizamettin Ariç, a popular Kurdish musician, was forced to flee the country in 1981 after he sang a love song in his native language.

Moreover, Kurds still face a continuous barrage of propaganda, in both schools and the media, asserting that their culture does not in fact exist. Officially "mountain Turks who have forgotten their language," they are told, despite virtually all non-Turkish scholarship to the contrary, that they are a Turkic people and that their language is a mere dialect of Turkish. Schoolchildren are forced to memorize and recite various dictums of Ataturk, such as "a Turk is worth more than the universe," and "happy is he who can call himself a Turk."

These restrictions and indoctrination were and are based, according to the Turkish government, on the need to establish one language and one culture in a multiethnic state threatened by foreign powers who would use minorities to divide the nation. But, of course, they also were and are hard to enforce. Kurdish continued to be spoken, to use a Kurdish expression, "off the tarmac," that is, throughout the countryside, in Kurdish enclaves in Turkish cities, in private and in other areas remote from Turkish officialdom. Cassettes of Kurdish music have had a mass underground circulation since the technology was introduced in the early 1970s. Radio broadcasts in Kurdish from Iraq, Iran and Armenia are picked up in much of Turkish Kurdistan. Even printed material in Kurdish, including the writings of Abdullah Ocalan, was available, sometimes even sold on the street at informal bookstalls. As a former member of the PKK noted, "Turkey is not a very efficient totalitarian state."[27] Perhaps not, but the continuing arbitrary imposition of fines, imprisonment and, according to most human rights organizations, torture, is effective in limiting Kurdish cultural expression.

Since the late 1980s, the prohibitions of Kurdish cultural expression have eased somewhat, partly as a response to the unofficial reality described above. Kurdish concerts are now permitted, though still rare enough to be mentioned in the international press, and at least four Kurdish-language newspapers are printed in the country. Recent opening sessions of the Turkish parliament have witnessed the presence of Kurdish delegates in their national dress, and official Turkish tourist literature, designed to lure visitors from the popular Mediterranean Coast to the Turkish east, lists among its highlights Kurdish customs and festivals.

Yet restrictions remain. All Kurdish newspapers, and Turkish-language ones as well, are monitored closely for political content. This is because both the 1982 Turkish constitution and a 1991 antiterrorism law have broadly worded proscriptions on any statement advocating separatism, autonomy or anything else that "weakens" or "threatens" the integrity of the Turkish state. Under these provisions, says a Turkish human rights lawyer, a person could go to jail just for mentioning that the wheat crop was especially poor this year. Police continue to seize the assets of newspapers that report on Kurdish cultural events. As one Kurdish artist noted, not only it is hard to draw the line between discussing Kurdish culture and promoting it, but it is crucial to do so, since the former is permitted while the latter, legally considered a form of advocacy of Kurdish separatism, is forbidden.

The issue of Kurdish cultural and linguistic freedom has divided the Turkish political establishment. Hard-liners, who want to see constitutional and statutory provisions against the cultural expression of Kurdish ethnicity interpreted as broadly as possible, continue to cite the dangers to the unity and integrity of the Turkish state. Others, like Ozal and the current president, Suleyman Demirel, justify a more liberal approach, based on the argument that the government should only enforce monolingualism and monoculturalism to the extent necessary for the smooth functioning of the Turkish state. That is to say, they believe it is impractical to have schools teach and TV broadcast in more than one language. But in the print media and in live cultural events, where a smaller and more homogenous audience can be addressed, other languages should be permitted.

While Kurdish freedom of expression divides the Turkish government, virtually all Kurdish political organizations, including both the PKK and the leftist parliamentary parties that support Kurdish rights, agree that Kurdish cultural freedom is a *sine qua non* for Turkish democracy, though the extent to which the government should promote it is hotly debated. It is in dispute, to take one example, whether private stations should be allowed to broadcast in Kurdish or whether the government channels should reserve broadcast time for Kurdish-language broadcasts. Even some members of the centrist parties argue that the arbitrary imposition of fines and imprisonment for cultural expression only strengthens support for the PKK. For its part, the PKK argues that the relaxation of the total ban was meaningless because it only legalized what was already going on, the widespread use of spoken Kurdish. The PKK also claims that the continued existence of the partial ban on Kurdish cultural expression, despite widespread opposition across the political spectrum indicates that hard-liners in the military continue to formulate state policy, despite the facade of democracy.

IRAQ

Baghdad and the Kurds

Iraqi Kurdistan has been at war for most of the past three decades, and at war with the Baath regime for much of the past two. Nowhere else in the Middle East have the Kurds fought longer and harder to break the grip of state administration, control and sovereignty. There are several reasons for this. First, the tribal confederations of the nineteenth century have survived into the present day. Allegiances to paramount leaders like Massoud Barzani and Jalal Talabani remain powerful, as does the Kurdish ethos of armed resistance to the state as a legitimate expression of the people's political will. Over the years, Kurds have survived numerous military campaigns against them and several catastrophic defeats. Thus, when considering the issues that have divided and continue to divide the Kurds and the Iraqi government, it is important to keep the structure, methods and aims of Kurdish tribalism in mind.

Equally important has been the government's approach to Kurdish unrest. Like all previous governments, the Baath government has tried to manipulate Kurdish leaders and instigate intratribal feuding. When that has failed, the Baath has, over the past 20 years, employed ever more effective and ruthless military means for suppressing the Kurds and their armies of *peshmerga*, methods that culminated in the use of chemical weapons at the end of the Iran-Iraq War and the *anfal* campaign immediately after. (For more on these methods, see the "Tactics" section of this chapter, below.)

Hence, many of the divisive issues in Iraq concern the war itself, as well as the distrust that the war has engendered among most Iraqi Kurds. This recent history, combined with the ancient and relatively unbroken tradition of tribal sovereignty, has created a vicious cycle of violence between the government and the Kurds, a cycle that has been broken, at least for the moment, by the establishment of the UN safe haven.

Like their Turkish brethren, the Kurds of Iraq have been politically repressed, economically shortchanged and culturally stifled. But with the exception of the political, the repression has never approached the degree of that faced by the Turkish Kurds. On several occasions over the past 20 years, the government in Baghdad has offered what appeared to be generous concessions on self-determination, economic development and cultural freedom: once in 1970, again in 1975, during the mid-1980s and most recently in the early 1990s. Usually these offers to negotiate have been turned down by the Kurdish leaders; in other cases, when negotiations did ensue, they broke down within a year or two. Why? First, Kurdish leaders have little faith in the Baghdad government, accusing it of bargaining in bad faith by using temporary cease-fires to position itself militarily. It should be noted, however, that Baghdad, unlike Ankara, has been willing to talk to Kurdish rebel leaders and to place concrete proposals on the negotiating table.

But putting aside for the moment accusations of duplicity and brutal methods of suppression, responsibility for the ongoing hostility lies with the Kurdish leaders as well. Like Saddam Hussein, Barzani and especially Talabani have frequently upped the ante of demands when they felt they were in a relative position of strength. In 1970, for example, Baghdad offered a comprehensive plan for Kurdish self-administration and cultural freedom. This plan was the basis for a series of cease-fire negotiations that eventually succumbed to mistrust. For their part, the Kurds believed they could not be defeated militarily, and they held out for greater concessions.

Again in 1985, at a time when Baghdad had been forced to withdraw most of its troops from Kurdistan, a similar proposal was made and turned down by the Kurds. "Autonomy," said Talabani at the time:

> is a very limited form of self-rule. We are not content with it. We don't think autonomy can solve the Kurdish problem in Iraq. At this moment, the continuing war between Iran and Iraq is paving the way for certain changes which we expect to be (perhaps) favourable to new slogans for the Kurdish national movement.

He added that what the Kurds were fighting for was "self-determination . . . [including] an independent state, a federal state, and Autonomy (real autonomy)."[28] While the problem of deciphering the terms is evident (how, for example, can one simultaneously fight for an "independent state" and a "federal state" with Arab Iraq?), the strategy is clear: to escalate demands, ultimately culminating in a demand for an independent state, based on the relative strength of the Kurdish negotiating position.

In 1990, Kurdish leaders saw an opportunity to push their agenda within days of the Iraqi invasion of Kuwait. There were overtures made by Talabani to the US government offering Kurdish help against Saddam Hussein in exchange for a recognition of some kind of sovereignty for Kurdish Iraq, and by both Talabani and Barzani to the Turks. These latter discussions also involved a *quid pro quo* deal: Turkish recognition of Kurdish sovereignty in northern Iraq in exchange for Iraqi Kurd help in fighting the PKK (see Chapter Six for a further discussion of these events). After the establishment of the safe haven in 1991 when Kurdish tribal leaders felt especially invulnerable, their negotiations with Baghdad once again fell through. It was clear from the beginning of these most recent overtures that the Kurds were not negotiating in good faith, and that the only issue they would consider was the southern limits of the Kurdish zone, especially in regard to the oil city of Kirkuk, and not the political relationship with Baghdad or the degree of sovereignty within the safe haven.

Moreover, the leaders of the Kurds of Iraq, though heading the smallest Kurdish population in the three countries under consideration, have tried to assume a leadership position throughout Kurdistan. Their agreement with Turkey during the Gulf War was based, in part, on their hostility to the PKK as a rival organization. In recent years, they have attempted to place a loyal supporter at the head of Iran's KDPI. These efforts are reflected in some of their statements on Kurdish unity. When asked why he calls his organization the Patriotic Union of Kurdistan, Talabani cited the historical division and annexation of Kurdistan by three separate states:

> If we say "PUK" of Iraqi Kurdistan, this means that we accept that annexation and recognize it to belong to Iraq. This is Kurdistan, and we think that Kurdistan is divided. We believe in the unity of the Kurdish nation.[29]

Of course, much of the blame for divisions between the Iraqi Kurds and Baghdad lies with the latter. The Iraqi government's offers of limited Kurdish self-rule and cultural freedom are not supported by its actions. Baghdad has engaged in a policy of massive relocation of Kurds to Arab areas. This has been done for immediate security reasons, but, say Kurdish leaders, it has also been part of a larger policy of forcibly "assimilating" and "annihilating" Kurdish culture, by breaking up Kurdish society into small and isolated groups that will be unable to preserve their language and culture. Baath scorched-earth policies have left much of the once agricul-turally rich region in ruins and, before the Gulf War, poverty and unem-ployment had become acute. And while Baghdad has never shown the kind of hostility to Kurdish culture evident in Ankara, its various campaigns against both Kurdish guerrillas and Kurdish civilians, culminating in the *anfal* campaign, have been characterized by Human Rights Watch as "genocidal."

The Kurds' fears of the Baath government are based on very real memories of Baath atrocities. Nevertheless, the Kurdish leaders of the safe haven evoke skepticism among many observers with their convoluted position on negotiations with Baghdad. On the one hand, they say they will never accept a political reintegration with the Iraqi state as long as a totalitarian regime rules in Baghdad—a position that implies that they would accept reintegration under other circumstances. On the other hand, the election of a provisional government in the safe haven, an election held against the advice of the UN Coalition, indicates that the Iraqi Kurds have something more permanent in mind than simply a temporary holding status until a democratic government emerges in Iraq.

Intra-Kurdish politics
Strictly speaking, the safe haven was established in the wake of the Gulf War as a way to solve the massive refugee problem confronting Turkey and, more or less incidently, to alleviate the problem in Iran as well. Over a million and a half Kurds had fled from Iraq after a failed uprising in the late spring of 1991 and in the face of a threatened Iraqi military offensive. After most of the refugees had returned to Iraq, however, the PUK and the KDP, yoked to one another since 1986 in the Iranian-brokered, anti-Baath Iraqi Kurdistan Front (IKF), made plans to hold elections and organize a provisional government in the safe haven.

Despite evidence of widespread intimidation and violence, the elections were declared binding by both parties, with both sides getting just under 50 percent of the vote. A runoff, stipulated in the original provisions for the election, was called off. Instead an agreement was worked out whereby each party would take 50 seats in a new parliament, the executive branch would be ruled by a "high committee" of two, Talabani and Barzani, and the various ministries, media facilities and military commands would be shared by both sides. "In all likelihood," reported *Kurdish Life*, "there was no run-off election because it was already clear that such a move might precipitate conflict between the two leaders" and their followers.[30] In fact, both parties continued to control their own regions like fiefdoms and, in the bureaucratic and military institutions of the modern state they were trying to create, they divided power and positions nearly evenly between them.

Rifts began to develop almost immediately, resulting from the long-standing rivalry between the two parties and the tribal confederations behind them, as well as new problems peculiar to the safe haven. It was not just that the two sides had to share revenues and power, but also that these were shrinking. The safe haven has been beset by double sanctions, those imposed on Iraq as a whole by the Coalition and those imposed on the safe haven by Iraq. The economy is in tatters, unemployment is almost universal, and urban Kurds have been reduced to selling family possessions on the street to survive. The *New York Times* reported a 95 percent drop in Kurdish income in 1994 from pre–Gulf War levels.[30a] Furthermore, what aid has come in has been siphoned off by the two sides, with virtually no revenue going to the Kurdish Provisional Government (KPG; usually referred to by the international community as the Kurdish Regional Administration, or KRA). In short, a crisis emerged over revenues and eventually led to a civil war.

When the Turks invaded the safe haven in 1992 in pursuit of PKK guerrillas, they caused enormous grief in Barzani's fiefdom along the Turkish border, but also created great opportunities. Most of the goods that entered Iraqi Kurdistan legally, such as food and medical supplies, and everything else that got through despite the sanctions, entered through Barzani territory. Situated along the Iranian border, where cross-border trade had always been and continued to be less substantial (even though Iran did not participate in the international sanctions against Iraq), Talabani could not skim off the same kind of income from tariffs and customs. While the KDP claimed it was turning over the collected sums to the provisional government, it was, says the PUK, actually keeping the millions for itself.

Moreover, Talabani was facing a challenge along the Iranian border from Iraqi Kurdish Islamist militants presumably supported by Tehran. As devout Muslims, these Kurds found the collection of customs and tariffs unacceptable. They refused to collect them and they refused to let Talabani's PUK collect them (the government in Tehran, it should be said, avoids this problem by collecting "fees" rather than tariffs). In the autumn of 1993, the two forces clashed. Hoping to maintain the fragile unity of the provisional government, Barzani sided with Talabani and issued a statement of support in December. But faced with dwindling cross-border trade and challenges from the Kurdish Islamist party, Talabani was not collecting the kind of money he had expected and needed to run his organization.

Not only was Barzani collecting revenues on imports, he had imposed a $500 fee on Iraqi Kurds going abroad. This allowed Barzani to maintain his organization and, with elections scheduled for May 1995, to resolve the 50–50 impasse in parliament, it looked increasingly likely that he would win a majority of seats and take control of the provisional government. And despite claims to the contrary, the provisional government was not a democracy.

Moreover, says Kurdish writer Azad Sulaiman (a pseudonym; his family still lives in the safe haven), "like Saddam, neither leader can take criticism. They dismiss everything they dislike as lies, fabrications of sick and inferior minds."[31] In an interview with *Hawkar*, Kurdish intellectual Fouad Majied Mesry concurred. "When democratic people are not allowed to express themselves, we must ask ourselves what is the principle of democracy. Achievement of a democratic system is not only slogans. . . ."[32] According to Saeedpour, the current struggle in the safe haven is due neither to Baghdad nor to the recent impoverishment of the region. It is the result of poor leadership, a legacy of the Kurds' tribal past. "You have to understand the Kurdish leaders' mentality," says Saeedpour:

> It all comes down to vanity and pride and who can make others think they're more important. By making deals with the West (which the Kurds look upon with awe), they can make other Kurds think they've got all the chips. And that's what's really important to them, that's what's always mattered to these guys [Barzani and Talabani].[33]

The problem is a perilous one, and not confined to Kurdistan alone. As Mideast historian Mordechai Nisan notes, "majority rule without minority rights is a prescription for repression or rebellion." Both the tribal framework of Kurdish society and the dictatorial nature of the Iraqi regimes under which the Kurds have lived insure that an opposition party will interpret an electoral loss not as a political set back, but as "a veritable . . . [final judgment of a] law of history in the eyes of the weak."[34] In other words, the PUK feared that a KDP victory would be permanent and would mean the PUK's ultimate destruction. The land dispute between two minor chieftains allied to Barzani and Talabani, obtensibly the immediate cause of the civil war, was really an effort by the PUK and the KDP to establish control over a greater portion of the safe haven in order to control the voting in their sphere of influence. The PUK realized that what it could not win with money, it would have to win with the gun.

IRAN

During the height of the Iranian revolution, there were large anti-shah demonstrations in most Kurdish towns. But, says anthropologist Martin van Bruinessen, "these were not noticeably different from those elsewhere in Iran."[35] The demonstrators demanded the release of political prisoners and an end to human rights violations and government corruption, and eventually called for the removal of the shah's government and its replacement by a revolutionary government dedicated to social justice and democracy. Once the shah had fallen, however, Kurdish demands began to deviate from those in the rest of the country. While leftists, Islamists and ethnic minorities such as the Azerbaijanis and Arabs tried to find a place at the political table in revolutionary Tehran, the Kurds began to insist on going their own way, at least to a degree.

Within days of the shah's fall from power in February of 1979, representatives of various political groups in Iranian Kurdistan, led by the KDPI, met to discuss their demands. They came up with an eight-point program involving economic and cultural issues, and one demanding Kurdish self-determination within a federal Iran. All of these demands, however, were vague and were frequently changed, reflecting the fluid political situation in the region. Clearly, however, the nationalist overtones in the rhetoric and the increasingly strident demands pointed to a growing Kurdish desire for a rather liberal federalism, though no political leaders were asking for independence.

At the same time, Tehran was drifting in another direction. As hard-line Islamists began to assert greater control over the government, especially in the wake of the US embassy seizure in November 1979, the line on Kurdish rights hardened. In December of 1979, following the referendum on the Islamic republic—widely boycotted by the Kurds—Tehran proposed a 14-point program to the Kurds of Iran. The government offered locally constituted "provisional councils" to administer issues of local concern, though what exactly those concerns were was left unclear. Tehran said it was willing to declare the Kurds an official religious minority as Sunni Muslims, but not to allow self-administration or autonomy as an ethnic group within a federal Iran.

The differences were rather academic, since Kurdistan had already risen up against both Tehran and local elites, including large Kurdish landholders, and fashioned a radical regime of peasants and workers. "Of course, we may be short of food and other necessities," one Kurdish farmer said,

> but we have our own councils, language, schools, roads, a kind of medical service in some areas and the freedom of expressing ourselves and choosing our own organizations. All these mean a new quality in our lives and it means *AUTONOMY* [emphasis in original].[36]

This experiment in Kurdish revolutionary democracy came to an end in 1980 with a military offensive organized by Ayatollah Khomeini himself. There was a partial revival of this autonomy during the war with Iraq, but that too was crushed by the Iranian military in the final years of the war. In the wake of the war, negotiations came to nothing. A. R. Ghassemlou and his successor were assassinated before anything definite could be worked out.

Since the rise to power of President Hashemi Rafsanjani, however, there has been a growing liberalization on the Kurdish question in Tehran, though nothing beyond more calls to negotiate has been issued. However, there has been a hardening of position on the other side. The KDPI's current leader, Mustafa Hejri, is widely seen as a tool of the Iraqi Kurdish leaders who, of course, have their own agenda. They have offered Hejri the right to maintain bases in the safe haven, but they insist on dictating the terms of Iranian-Kurd dialogue. Moreover, they believe a demonstration of their hostility to the Iranian state is the best way for the Iraqi Kurds to keep in good standing with Western and Turkish allies.

Aside from the politics of the safe haven, there are still serious issues dividing the Iranian government and the Kurds. Hejri and other Kurds inside Iran insist that the Kurdish movement is a largely secular one. Thus, they say, they are not fighting as Sunnis against Shiites but, rather, as secularists against a theocratic state. Nevertheless, as one observer noted, it is not so much that many ordinary Kurds are averse to a limited application of *sharia*, or Islamic law, but that they do not like the fact that it is administered by government-appointed judges. This difference in attitudes toward the religious issue is probably due to the fact that much of the KDPI leadership, in the tradition of Ghassemlou and his successor, Sadeq Sharafkandi, is urban, secular and thus somewhat out of touch with many rural Kurds.

Kurds within Iran also claim that the government continues to maintain an arbitrary and arbitrarily enforced ban on Kurdish cultural expression. The KDPI has declared that the government is actually trying to undermine Kurdish society. "It has been proven that it is the regime's men," reads a 1991 KDPI document,

> who introduce and encourage the use of drugs. At present, drug sale has invaded the schools. . . . We wonder how the regime's representatives . . . can pretend not to know of the existence of alcohol production and the traffic which exists between neighboring countries and Iran, in spite of the imposing number of checkpoints and bodies [*sic*] responsible for fighting against smuggling.[37]

Perhaps, but any possible spread of drugs and alcohol might also reflect the growing economic frustration in the region. And the comment about smuggling may reveal deep-seated Kurdish frustration at efforts by the government to halt this traditional lucrative source of Kurdish income. Other complaints are not unique to Kurdistan. The KDPI complains that civil rights are routinely violated. Government agents, says another Kurdish communiqué, "enter everywhere without permission to look for political documents (which could send their owner to the gallows.)"[38]

Finally, say Iranian Kurds, the current government in Tehran is following the same policies toward them as did Khomeini and, indeed, the shah. During a 1991 visit by high government officials to Kurdish areas of Iran, whose ostensible purpose was to assess the postwar rebuilding process, the KDPI issued a statement which it claimed revealed the real reason for the visit. The government, it said, "is trying to find ways to divide the Kurds so that the 200,000 soldiers can leave."

> It is an embarrassment that they are there since there is no longer the excuse of the Iraq war. They are trying to promote old feudal landholders, ex-Savak [the shah's secret police] and turn them into a new *jash* [progovernment Kurdish militia], but this hasn't worked.

Now, the Kurds said, the government is trying mass conscription so as to be able "to send Kurdish youth back to repress their own people."[39] The government responded by making charges of its own, calling the KDPI "counter-revolutionaries" who work with foreign agents and governments against the "will of the Islamic Kurdish people." To which one Kurd responded, "it sounds like the Shah who used to call Kurdish rebels 'agents of red imperialism'."[40]

TACTICS

The Kurds are legendary guerrilla fighters with an ancient reputation. Greek historian Diodorus, writing in the fourth century B.C., said that the Kurds "in their highland fastnesses were more trouble than they were worth to the foreign armies and empires." It was, he advised, "sufficient to keep them by force or agreement from troubling the plain."[41] It has not been sufficient, however, for the modern states that include Kurdish populations in their territories. Turkey, Iraq and Iran have been trying to assert their administrative, judicial and fiscal authority over Kurdistan for much of this century. In this seemingly Sisyphean task, they have tried assassination, tribal manipulation and negotiation. Ultimately, all three states have resorted to military force, often on a large scale and often employing advanced military hardware acquired in the international arms market.

Their success has been mixed. They have at times temporarily halted Kurdish unrest and reasserted government authority, but over a longer time frame the military approach has been largely a failure. The reasons are simple. Not only are Kurdish fighters successful at guerrilla warfare, but their culture, particularly among highland Kurds, is imbued with the warrior ethos and a jealous regard for their independence from lowland regimes. Not for nothing do traditional Kurdish guerrillas call themselves the *peshmerga*, "those who stare death in the face" and turncoat Kurds *jash*, or "little donkeys." Kurdish territory is also difficult to access and riddled with isolated valleys and hidden caves. Unlike the armies that come to fight them, they know the territory and often receive material support and information from their civilian fellow Kurds. That is why the various regimes have tried to use Kurds to fight Kurds, either through conscription or alliance with loyal tribes. But the vagaries of tribal politics and the intense national feeling of the Kurds have often made these efforts, to quote Diodorus again, "more trouble than they were worth."

TURKEY

The Government
There are an estimated 400,000-plus Turkish soldiers, security forces and local gendarmerie currently patrolling the southeastern provinces of the country. Their enemy, the guerrillas of the PKK, number approximately 20,000, with about 75,000 "sympathizers." So far, somewhere between 15

and 20,000 people on both sides have been killed in the 12-year-long war. Moreover, it is estimated that the Turks spend about $7 billion annually on their war against the PKK, contributing largely to Turkey's current (as of 1991) $70 billion debt. Turkey received over $350 million in military aid from the US in 1995, though Congress withheld 10 percent because of alleged human rights abuses by the Turkish army.

In the early years of the war, the Turkish military was ill-equipped to cope with the guerrillas. Established as a conventional army to protect NATO's southern flank against a possible Soviet invasion, the military was organized into large battalions and was trained for standard battle campaigns, with a heavy reliance on fixed-wing aircraft and tanks. None of this is particularly useful for counterinsurgency warfare in mountainous terrain. But since 1987, the army has adjusted, establishing elite "strike forces" of 5,000 men and adopting rapid-response Cobra helicopter tactics. In addition, the PKK has recently accused the United States of providing satellite intelligence on guerrilla movements to the Turkish military.

Beginning in the winter of 1994–1995, the army began year-long campaigning against the PKK, a change from its previous practice of withdrawing from the mountains during the winter when heavy snows make roads virtually impassable. The difficulties of winter campaigning were expressed by an army official during a typical rapid-response attack, part of a clash between guerrillas and soldiers in December 1994 when the army airlifted 10,000 men by helicopter to the Tunceli region. "The fighting is getting very intense in some points," he told a Reuters reporter at the time, "but although the rebels are still encircled, bad weather has slowed operations at times."[42]

In addition to the use of unconventional forces, the Turkish military may also be using unconventional weapons. According to the British-based Kurdistan Human Rights Project, the Turks have been using napalm against the PKK. After listening to Kurd civilians describe the bodies of guerrillas they had buried, the organization declared "there is nothing in the descriptions or the photographs [taken at the time the bodies were exhumed] to contradict the use of napalm."[43]

Turkey has also escalated the war by attacking PKK bases in the safe haven of Iraq, though this is nothing new. As early as 1983, during the Iran-Iraq War, Iraqi Kurds were complaining that Turkish soldiers and planes were killing Iraqi Kurd civilians and guerrillas. Turkey admitted that there might have been some accidental attacks; the Kurds said they were deliberate, part of a deal between Ankara and Baghdad. It has been alleged that, in order to gain the permission of the Iraqi government to enter its territory in pursuit of the PKK, the Turks offered to go after KDP and PUK guerrillas, who were fighting the beleaguered Iraqi military at the time. The attacks continued through the war and after, though it was no longer in Ankara's interest to attack Iraqi Kurds, since Turkey is no longer allied with

Baghdad. Yet as late as 1991, KDP leader Barzani charged Turkey with attacks on Iraqi Kurds. "We confirm that the bombed targets are purely civilian and residential areas," he said, adding, "we also catagorically [sic] deny the presence of any PKK bases in the affected areas."[44]

The protestations have not changed Turkish policy. They claim that so-called Iraqi Kurds and Turkish Kurd refugees in Iraq are actually PKK guerrillas. Thus they have escalated their offensive in northern Iraq. In March of 1995, the Turks sent in 35,000 troops against an alleged force of 2,000 guerrillas, in what the government admitted was the largest Turkish military campaign in the history of the republic. Despite its size, most experts said the offensive was ineffectual. The huge preinvasion buildup, they say, tipped off the guerrillas. "This kind of thing, with pincer movements and tanks, looks good in the cabinet room or on a World War One map," commented one military analyst, "[but] it will accomplish nothing significant against the PKK. Most guerrillas probably melted away before the assault, leaving Kurdish civilians behind."[45] In July, the Turks again launched a major offensive into the safe haven, though it did not match the March incursion in number of troops or intensity of the fighting.

Frustrated in its efforts to defeat the guerrillas militarily, the Turkish government has tried to neutralize their civilian base. Local human rights officials estimate that over 4,000 villages in the southeast have been forcibly evacuated. PKK representatives in the US claim that between 1.5 and 2 million Kurdish civilians have been coerced "to flee their millennium old homes to the large cities with neither shelter or jobs."[46] Kurds and human rights observers say that many of the villages have been burned to prevent the inhabitants from returning. The choice of villages is not accidental, say Kurdish rebels. The government has created a *cordon sanitaire* of free-fire zones and minefields along its borders with Iraq, Iran and Syria. Originally planned to encompass 600 square kilometers, it was scaled back after protests from European governments. However in 1992, the Turks established a smaller zone inside the safe haven—that is, on the Iraqi-Kurdish side of the Turkish border.

In villages that remain, the Turkish military has established village militias, or village guards, that patrol the surrounding areas, engaging the PKK in firefights and reporting guerrilla movements to the military. Kurdish villagers say and human rights observers confirm that villagers are usually conscripted into the militias against their will. If they refuse, their villages are shelled by the military or placed under quarantine. "Our village of 400 families was subjugated to an economic embargo for 12 months," said a Turkish Kurd refugee in Iraq:

> We ran out of food and were not allowed to obtain food from the city. We could not take our livestock for pasture because of mines planted around our village. They then surround our village with tanks made in Germany and

asked us to become village guards. When we refused their offer, we were taken to Diyarbakir [a large Kurdish city] to be tortured.[47]

Indeed, torture is believed to be widespread in Turkish prisons. According to a Human Rights Foundation of Turkey Report, 2,689 prisoners were tortured between 1989 and 1994, the latest year for which statistics are available. In 1994, the figure was 387, including 117 women and 16 children. Turkey has admitted to the European Convention for Prevention of Torture that cases do exist, but they claim they are isolated incidents by overzealous jailers and military personnel. In addition, the government claims that it investigates every case that is brought to its attention and that it has paid compensation to victims and their families on many occasions.

More common than torture has been imprisonment without due process. After the military coup of 1980, an estimated 48,000 people were arrested for political crimes, most of whom, said Amnesty International, did not receive fair trials, if they received trials at all. According to the Kurds, Turkish prisons hold, at any given moment, thousands of people who have never been indicted or convicted of any crime. In its defense, the government claims that the charges of mass imprisonment have never been confirmed by independent organizations, though several attempts to conduct prison inspections have been turned away by Turkish authorities.

Higher-profile cases include the arrest, trial and conviction in 1994 and 1995 of six Democracy Party (DEP) members of parliament, who were denied parliamentary immunity for their statements on behalf of the Kurds. (DEP has since been banned and resurrected as the People's Democracy Party [HADEP]. DEP itself was formed after the People's Labor Party [HEP] was closed by the government in 1993.) The government claims that the lifting of parliamentary immunity was entirely legal, since the arrestees supported the separatist PKK in violation of the constitution, and was instituted by a parliamentary majority that included 100 Kurdish delegates. But, says HADEP, the arrests of the six parliamentarians are just the tip of the iceberg. Over the past several years, it claims, military-connected death squads have murdered almost 100 HEP, DEP and HADEP administrators and deputies. Demonstrations, party assemblies and even funerals, they add, have been attacked by security forces, with additional loss of life. Both DEP and HADEP assert that the government is engaged in a widespread campaign of terror "in order to isolate our deputies from the electorate."[48] The government denies all charges of complicity in these attacks, citing instead rivalries between the opposition parties and the PKK.

The PKK

As a guerrilla organization with a fraction of the personnel and resources of the Turkish military, the PKK prefers to attack isolated posts and bases, as well as border guardhouses. The *modus operandi* is usually the same. After cutting off communication, the guerrillas slip onto the grounds of the facility and attack quickly. Security personnel and soldiers are killed, food, weapons, and other materiel are seized before the guerrillas disappear back into the mountains, where they hide out and stash their finds in the labyrinthine caves that riddle the region. The PKK also targets convoys. In late May of 1993, for instance, a PKK unit attacked a bus full of off-duty soldiers in eastern Bingol province. According to one British journalist who later visited the area, "thirty-three unarmed men were dragged from the bus and shot dead at point-blank range."[49] By 1994, says the government, over 4,000 security personnel had been killed by the PKK in the 10-year war.

While attacks on security personnel are acknowledged by the PKK, government and human rights organizations' charges that the PKK targets civilians as well are denied. According to these sources, the PKK targets "civilian" members of the village guard, as well as their families and neighbors, sometimes targeting entire villages believed to support collaborators. After an alleged PKK attack on the village of Hamzali in 1995 that killed 19 people, including eight women and seven children, a government official said, "they attacked Hamzali because the village did not support them. It was a guard village."[50] According to Britain's *Financial Times*, the PKK has burnt villages and killed villagers as warnings against providing information about guerrilla movements to the government. "If we support the government, the PKK will kill us," one villager told a journalist.[51]

Furthermore, the government claims that the PKK targets anyone Ankara sends to improve the lives of Kurdish villagers, including teachers, health care personnel and construction crews. In September of 1994, for instance, the government reported that PKK guerrillas killed six elementary school teachers. And according to Reuters, over 3,000 schools in the southeastern provinces "were forced to close down last year because of PKK attacks and threats."[52] In addition, says the government, the PKK has declared that all political candidates are "military targets," a declaration that Human Rights Watch "called on the group to disavow."[53] It is the PKK, the government asserts, that has sent 30,000 Kurdish villagers fleeing to Iraq and 300,000 more to Turkish cities for safety, and that has systematically attacked mosques and worshippers.

The PKK admits it attacks village guards in self-defense, but says it stopped attacks on families and neighbors in the early 1990s, when it became clear to them that the government was forcing people to participate in the militia under threat of imprisonment and torture. As one PKK spokesperson said, "if we did everything the government said we did, we'd get no help from the villagers. And without their support the government would have annihilated us long ago."[54] As for the charges of attacking mosques, the PKK says that originally the organization was anti-Islamic because it felt Kurdish religious leaders were largely apologists for the government. However, it says, the depth of religiosity among rural Kurds convinced it to change its position. But, a spokesperson adds, the official position of the PKK never included physical attacks on mosques, religious leaders or worshippers.

These disclaimers are meaningful only if they accord with what is going on in the field. As journalist Colin Barraclough notes, "the severity of recent PKK attacks has convinced some observers that [Ocalan] no longer has full control of his commanders in the field."[55] To that, the PKK's former American spokesperson Kani Xulum responds, only those who understand "our strategies and aims" are recruited and "we're careful to keep psychopaths" out of the organization. For the PKK, he says, recruitment is both a "political and a character issue."[56]

Recruitment and training is another source of dispute between the government and the PKK. The government maintains that the PKK recruits its guerrillas forcibly, then subjects them to "brainwashing" sessions at training camps in Lebanon. And, the official Ankara Journalist Association reports, "members of the organization are sent into armed clashes under the influence of drugs. [PKK leaders] keep them under the influence of drugs so as to prevent them from seeing the reality."[57] Unlikely as this last claim may be, there have been PKK defectors, presumed genuine, who have spoken of intimidation of guerrillas within PKK camps and units in the field. According to one such defector, "if anyone crosses [Ocalan], either with eyes or attitude, he is accused of creating conflict. The sinner is then declared a contra-guerrilla, and his punishment is death."[58] The PKK dismisses such charges, saying no one is executed and those who do not get along with others or oppose the basic principles of the revolution are simply drummed out of the organization.

Finally, there have been numerous charges and countercharges made about PKK terrorism. The government routinely labels the PKK a "terrorist" organization. On December 25, 1991, members of the PKK shouting "Long live Kurdistan!" threw several firebombs into an Istanbul department store, killing 11 people, according to Turkish authorities. And an alleged member of the PKK told the Swedish newspaper *Aftenbladet*, "we are going to kill Swedish tourists [in Turkey]," a report confirmed by Ocalan, who said "tourists have now been warned. If they continue to come here, they support the Turkish government."[59] Indeed, in the past several years, several bombs have gone off at tourist resorts along Turkey's Mediterranean coast, though so far no foreigners have been killed. The Turkish government has also published documents it claims link the PKK to the 1986 assassination of Swedish Prime Minister Olaf Palme, a charge the PKK says is ridiculous, citing the steady support the Swedish government has shown the Kurdish cause. Instead, it hints, Turkish security forces may have been behind the assassination.[59a]

IRAQ

The government

In the spring of 1987, Iranian and Iraqi Kurdish forces launched their last offensive of the Iran-Iraq War, a drive through the mountains of Iraqi Kurdistan. The fighting was some of the bitterest and bloodiest in a long and bloody war. It was a decisive moment. Baghdad itself was threatened, the terrain was treacherous and Kurdish guerrillas had already proved themselves notoriously difficult to defeat by conventional means. Saddam Hussein needed a shortcut to victory over Iranian and Kurdish forces, and he found it in the mustard and nerve gas, or rather the technology to make them, supplied to him by West Germany.

Chemical attacks against Iranians and Kurds may have begun as early as 1983, though the first internationally verified use of chemical weapons dates from the late winter and early spring of 1987. First several villages allegedly harboring Kurdish guerrillas were attacked in early March. The Kurds protested but, hoping for an Iraqi victory over the feared Shiite Islamic fundamentalists of Iran, the world's governments and media largely chose to ignore the story. But when the Iranian offensive began, Baghdad decided a greater use of chemical warfare was in order, and on March 16 the Iraqi air force dropped chemical canisters on the Kurdish-occupied city of Halabja. These attacks represented the first use of chemical weapons since World War I and their first use ever by a government against its own people.

Nerve gas smells like rotting apples, some of the Kurds in Halabja said. Others compared it to garlic. "Like the mist of winter a cloud of milk smelling of garlic perfumed and permeated the air," a Kurdish survivor recounted.

> We used our clothes to prevent our lungs from invasion. I saw people going blind, their faces burned black and blue. They were vomiting. People were dying in the center of town where the rockets landed. The people fled the town climbing the eastern mountains toward Iran's border. . . . On the next day we arrived in Khorramshahr [Iran]. My daughter came later and told me there were hundreds of people dead in the streets of Halabja. In their fear people had jumped into cars asking drivers to take them away. But the drivers were already dead in their cars, lifeless like statues.[60]

Halabja is an ancient cultural center in eastern Kurdistan. It was also the first major town captured in the last joint Iranian-Kurdish offensive of 1988, hence the Iraqi attack. But the troops escaped; few were among the 6,000 or so victims. The Iranians, eager to prove their earlier charges that Iraqis had employed chemical weapons against them, invited a British film crew to record the devastation. But while human rights organizations did their utmost to publicize the attacks, they achieved precious little for their efforts: condemnations by the UN and Western governments, but no sanctions against Baghdad. For the Kurds, worse was yet to come.

Like so many of his predecessors in Iraq, Turkey and Iran, Saddam Hussein was determined to find a final solution to his Kurdish problem in the months following the end of the Iran-Iraq War. It was called *anfal*, the Koranic word for the "spoils of war." The thrust of the *anfal* campaign involved the "cleansing" of Kurdistan, the removal of hundreds of thousands of Kurds from their mountain fastnesses and the destruction of strategic swaths of their homeland. Moving from region to region, the Iraqi military employed vast pincer movements to surround the villages and valleys of Kurdistan, flushing out guerrillas and civilians with chemical and conventional weapons.

Most of the women and children were packed into buses with the windows painted over and transported to concentration camps in the Iraqi desert. According to a Human Rights Watch report, conditions in the camp were almost beyond imagination.[61] Torture, rape, starvation and thirst thinned the ranks of Kurdish prisoners. As for male Kurds of fighting age, anywhere from 15 to 50 years old, many were simply hauled off into the desert and shot, or dumped into mass graves and buried alive. Survivors were not allowed to return to their villages, but were placed in dilapidated housing developments in northern cities, where they were surrounded by barbed wire and guard towers, required to get passes simply to do their shopping, attend school or go to their jobs. Some escaped and returned to their villages only to discover that the Iraqi military had methodically leveled their houses, plugged their wells with concrete and even salted their fields. One can get some sense of the scale of the disaster from statistics: 4,000 villages destroyed, according to Human Rights Watch; 50,000 to 100,000 dead; half of the Kurdish farmland laid to waste.

Approximately 100,000 Kurds escaped this nightmare only to find themselves in another of the refugee camps in Turkey. Fearful of drawing any international attention to the Kurds generally, the Turks tried to cover up evidence of chemical attacks, listing the obvious symptoms under headings like "pneumonia," "exhaustion" and "injuries due to sudden flight." Eventually, the refugees returned after the Iraqi government, convinced of *anfal*'s success, issued a general amnesty to Kurds on September 6, 1988. Refugees were given until October 9 to return to Iraq. Any Kurd attempting to return after that would be arrested and dealt with in ways unmentioned by the government's decree. While they could return to Iraq, many areas of Kurdistan remained off-limits.

Despite the death and destruction wreaked on Iraqi Kurdistan, the Kurds had not been beaten in spirit. When the Gulf War ended less than two and a half years later, and President George Bush (and Kurdish leaders on CIA-funded radio broadcasts) urged the Kurdish people to rise up against Saddam Hussein's dictatorship, they were seemingly once again ready to do battle. This time, though, the confrontation was a nonstarter. The vast majority of Kurdish *peshmerga* and about half the civilian population had fled to Turkey and Iran. Villages, towns and military bases that were so easily overrun by the Kurds in mid-March 1991 were retaken by Iraqi forces without a fight several weeks later.

When the Kurds returned in the late spring, they came back under Coalition protection. With a UN-sponsored no-fly zone established above the 36th parallel and 11,000 Coalition troops on the ground (half of whom were from the US), Operation Poised Hammer made sure Baghdad's remaining forces could not attack northern Iraq. But after the Coalition troops pulled out in July (the no-fly zone was maintained and allied leaders promised to return if Iraq invaded), fighting between Kurds and Iraqi forces recommenced. It was a territorial dispute. Large parts of Kurdistan, including the PUK's headquarters in Sulimaniye were south of the 36th parallel, and Talabani was determined to retake the city. By November, Saddam Hussein was forced to withdraw.

In the years since, Baghdad has tried several strategies to wrest back control of the Sulimaniye area, as well as to pressure all safe-haven Kurd leaders to return to the negotiating table. Kurdish leaders claim that Iraq has frequently bombarded Kurdish-controlled territory with artillery, and that Baghdad ground troops have reoccupied parts of it incrementally, so as not to attract the attention of the Coalition. The Iraqis counter that their actions have been purely defensive. For the most part the West has accepted the Kurdish view. But when fighting between the two commenced again in March of 1995, the international press began to question Kurdish claims in light of the ongoing struggle amongst the Kurds themselves. "It is not clear," the Associated Press reported, "why Saddam would launch an assault now," since he was trying to get the UN to lift the economic sanctions imposed on Iraq since its invasion of Kuwait over four years earlier.[62] Since then, clashes between the Iraqi military and the Kurds have continued. In July, an estimated 300 people were killed or wounded near Sinjar, about 250 miles north of Baghdad. The KDP has blamed the fighting on Saddam Hussein.

Iraqi Kurds have also complained that Saddam Hussein has launched a campaign of terror in the safe haven. Agents of the Baghdad government and Kurdish *jash*, they say, have set off numerous bombs and have systematically engaged in the assassination of international advisors and journalists. The Iraqi government insists that this is "pure fabrication" and that the bombings and assassinations are a result of intra-Kurdish feuding.

While it is difficult to determine the veracity of each side's claims given the current unstable climate in northern Iraq, another tactic employed by Baghdad against the Kurds is acknowledged by both sides. Since the summer of 1991, the Iraqi government has engaged in economic warfare with the Kurds in the safe haven. Beginning in October of 1991, Baghdad has attempted to cut off electricity and water to parts of northern Iraq. That same month the Iraqi government cut off all payments to civil servants in the safe haven, informing them that they must return to Iraq proper to keep their jobs. In May 1993, Baghdad invalidated all 25-dinar notes and issued new ones, knowing that these notes were a popular form of savings in Kurdistan and that Kurds were unlikely to make it to Iraqi banks to redeem them for new ones.

Meanwhile Baghdad imposed its own sanctions against the Iraqi Kurds, though they have been of little consequence since both Arabs and Kurds continually violate them. Even with the internal frontier established under the safe haven, the level of agricultural and other trade between the Kurdish and Arab regions of Iraq remains significant. In fact, the United States was forced to purchase $10 million in surplus wheat from the Kurds in 1994 in order to prevent them from selling it to Baghdad in contravention of UN sanctions.

The Kurds

The establishment of the safe haven in 1991 has not brought peace to northern Iraq. Over the past several years, three separate but interrelated conflicts have periodically flared up in the region (not to mention the occasional firefights between Iranian military forces and Iranian Kurds based in northern Iraq; see "Iran" below). First, there has been the war of nerves, sanctions and occasional military engagements between Baghdad and the Iraqi Kurds, described above. Second, an alliance of the Turkish military and the Iraqi Kurds has been at war with PKK guerrillas based in the safe haven. And finally, the bloodiest of all involves the two main political parties-cum-tribal confederations of Kurdish Iraq, the KDP and the PUK, who have been fighting a civil war in the safe haven, with periodic cease-fires, since May of 1994.

Each conflict has involved different tactics and methods. The Turkish-Iraqi Kurd campaign against the PKK, a continuation of Turkish incursions that have been ongoing since the mid-1980s, began in earnest in the fall of 1992 in what was called a "final offensive" against the Turkish guerrillas. The fighting was furious, though it took three days before Turkey and Western military sources acknowledged that the Turks were involved. At first, Turkey's chief of staff, General Dogan Gures, said Turkey's role was limited to flying reconnaissance for the Iraqi Kurds. "We have been establishing targets with armed reconnaissance flights for the last year," he told Reuters. "When they [Turkish pilots] see a target, they [the Iraqi Kurds] strike." But a Talabani aide contradicted Gures. "We drive them to the mountains," he told newsmen, "and Turkish jets blast them there." As one Iraqi *peshmerga* observed "they [the Iraqi Kurds] gave the army the coordinates of the PKK camps. How else could the planes have distinguished PKK camps . . . which are just 500 meters from *peshmerga* camps? Why do they never miss their aims?"[63]

The joint campaigns, some extensive and some limited, continued into 1994 despite a growing rift between the Iraqi Kurds and Ankara, and increasing tension among the Kurds themselves. While both Ankara and the Iraqi Kurds shared the same aim, the elimination of PKK bases in northern Iraq, they disagreed over methods. In their quest for a final victory over the PKK in Iraq, Turkish forces have been employing overwhelming firepower and have increased the duration of their incursions. Iraqi Kurdish leaders, however, have insisted that the offensive be kept short, to avert growing hostility from their own people and increasing scrutiny from the press. "It's a crime," said one Iraqi Kurd in Arbil:

> Our leaders are mistaken. The PKK are fighting for their rights in Turkey, just as we are fighting for our rights. We should be helping them in every way we can, not killing them. If this war goes on, there could be demonstrations in the streets. We won't accept it.[64]

And, in fact, Barzani, whose sphere of influence near the Turkish border has been under attack by Turkish forces, has periodically closed his offices in Ankara in a protest over Turkish military attacks on Iraqi Kurds. But fearing this might alienate the Turks and give his rival Talabani the upper hand, he has always backed off and reopened the offices. Meanwhile, both Ankara and the Iraqi Kurdish leaders remain optimistic, at least in public, that the PKK will be destroyed in the safe haven. After the 1992 raids, for instance, Turkish Interior Minister Ismet Sezgin declared that PKK fighters had been trapped on mountaintops, while a KDP official announced "the work is 70 percent finished."[65]

It was not. The PKK has put up fierce resistance against Turkish attacks, or avoided engagements by slipping back into Turkey. Meanwhile, between the 1992 offensive and the beginning of the Iraqi Kurd civil war, the Iraqi *peshmerga* have grown wary of PKK capabilities, though they claimed their growing hesitation to attack the PKK head-on has been an attempt to avoid a "large loss of life."[66] In fact, the *Associated Press* reported "fierce hand to hand fighting on bloodied rock hills" in 1995. Moreover, Iraqi Kurds have been shocked at the forces they were fighting. "They are mostly children, and fighting with their fanaticism," said one Iraqi tribal chief, during a firefight in 1992. "I saw the one who threw that grenade," said an Iraqi *peshmerga* in the heat of battle. "It was a girl!"[67]

Meanwhile violence between Iraqi Kurd factions emerged in 1992, as the two parties prepared for elections in May. In the spring, Amnesty International reported voter intimidation by the *peshmerga* of both the KDP and the PUK in their respective regions. The worst act of violence occurred on May 7, when six PUK members and 17 passersby were killed in Chamchamal, halfway between Kirkuk and Sulimaniye, outside the safe haven. IKF leaders quickly blamed the incident on local tribal chiefs and said it had nothing to do with the elections. Other incidents, like a car bomb in Dohuk, were blamed on Saddam Hussein, though fears of a major act of sabotage by Baghdad proved unfounded, and the elections were held.

Tensions increased after the elections, with political power struggles both in rural areas and the provisional capital of Arbil. In the spring of 1994, the two sides were busily arming themselves for an expected showdown when, in late April, a minor land dispute between rival tribal chieftains escalated into a full-scale armed confrontation between Massoud Barzani's KDP and Jalal Talabani's PUK. As in all civil wars, the fighting—from May of 1994 to April of 1995, when a cease-fire went into effect—has been fierce, vicious and costly in lives and resources. It has also severely damaged the credibility of Kurds' capacity to govern themselves. According to one American Kurd who visited the region in 1994, both parties, like the gangs of American inner cities, have appropriated colors for themselves, attacking anyone wearing the wrong color in the wrong place. Moreover, independent human rights monitors have alleged that both sides are killing prisoners.

The announcement of a peace plan in November 1994, and a renewed joint commitment to hold parliamentary elections on schedule in May, 1995, did nothing to stop the fighting, which in fact only intensified. In early 1995, the fighting arrived at the provisional capital, a supposedly neutral enclave between KDP and PUK zones, and by the end of January the city had fallen to the PUK. The death toll was almost 500, including over 40 children. Estimates are that over 5,000 Kurds have died since the fighting began in May 1994, a total greater than the number of Kurds killed over the same period by military forces in Turkey.

Retaliation and counterretaliation escalated in early 1995. In March, a bomb went off, killing 18 civilians, in the town of Zahko. Both sides claimed that Saddam Hussein was behind the attack. For fear of bad publicity, both sides continually downplay the ferocity of the conflict, but inside sources have told *Kurdish Life* that the bombing was the doing of Talabani. According to Saeedpour, the fact that the bomb was set off among the oil trucks and truckers who are such an important source of Barzani's income points to the PUK, though it should be noted that Saddam Hussein also has an interest in destroying Kurdish resources. Perhaps because of the ferocity of this attack, a cease-fire was declared by both sides in April 1995, and was largely holding some months later, though tensions between the two sides remain high.

IRAN

Iranian Kurdistan has been more or less at peace since the Iran-Iraq War ended in August 1988. The KDPI has moved its headquarters to the safe haven, about 60 miles west of the Iranian border in the PUK sphere of influence. The Tehran government asserts that the KDPI is receiving arms from Turkey via Talabani's organization. So far, these weapons have not figured much, since the KDPI has been limited or has limited itself to brief cross-border raids on Iranian military outposts and border stations.

Tehran has also limited its response to KDPI raids to periodic air attacks. The most recently verified encounter involved Iranian jets and three Scud missiles fired at what Tehran called "joint concentration centers of the counter-revolutionary agents" inside Iraq.[68]

In fact, the leftist Islamic *mujahideen* Khalq, headquartered in Baghdad, is widely considered to be a more serious armed threat to the Iranian government. In July 1995, the Iraqi government charged Tehran with launching rockets against *mujahideen* bases inside Iraq; Iran maintains that it has never violated the 1988 peace treaty with Iraq by attacking the so-called "counter-revolutionary" bases inside its neighbor's borders.

NEGOTIATIONS

While none of the three states is currently negotiating with its Kurdish population, recent history reveals a markedly different approach to talks by Ankara, Baghdad and Tehran. Turkey has pursued a no-dialogue policy with the PKK, though it has offered limited amnesty to guerrillas and supporters who turn themselves in. Iraq maintains an open invitation to negotiate with both the KDP and PUK, and has engaged them in a series of negotiations both before and after the establishment of the safe haven. Iran and the KDPI have not seriously sat down at the negotiating table since the assassination of KDPI leader A. R. Ghassemlou by Iranian agents posing as negotiators.

TURKEY

There have never been negotiations between the PKK and the Turkish government, official or unofficial. However, there have been several unilateral cease-fires declared by the PKK, the most recent being in May of 1995. The previous unilateral cease-fire, in March of 1993, was ignored by Ankara and then declared null and void by the PKK after one of its units attacked an army convoy in May, killing 33 off-duty soldiers. In March of 1994, Ocalan told an international conference on northern Kurdistan that the PKK is "ready for a bilateral cease-fire followed by talks under international supervision."

> I would like to state as clearly as possible that we absolutely do not have the partition of Turkey as our goal, and the propaganda which says that we do, does not reflect our reality. . . . I commit myself to accepting any decision on possible solutions adopted by your conference. I declare moreover that if the way is cleared for a political settlement and free political action, I will act to end the armed struggle definitively.[69]

The sticking point has been the government's distrust of PKK intentions; it believes that "the PKK is not in favor of a solution [and] refuses any approach other than the creation of an independent Kurdistan,"[70] a position which, Ankara says, no sovereign government could accept. Some observers have suggested that the recent Turkish escalation may actually represent a prelude to negotiations; by this logic, military hard-liners have to be placated before advocates of negotiation can move forward. No statement from the government indicates that this is in fact the case.

Nevertheless, Ankara has offered an amnesty law for repentant Kurdish rebels. There have been several amnesties offered over the years, the latest coming in May of 1995, extended in July for two more months. The law offers PKK members who have not taken part in acts of violence full immunity from prosecution and offers guerrillas lighter sentences if they give themselves up. According to the semiofficial Anatolian news agency, approximately 200 PKK members have surrendered and taken advantage of the amnesty law in its first two months. Meanwhile, outside efforts such as that of Danielle Mitterrand, wife of the late president of France, who in 1994 called for a dialogue, have failed to bring the two sides to the negotiating table.

IRAQ

As there are several wars currently being fought in northern Iraq, so there have been several attempts at negotiations, that is, between Baghdad and the Kurds and between the PUK and the KDP, though neither is entirely independent of the other. Talks between the government and the Kurds are hampered by a decades-old distrust between rival Kurd factions. To put it simply, Talabani's PUK has always been, until recently, more willing to bargain with Baghdad than is Barzani's KDP. From Talabani's point of view, negotiating with Baghdad is a better method of achieving Kurdish goals than fighting it, though this is in part due to the fact that Talabani's largely urban following has been militarily and geographically more vulnerable. In May of 1991, Talabani explained why he had met with Saddam Hussein to work out a federal plan for Iraq. "There was no regularized form of cooperation among the clans," he told historian Moti Zaken. "They did not know how to operate the tanks, planes, and helicopters they seized from the Iraqis."[71]

However, from Barzani's viewpoint, Talabani has been more willing to negotiate with Baghdad as a means to strengthen his position vis-à-vis the KDP. Ever since Talabani tried to cut a deal with the pre-Baath government, his organization has been brushed with the pejorative label "66er traitor," after the year in which the aborted deal took place. This reputation, says the KDP, was confirmed in 1983 when, in the midst of the Iran-Iraq War, Talabani negotiated an alleged *quid pro quo* deal with Baghdad in which PUK forces would aid the Iraqi army against Iran in exchange for the Iraqi government's help in the PUK's struggle with the

KDP. When the negotiations failed, says Zaken, "Talabani became the most notorious enemy of the Baath regime."

In the past, he had spoken of mere autonomy for Iraqi Kurdistan, but after his 1985 disappointment [over a failed general Kurdish uprising in Turkey] he changed his objective to national self-determination leading to an independent Kurdish state.[72]

That about-face paved the way for the establishment of the Iraqi Kurdish Front (IKF) two years later—an umbrella organization for the PUK, the KDP and several smaller Kurdish parties. However, the utter annihilation of Kurdish resistance in the wake of the *anfal* campaign killed all chances at negotiations, at least involving two relatively equal parties, until after the Gulf War.

Even so, the history of negotiations between Baghdad and its Kurds has been more encouraging than those between the PKK and Turkey. As early as 1970, the Baath government had offered a comprehensive peace plan to a coalition of Barzani (the father, Mustafa) and Talabani negotiators involving Kurdish administration, expanded economic investment and total cultural freedom, including the establishment of Kurdish media and the use of the Kurdish language in northern Iraqi schools. Those negotiations eventually came to naught because of increasing distrust between the two parties, including an assassination attempt against Barzani involving *mullahs* who had unwittingly had explosives planted on them by Baghdad security forces. They were blown up when they sat down with the KDP leader, who himself escaped serious injury.

After the end of the 14-year Iraqi-Kurd war and following the debacle of 1975 in which Kurds were betrayed both by the shah and his US backers, Baghdad claimed that it would fulfill the terms of the March 11, 1970 accords. The government has asserted ever since that those terms were carried out, at least in part, until the Iran-Iraq War and new hostilities between the government and the Kurds made further efforts impossible. This scenario is dismissed by Iraqi Kurds, and by the human rights organizations that unofficially tried to monitor the implementation of the terms in the 1970s and 1980s.

Since the establishment of the safe haven, Baghdad has been extremely anxious to achieve a negotiated settlement with the Kurds so that Iraq could reexert its sovereignty over the north of the country. As early as May 1991, Barzani was claiming he had negotiated a 20-point agreement with Saddam Hussein. Its provisions included the right of Kurdish *peshmerga* to keep their arms and serve as the government's security force in Kurdistan. In addition, the agreement called for the demarcation of an autonomous Kurdistan and "democracy throughout the country." The deal, if it was a deal, was another nonstarter. Each side blamed the other. The Kurds say Baghdad secretly added another demand, that Kurds cut their ties to the

West, while Saddam Hussein says the Kurds were simply unwilling to negotiate in good faith as long as they felt they had the support of the Coalition. In fact, say observers of the talks, the real issue involved the extent of the autonomous zone. Kurds demand that it include the once largely Kurdish city of Kirkuk, now more than half Arab due to the government's policy of relocating Kurds by force, while Baghdad insists that the oil-refining center remain part of the Arab section of the country.

In 1992, it was Talabani's turn to announce a negotiated settlement with Baghdad, based on provisions similar to those of the 1991 agreement, but that too failed. In the years since, there has been a series of desultory efforts to find an agreement, but nothing even remotely like a settlement has been reached. Fighting between the rival Kurdish factions has closed off the possibility of negotiations with the government for the moment, though in January 1995, Baghdad said that it was willing to sit down with both parties to achieve a "peaceful solution" to the Kurdish struggle. It is time, announced Baghdad radio, to "learn from the lessons of the past years and lean toward national solutions to put a final end to these painful situations and events."[73]

Meanwhile, a cease-fire negotiated in April between the PUK and KDP seems as if it might be leading to a peace settlement. In May 1995, members of the Iraqi Kurdish parliament, meeting in the neutral village of Daraban, voted to extend the assembly's mandate. And in June, Barzani and Talabani announced their respective prerequisites for coming to the bargaining table. The KDP leader insists that Talabani's forces evacuate the provisional capital of Arbil and surrender the $14 million it claims the PUK pilfered from the treasury during its occupation, while Talabani demands that Barzani agree to share in the customs and duties he collects on goods coming over the Turkish border, probably the most lucrative source of revenue in the safe haven. Turkey, hoping to get the Iraqi Kurds' help in combatting the PUK, is urging the two sides to negotiate.

IRAN

Negotiations between the Islamic government of Iran and the KDPI have a tortured history, especially since the end of the Iran-Iraq War, though the troubles date from the first year of the revolution. In 1979 and 1980, Iran was forced to negotiate a broad set of reforms in its relations with the Kurds, reforms that essentially granted the Iranian Kurds partial autonomy within a federal Iran. The war with Iraq, however, prevented the agreement from ever being ratified. Instead, Iran settled its Kurdish problems by overrunning the region militarily early in the war. Khomeini, however, never forgot the humiliation of conceding autonomy to the Kurds in that first year of the revolution. Kurdish autonomy was an affront to the ayatollah's vision of a united Islamic community in Iran.

Unlike Iraq, which, due to the military aid it received from Arab countries and the West, ended the war in a position of strength, the government in Iran was in no position to launch an Iranian *anfal* against its own Kurds. Nor did it need to. Resistance continued, but no great postwar offensive was launched by the KDPI. Moreover, KDPI leader A. R. Ghassemlou maintained that the aims of the organization and the Kurdish community had not changed. The KDPI, he said in 1989, had never been and would continue not to be interested in an independent Kurdistan, opting for autonomy along the lines offered by Tehran in 1980. Ghassemlou also felt that the Iranian government was in no position to deny the Kurds what they wanted:

> Looking at Iran overall, we see that the condition of the Iranian Kurds is not as serious as one might think. On the military level, the morale of the *pasdaran*, who symbolize the regime's power, is at its lowest ebb. Their vulnerability has grown in proportion to the number of operations carried out by the *peshmerga* in Iranian Kurdistan after the cease-fire [with Iraq].[74]

Still, Ghassemlou was a pragmatic politician. He recognized that, despite heroic Kurdish claims to the contrary, any fighting in Kurdistan would hurt his people more than it would Tehran. And, he believed that, once the Islamic government had recovered sufficiently from the war, it could launch another offensive which, with its army no longer pinned down against Iraqi forces, would be devastating.

Thus, in the summer of 1989, he accepted an Iranian initiative to negotiate in Vienna. Ghassemlou publicly claimed that he would not back away from the original Kurdish demands for autonomy, but privately he expressed a willingness to consider other options. Tehran, however, had no intention to negotiate. On July 12, Ghassemlou, KDPI (Europe) head Abdullah Qaderi-Azar and Fadhil Rassoul, a professor of Iraqi-Kurdish origin, met with Iranian negotiators Hadji Mustafawi and Mohammed Jaraf Sahraroudi at the home of Rassoul's friend Renata Faistauer. At the negotiating table, the two Iranians and a bodyguard, all agents of SAVAMA (the Islamic government's secret police), drew guns and shot the three Kurdish negotiators dead. While Austrian authorities dithered, the three Iranians fled the country under diplomatic passport. They have yet to be captured and tried.

The effect of Ghassemlou's assassination was predictable. The Kurds vowed never to trust the government again. Ghassemlou's words of warning from an interview in the mid-1980s spoke prophetically from the grave.

> I visited Khomeini in Paris. I was not very optimistic because I knew him to be a reactionary and tyrannical man, but I did not think then he would prove so pitiless and sanguinary.[75]

Still, events and circumstances have a way of changing what seem like irreversible decisions. The death of Khomeini in June 1989, while not affecting the government's decision to assassinate Ghassemlou, nevertheless elevated parliamentary speaker Ali Akbar Rafsanjani, a relative moderate on the Kurdish question, to power. These two deaths, so contradictory in their consequences, prepared the stage for the new, post-Khomeini era in Kurdish-Iranian history.

However, the situation did not improve when Ghassemlou's successor and political heir, Sadeq Sharafkandi, was assassinated in a Berlin restaurant on September 17, 1992. Tehran denied any involvement in the murder. "Why would we be crazy enough to organize such insane acts in the very country (Germany) which is our major trading partner and with which we have such excellent relations?" asked Iran's ambassador in Bonn. In a meeting with German government officials, the ambassador hinted at "foreign hands working to disturb Tehran-Bonn relations."[76]

Unlike Ghassemlou and Sharafkandi, the KDPI's current leader, Mustafa Hejri, does not appear to be interested in negotiating with Tehran. From the very beginning of his control of the organization, he established Iranian Kurdish bases in northern Iraq and has largely allied himself with Iraqi Kurds, especially Talabani's PUK. Neither the Iraqi Kurds nor the KDPI now has any real interest in negotiating with Iran. The KDPI has largely removed itself from Iranian Kurdistan and so does not have to answer to popular will there, and the Iraqi Kurds, allied with the West, believe it is in their interest to support opponents of the Islamic regime in Tehran.

NOTES

[1] Izady, Mehrdad, *The Kurds: A Concise Handbook* (Washington D.C.: Taylor and Francis, 1992), p. 50.

[2] Cited in McDowall, David, *The Kurds: A Nation Divided* (London: Minority Rights Publication, 1992), p. 23.

[3] Anonymous, interview with author, March 25, 1995.

[4] "An Interview with Mustafa Tasar," excerpted from *2000'E Dogru*, June 12, 1988, unpublished manuscript, provided to author by Kurdish Cultural Institute, no pagination.

[5] Kandemir, Nuzhet, unpublished letter to the *Washington Post*, November 14, 1994, provided to author by Turkish Embassy, Washington D.C., no pagination.

[6] *Los Angeles Times* (May 15, 1992), p. 22.

[6a] Xulum, Kani, interview author 11/21/94.

[7] Lazier, Sheri, *Into Kurdistan: Frontiers Under Fire* (London, Zed Books Ltd., 1991), p. 64.

[8] Marcus, Aliza, "In Kurdistan," in *Dissent*, July 1994, p. 42.

[9] "Abdullah Ocalan: 'We Put our trust in the Kurdish people" in Kurdistan Solidarity Committee, *The Workers' Party of Kurdistan*, London: Kurdistan Information Centre, 1992, p. 2.

[10] Marcus, Aliza, "Turkey's Kurds After the Gulf War: A Report from the Southeast," in Chaliand, Gerard, ed., *A People Without a Country: The Kurds and Kurdistan* (New York: Olive Branch Press, 1993), p. 241.

[11] "Towards a National Assembly," in Kurdistan Solidarity Committee, *The Workers' Party of Kurdistan* (London: Kurdistan Information Centre, 1992), p. 15.

[12] "Kurdistan and the Kurdish people are not for sale! The march to freedom continues!" in Kurdistan Solidarity Committee, p. 9.

[13] Marcus, *op.cit.*, p. 41.

[14] Hottinger, Arnold, "Forbidden Identity: The Kurds in Turkey," in *Swiss Review of World Affairs*, vol. 39 (June 1989), p. 23.

[15] Kandemir, unpublished letter, November 14, 1994, no pagination.

[16] Ankara Journalist Association, *PKK Reality in Turkey and in the World* (Ankara: Gazeteciler Cemiyet Yayinlari, 1994), p. 8.

[17] Corbin, Sam, "Turkey: The Oppressed Kurds," in *AfricAsia* (March 1985), p. 19.

[18] "Guarding Turkey's Eastern Flank," in *The Middle East* (April 1986), p. 10.

[18a] see note 17.

[19] Kandemir, Nuzhet, unpublished letter to the *Washington Post*, May 27, 1994, provided to the author by the Turkish Embassy, Washington D.C., no pagination.

[20] Corbin, *op.cit.*, p. 19.

[21] Marcus, *op.cit.*, p. 41.

[22] Kandemir, Nuzhet, unpublished letter, May 27, 1994, no pagination.

[23] Saeedpour, Vera Beaudin, interview with author, March 14, 1995.

[24] "Guarding Turkey's Eastern Flank," in *The Middle East* (April 1986), p. 10.

[25] Ozal, it should be noted, is of partial Kurdish descent by way of his mother's family.

[26] "The Trial of Ismail Besikçi," in *Kurdish Times*, vol. 1, No. 2 (Fall 1986), p. 14.

[27] Anonymous, interview with author, March 25, 1995.

[28] "Interview with Mr. J. Talabani," unpublished manuscript, September 1985, Brooklyn, Kurdish Cultural Institute, p. 8.

[29] *Ibid.*

[30] "A Conflict of Interests," in *Kurdish Life*, No. 4 (Fall 1992), pp. 2–3.

[30a] Cited in "Kurdish Regional Government Revenues" in *Kurdish Life*, No. 13 (Winter 1995), p. 4.

[31] Sulaiman, Azad (pseud.), "The Politics of Green and Yellow," in *Kurdish Life*, No. 11 (Summer 1994), p. 2.

[32] "Thought Waves" in *Hawkar: Newsletter of Hawkarani Kurdistan*, No. 12/15 (January/February 1994), p. 4.

[33] Saeedpour, Vera Beaudin, interview with author, March 14, 1995.

[34] Nisan, Mordechai, *Minorities in the Middle East: A History of Struggle and Self-Expression* (Jefferson, N.C.: McFarland and Company, 1991), p. 22.

[35] van Bruinessen, Martin, *Agha, Shaikh and State: The Social and Political Structures of Kurdistan* (London: Zed Books, 1992), p. 35.

[36] Kurdistan Democratic Party of Iraq, unpublished document, 1980, Brooklyn, Kurdish Cultural Institute, no pagination.

[37] Kurdistan Democratic Party of Iraq, unpublished document, 1991, Brooklyn, Kurdish Cultural Institute, no pagination.

[38] *Ibid.*

[39] *Ibid.*

[40] "Hygiene and Public Health under Khomeini," in *News from Kurdistan*, No. 36 (January-February 1989 [*sic*; an apparent error, actual date unknown]), p. 14.

[41] Izady, *op.cit.*, p. 35.

[42] Reuters on-line wire service, C-reuters@clarinet.com, December 2, 1994.

[43] Kurdistan Human Rights Project, *A Delegation to Investigate the Alleged Use of Napalm or other Chemical Weapons, by Turkish Security Forces in South East Turkey* (London: KHRP, 1993).

[44] Barzani, Massoud, "A Statement by Massoud Barzani on Recent Turkish Attacks on the Kurdish Region in Northern Iraq" (London: KDP, October 10, 1991).

[45] Reuters on-line service, C-reuters@clarinet.com, March 22, 1995.

[46] American Kurdish Information Network, "An Open Letter to the President of the United States" (Washington D.C.: AKIN, December 9, 1993).

[47] Democracy Party (DEP), "Democracy Party Fact Finding Mission on Recent Kurdish Exodus from South East Turkey into Iraqi Kurdistan" (DEP, May 16–24, 1994).

[48] Party Assembly of the Democracy Party, "From the Democracy Party to the Public," Kurdish Cultural Institute, Brooklyn, no date.

[49] Barraclough, Colin, "The Kurds: A Fire in Turkey's Underbelly," in *Insight* (October 25, 1993), p. 10.

[50] Reuters on-line wire service, C-reuters@clarinet.com, January 2, 1995.

[51] *Financial Times* (August 16, 1989), p. 7.

[52] Quoted in Turkish Embassy, "Fact Sheet: PKK Terrorists Kill Six Teachers in Turkey" (Washington DC: Turkish Embassy, September 23, 1994).

[53] Quoted in Turkish Embassy, "Fact Sheet: PKK Threatens Candidates for By-Elections" (Washington DC: Turkish Embassy, November 8, 1994).

[54] Xulum, Kani, interview with author, November 21, 1994.

55 Barraclough, *op.cit.*, p. 10.
56 Xulum, interview, November 21, 1994.
57 Ankara Journalist Association, *op.cit.*, p. 33.
58 Villemoes, Lars, "I Helped Olaf Palme's Murderer," in *Weekendavisen* (Copenhagen, July 8–15, 1994).
59 *Aftenbladet* (Stockholm, November 5, 1990).
59a See note 58.
60 Middle East Watch, *Genocide in Iraq: The Anfal Campaign against the Kurds*, New York: Human Rights Watch, 1993, pp. 71–73.
61 Several experts who follow the Kurdish situation closely are not in full agreement with the Human Rights Watch Report. The organization, they say, refuses to allow outside experts to examine their "60 tons" of documents, currently held under lock and key in a Bronx, N.Y. warehouse.
62 Associated Press on-line wire service, C-ap@clarinet.com. March 10, 1995.
63 "Conflict of Interests," pp. 2–3.
64 *Ibid.*, p. 3.
65 *Ibid.*
66 *Ibid.*
67 *Ibid.*, p. 2.
68 Reuters on-line wire service, C-reuters@clarinet.com, November 9, 1994.
69 "International Conference Held on North West Kurdistan," unpublished transcript, March 12–13, 1994, no pagination.
70 Ankara Journalist Association, *op.cit.*, p. 7.
71 *Christian Science Monitor* (May 8, 1991), p. 19.
72 *Ibid.*
73 Reuters on-line wire service, C-reuters@clarinet.com, January 17, 1995.
74 "Interview of Dr. Ghassemlou" in *News from Kurdistan*, No. 36 (January-February 1989), p. 1.
75 "KDP's Qassemlu: 'The Clergy Have Confiscated the Revolution'," in *MERIP Reports* (July/August 1981), p. 18.
76 "Iraqi Kurdistan's Misbegotten Mission," in *Kurdish Life*, No. 8 (Fall 1993), p. 5.

6

KURDISTAN SINCE THE GULF WAR

When one wolf becomes a thousand wolves,
  woe unto the poor.

The owner said, "God, I'm counting on you."
The thief said the same thing.
  ——Kurdish proverbs

IRAQ: ESTABLISHING THE SAFE HAVEN (1990–1991)

THE INVASION OF KUWAIT

Opportunity, it is said, seldom knocks twice. But that has not been so for contemporary Kurdish leaders. On at least four occasions in the past 20 years, they have been drawn to the door. Iraqi Kurds heard a rapping in the 1970s, when the shah and the CIA visited with financial and military aid. Iranian Kurds heard it in 1979, when the shah fell. Both Iranian and Iraqi Kurds heard it in the thunder of artillery during the Iran-Iraq War. Then on August 2, 1990, the Iraqi Kurds heard it again as Iraqi troops occupied Kuwait. But each time the Kurdish leaders tried to exploit these opportunities, they failed.[1]

The leadership in Iraqi Kurdistan, both Massoud Barzani of the Kurdish Democratic Party (KDP) and Jalal Talabani of the Patriotic Union of Kurdistan (PUK), immediately recognized in the Kuwaiti invasion an opportunity for themselves, their organizations and their people. More attuned to the geopolitical maneuverings of the region, or simply more opportunistic, according to his detractors, Talabani moved first. Within days of the invasion, he was holding strategy sessions in Damascus with Iraqi opposition leaders and representatives of the Tehran government. Then he went to Washington with an offer to raise a 30,000-man army within Kurdistan, and even to assassinate Saddam Hussein. Barzani was also maneuvering. In late August, Hoshyar Zibari, officially a spokesman for the Kurdish Democratic Front—a coalition of Kurdish parties formed during the Iran-Iraq War—but in fact an aide to Barzani, told the *Washington Post*, "there is an existing internal opposition to Saddam Hussein. If the United States and the West want to see democratic change [in Iraq], they must recognize the opposition and understand our objectives."[2]

Barzani's and Talabani's eagerness to take advantage of the invasion is understandable, even if their failure to learn from experience and history is not. After all, it had been only fifteen years since the shah and the United States had abruptly abandoned them with the Algiers Accord, and exactly two years since the ayatollah had let them down by agreeing to a cease-fire with Iraq. Still, the Iraqi Kurds and their leaders were in a very tough position in the summer of 1990, regardless of who was at fault. Cut off from Iranian arms and logistical support, the Kurds had been crushed when Saddam Hussein turned the full force of his military machine on them in the months following the Iran-Iraq War. The *anfal* campaign had decimated Iraqi Kurdistan. Thousands of villages had been destroyed, tens of thousands of Kurdish *peshmerga* and civilians had been killed, and hundreds of thousands displaced from their homes. Kurdish opposition had been broken and Saddam Hussein looked more secure in power, and hence less likely to compromise on Kurdish issues, than at any time in the past.

Kurdish disappointment with the West was also running high. "The Western world and the Soviet Union must stand in the dock with Saddam Hussein," a Kurdish spokesman told the British press in March, 1990. "There are countries in this world with the power to have acted against him, to have forced his hand" for using chemical weapons against the Kurds. Yet characteristically, the Kurds were willing to forgive and forget in the wake of the Iraqi invasion of Kuwait in August. With renewed hope, Iraqi Kurdish leaders believed the invasion of Kuwait, bringing with it the possibility of Western intervention against Iraq, might rescue them from their latest predicament.

As the coalition of forces against Saddam Hussein began to come together during the late summer and fall of 1990, the Kurds of Iraq tried to ingratiate themselves with the American-led Coalition. Yet neither the Pentagon nor the State Department would meet with Talabani when he traveled to Washington that August. As the US government began formulating its response to the Kuwaiti invasion, the Kurdish issue, at least officially, was considered irrelevant. "Our concern for the Kurds is for their human rights," a State Department official told newsmen, "and not as a nationality to be broken off from a republic."

The Kurdish offer of aid was dismissed. The State Department wrote off the Kurds as too weak to play a significant role in "overthrowing" Saddam Hussein or "destabilizing" his government. "We don't see them as particularly effective," a State Department spokesperson explained.[3] This was an entirely different assessment from the one made by the Nixon administration in the early 1970s, when it backed the shah's effort to use Iraqi Kurds to keep the then-pro-Soviet Saddam Hussein off-balance. But the Kurdish leaders got the message, assuring Washington that their ambitions were limited to the elimination of Saddam Hussein and "the establishment of Kurdish rights within a democratic Iraq."[4]

Faced with seeming indifference, Talabani tried to put the best light on things. Over and over again, he told whoever would listen that the Iraqi opposition forces, by which he meant the Kurds, were the only potentially serious antigovernment fighting force in the country, and were the West's best bet to rein in Saddam Hussein. "We prefer to unite our forces and do it by ourselves. The regime of Saddam Hussein should be overthrown by Iraqi forces," he told reporters, adding that gas masks and antitank and antiaircraft Stinger missiles from the West would help.[5] But while Washington initially dismissed any consideration of a Kurdish role in the conflict, Ankara, fighting a Kurdish rebellion of its own since 1984, recognized the potential of the Iraqi Kurds for Turkish interests.

THE TURKISH CONNECTION

According to a number of scholars and journalists who have studied Turkish foreign policy closely over the years, Ankara provides a very important key to understanding the 1991 Gulf War and its aftermath, in both Kurdistan and the region generally. After the fall of the shah, the pillar of US policy in the Persian Gulf for at least a decade, Turkey loomed ever larger in US strategic thinking. In 1980, the two countries signed the Defense and Economic Cooperation Agreement, a *quid pro quo* deal whereby Washington would modernize Turkey's military in exchange for bases and listening posts. "With the fall of Iran," writes Middle East economist Peter Thompson, "it was recognized that [radical political] Islam . . . was the single biggest threat to US [Middle East] interests. In the battle against this new adversary, Turkey . . . [became] a key component in the building of a military alliance structure to 'contain' Islam and 'roll back' Iran. Although Turkey was peripheral to US and NATO strategy during the Cold War, the situation changed dramatically with the collapse of the Soviet bloc."[6]

Not surprisingly, Turkey's defense minister in the early 1990s agreed with this assessment. "With the end of the Cold War," wrote E. Nevzat Ayaz, "Europe's center of gravity for risks and instabilities shifted from the center of the continent eastwards, that is to the Balkans, the Middle East, and Central Asia."[7] The one discrepancy between the views of these two military analyses, the inclusion of central Asia by the Turkish minister, is quite significant. Since the establishment of the post-Soviet Muslim republics in central Asia, Turkish leaders had begun to envision a Turkish sphere of influence there, though subsequent events in central Asia and Turkey's nearly bankrupt treasury have put their plans on hold. Nevertheless, by the end of the 1980s, Turkey, along with Egypt and Israel, had become one of the pillars of US strategy in the Middle East. Not coincidentally, they were and are the three biggest recipients of US military aid as well.

As noted in Chapter Five, the Turkish military and the Turkish right have long harbored ambitions for a restoration of the oil-rich former

Ottoman *vilayet*, or province, of Mosul, in southern Kurdistan, now a part of northern Iraq. While Turkey remained officially neutral during the Iran-Iraq War, it reconsidered its position in light of Iranian victories in 1986. Speaking to the *Christian Science Monitor*, a ruling party spokesman claimed that Turkey had "historical and economic rights in that region [northern Iraq]," and the press was filled with possible scenarios whereby the Turkish military might intervene to prevent the "the fall of Kirkuk to Kurdish-Iranian forces." To counter the US tilt towards Iraq, the Turkish government argued that with the oil of northern Iraq, Turkey would "no longer be in need of US or other foreign aid."[8] But with Iraq unbeaten by Iran, the issue became moot, until the invasion of Kuwait. Like the Kurds, Turkish Prime Minister Turgut Ozal, a nominal liberal in Turkish political terms, though an ardent nationalist as well, heard opportunity knocking. In the weeks following the invasion, the government-dominated press published stories about Turkish rights to Kirkuk, the oil-refining city in southern Mosul.

To the rest of the world, Turkey's claims seemed implausible, based as they were on Ottoman claims that had been ended three-quarters of a century earlier. By that standard, said critics of Turkish foreign policy, the Turks could claim possession of much of the Middle East, and the Balkans as well. "If frontier settlements imposed by British imperialism after World War I were called into question," noted London's *Financial Times*, "both Saudi Arabia and Turkey could put forward claims to large and valuable areas of Iraqi territory."[9] Moreover, there was an inherent contradiction in Turkey's position. If violations of the territorial integrity of Kuwait, entirely a creation of British imperialism, were unacceptable, how could a Turkish landgrab in northern Iraq be any different? Turkey's answer, that the region around Kirkuk was inhabited by a Turkish-speaking majority (the Turcomans), was equally questionable. There was no Turcoman majority; Ankara had inflated the number by a factor of at least five. In fact, the Kirkuk region is roughly equally divided between Arabs and Kurds, with Turcomans making up a minority of about 350,000 people. In short, Turkish claims were mutually exclusive: claims grounded in previous Ottoman possession were based on the logic of empire, while the Turcoman argument was an ethnic nationalist one—the very antithesis of Ottoman imperial sovereignty.

As crucial as Turkey was to American strategy for the Middle East and for the coalition against Saddam Hussein, US and Coalition leaders would not accommodate Turkish ambitions, as they proved when they conspicuously established the southern border of the safe haven above the 36th parallel, well to the north of Kirkuk. In fact, the Turkish people themselves were not particularly enthusiastic about their government's ambitions. While right-wing papers called for the "restoration of northern Iraq to Turkish sovereignty as a reward for Turkey's participation in the Gulf War," a survey conducted by the leading Turkish daily *Milliyet* found that less than a quarter of the Turkish people agreed. A full 73 percent of the respondents said Turkey should "have no designs on the oil cities [that is, Kirkuk and surrounding towns]."[10]

Ozal and his ruling Motherland Party, however, were not deterred. They allegedly drew up a plan involving a division of Iraq into a weak federation of three autonomous regions, including a Kurdish entity in the north, a Turcoman region in the middle around Kirkuk, and an Arab province in the south. Existing borders would remain intact, in deference to the aims of the Gulf War Coalition. For the plan to work, Iraq's Kurds would have to be won over, and so they were. Publicly, the Turkish government began to hint that Kurdish autonomy in northern Iraq was on the table. Interviewed on National Public Radio before the beginning of the Gulf War, Motherland Party spokesman Kaya Toperi said "that under certain circumstances" Turkey "might not look unfavorably" on the idea.[11]

This implied offer was, of course, a total departure from Turkey's previous policy on Iraqi Kurds and autonomy. "Prior to Iraq's invasion of Kuwait," *Kurdish Life* noted, "Ankara and Baghdad had eagerly collaborated to repress Kurdish political activities." In 1984, Turkey and Iraq had signed a pact allowing for hot pursuit of Kurdish rebels up to six miles into each other's territory. Since Iraq was hardly in a position to launch serious raids into Turkey during its war with Iran, the pact was clearly designed with Turkey's military in mind. Moreover, it was merely a legal nicety, since Turkey had been attacking Kurds in northern Iraq since at least May 1983, a year before the Kurdish Workers' Party (PKK) had launched its first attack on the Turkish military. Major incursions followed through the end of the Iran-Iraq War and after. "We are determined to follow these rebels [the PKK] to their lairs and smash them," Ozal announced after a 1986 raid. "Let this be a warning to those who shelter rebels."[12]

Furthermore, as far as the Turkish government was concerned, Iraqi Kurds were guilty of the offense just of being who they were. As the most rebellious and effective Kurdish movement in the Middle East, until the rise of the PKK in the mid-1980s, Iraqi Kurds represented a threat by example for Turkish Kurds. "The Turks," noted the *Financial Times*, "are terrified that any support for the aspirations of the Iraqi Kurds would have repercussions on their side of the border."[13] Thus, when thousands of Iraqi Kurds fled to Turkey during the 1988–1989 *anfal* campaign, Turkey first refused to let them in, citing the expense, then kept them isolated from Turkish Kurds who were more than willing to bear the cost of succoring their Iraqi brethren.

In the pro-Iraq climate of the mid-1980s, however, nobody was complaining about Turkish incursions except Iran, which understood the favor ostensibly neutral Turkey was doing for Iraq by attacking Iran's allies, the KDP and PUK guerrillas. With impeccable diplomatic reserve, Tehran pleaded with Turkey in 1986 "to refrain from hindering the movement of combatant Iraqi Kurds against the present regime in Baghdad."[14] The Iraqi Kurds themselves had no such reservations, announcing that "The continuation of this form of jungle-law behavior by the fascist juntas of Turkey and Iraq endangers the very existence of the Kurdish people and its just right for struggle, in achieving their national and democratic aspirations."[15]

In the first days of the Iraqi invasion, Turkey's first concern was the Kurds. "Initially," noted the London *Observer*, "Ozal feared that the US might back the [Iraqi] Kurds."

> American officials assured him the US would not even contact the Kurdish opposition within Iraq. . . . But as the crisis evolved Ozal himself, in a typical u-turn, decided to contact the Kurdish leaders, who secretly visited Ankara . . . something unimaginable at the start of the Gulf saga.[16]

To prepare the way and help soften Turkey's anti-Kurdish image, both with Iraqi Kurds and the Coalition, Ozal made a seemingly bold move, especially so in the context of Turkish politics. In early February of 1991, Ozal called for a lifting of the Turkish ban against the use of the Kurdish language. The law, which passed the Turkish parliament in April, had serious limitations, however. It did not, for example, allow publications or broadcasts in Kurdish, and it maintained the ban on all political discourse in Kurdish. Turkey's own Human Rights Association called the move "window-dressing" and an "insincere gesture." Moreover, an Ozal-sponsored antiterrorism bill, which passed the Turkish parliament in 1992, reinforced and expanded the penalties against Kurdish political activities, under the rubric of threatening the "indivisibility of the Turkish state."[17]

Iraqi Kurdish leaders, meanwhile, were more than ready to talk with Ozal. "Rebuffed by Washington," noted *Kurdish Life*, "representatives of the Iraqi Kurdistan Front [a coalition of the KDP, PUK and five minor parties created during the Iran-Iraq War] were more than ready to listen to anyone who would talk to them."[18] In a mid-February interview in the *Washington Post*, KDP chief Massoud Barzani said "if the Turkish government has a political program, then we are ready for discussion." Then, as if speaking to Turkish officials, he added that the Kurds had controlled the frontier to Ankara's satisfaction all during the 1960s and 1970s, hinting that they could be counted on to do so again.[19] On March 7, the new friends met in Ankara. The expected *quid pro quo* was arrived at almost immediately: Turkey offered to support an autonomous Kurdish region in northern Iraq in exchange for an Iraqi Kurdish "guarantee" to secure the border against PKK incursions. Within days, the deal was public knowledge, with reports circulating in the US and international press. Iraqi Kurds were elated. Talabani told *Milliyet* that the talks represent "a new page in the relations between the Kurds and Turkey." And to Reuters he confidently announced:

Ankara would do its best to make the Kurdish cause known in Europe and America and would support setting up direct political relations between the Kurdish movement in Iraq and the [Bush] administration.[20]

That Talabani had acquiesced to Turkish demands was made clear when he declared to the *New York Times*: "Kurdish opposition parties no longer regarded Kirkuk as an integral part of Kurdistan," a statement akin to a US politician saying Texas was not an integral part of the union. Still, in his excitement, Talabani did not forget to address the expected uproar among Turkish Kurds. "Democracy," he predicted, "would spread in Turkey and everyone, including the Kurds, would have the right to form parties." He was also careful to address US concerns about Iraq's territorial integrity, saying "other matters such as national rights and federalism were premature." Meanwhile, in expectation of flak from the Turkish right, Ozal blandly pronounced "there is nothing to be afraid of talking [*sic*]. We must be friends with them [Iraqi Kurds]. If we become enemies, others can use them against us."[21]

Neither of these arguments convinced its respective audience. The Turkish right was up in arms, sensing that a dangerous precedent had been set. "This will give false and wrong messages to those inside Turkey," a Turkish political scientist declared. "They too might ask for the same rights [to form] a federation." Even members of Ozal's Motherland Party were concerned enough to voice their opposition. "Ozal has made a historic mistake by holding secret talks with guerrilla leaders," a party leader said. "Such moves can be a serious threat to [Turkish] national unity."[22] As for the Kurdish resistance leaders, they were furious and worried. PKK leader Abdullah Ocalan told the *Washington Post* he was "suspicious and contemptuous of the more established Kurdish nationalist parties, especially in Iraq," and said that the meeting with Iraqi Kurds came "at the expense" of the PKK and the cause of Kurdish unity and freedom. Ocalan also hinted at retaliation. "Our struggle makes the Iraqi Kurds' own struggle easier today, but if we wanted, we could cause them problems."[23] Ocalan was not alone in his anger. Throughout Turkey, Kurdish demonstrators clashed with security forces in the days following announcement of the talks between the Turkish government and the Iraqi Kurds.

One needn't be a Kurdish separatist, however, to recognize the obvious contradiction in Turkey's new policy, in which it helped secure autonomy for the Kurds of Iraq while denying the same to its own Kurdish population, which numbered 15 million to Iraq's three and a half. "Europe does not understand the Kurdish problem," Ozal lectured reporters from the *Los Angeles Times* in May, 1991:

In Iraq, in Turkey, they are two different problems. . . . In Turkey, Anatolia is a melting pot for different nationalities. . . . When I talk about mass movement like there was in northern Iraq, I mean they took control of whole cities. . . . Once Turkey, after 1945, went into [a] democratic system, there is [*sic*] no uprising. Except a guerrilla movement, a small guerrilla movement, not a mass movement.

Asked to explain the demonstrations that swept Turkey with their chants of "Long live Kurdistan!" Ozal replied again that these were "small minorities . . . the main body of the Kurdish people is not in east Anatolia anymore. . . . It is integrated into this society [that is, in western Turkish cities]."[24]

On the face of things, Ozal's protestations contradicted his pro-Iraqi Kurdish policy. If the guerrilla movement was as insignificant as he made it out to be, why was he reversing decades of Turkish policy in order to gain Iraqi Kurd cooperation in crushing the PKK? While the reporters did not point this out, Ocalan did. Ozal's lifting of the decades-old ban on the Kurdish language, he argued, was "due to our seven-year struggle." He also claimed that Turkey was bankrupting itself in its struggle with the PKK, with little result, hence the need for "desperate" acts like the alliance with Iraqi Kurdistan Front.[25]

While Ozal's move caught the PKK and the Turkish right off-guard, the US government seems to have been aware of Turkish plans for months. As early as December of 1990, according to Kurdish scholar Vera Beaudin Saeedpour, the State Department was asking Iraqi Kurdish representatives how they "might react to a role for Turkey in northern Iraq."[26] In retrospect at least, US approval of Turkish strategy seemed natural, as long as Turkey did not make overt moves to incorporate Iraqi territory. By forming an alliance with Iraqi Kurds, Turkey obviated the need to occupy northern Iraq directly, though it might have done so if it had gotten the green light from the United States.

In short, US and Turkish interests coincided. Both countries envisioned Turkey as a source of stability in the Middle East and a bulwark against the Islamist politics of Iran. And both governments recognized that the main threat to Turkish stability was the guerrilla war in Turkish Kurdistan. Thus, any method that the Turks might employ to crush the PKK, short of annexation of Iraqi territory, would meet with the tacit approval of the United States. But that recognition of Turkish strategic needs, according to a number of observers, was not the only reason the US gave the go-ahead to the Turkish-Iraqi Kurd alliance.

Their hypothesis, according to Saeedpour and economist Peter Thompson, goes like this. Northern Iraq is situated in the heart of Kurdistan and the heart of the Middle East, with borders on Turkey, Syria, Iran and of course Iraq. By establishing a Kurdish autonomous region there, the United States was committing itself to protecting it. That commitment, however, was one the US was happy to make since it necessitated a permanent US presence in the region. The US could help Turkey fight its own Kurdish guerrillas, sponsor Iranian Kurdish guerrillas in their struggle against the Islamic government in Tehran, and keep Saddam Hussein under close watch. In fact, speculates Saeedpour, the US decision to leave Saddam Hussein in power after the Gulf War was part of the plan. The US commitment to protect the Kurds would be justified as long as its adversary Saddam Hussein was in power.[27] Whether planned or not, this is indeed how things worked out. Everyone benefited: the Turks received critical support in their struggle with the PKK; the US had a justification for continued military presence in the region; and the Iraqi Kurdish leaders got control over northern Iraq. Everyone benefited except, as it turned out, the Kurdish people themselves.

Not just the Turkish Kurds, but the Kurds of Iraq were made to pay for the deal with their intense suffering in the refugee camps along the Iraqi-Turkish and Iraqi-Iranian borders following the failed uprising in northern Iraq at the end of the Gulf War. As far as the international television-news-watching public was concerned, the Kurdish exodus following the war was an unmitigated tragedy. An international leader, in this case President George Bush, promised to support the Kurdish people in their struggle against the Baath government, only to renege when Iraqi forces reentered Kurdistan.

DESERT STORM AND THE KURDISH UPRISING

The tragedy, of course, was all too real, but it may not have been unforeseen. In fact, say some experts, it may very well have been orchestrated. Several salient facts seem to back up their opinion. To backtrack a moment, Iraqi Kurdish leaders had boasted of their prowess in the months following Iraq's invasion of Kuwait. Talabani even claimed that if Baghdad employed chemical weapons against them, the Kurds would retaliate by blowing up dams and flooding Baghdad. This was no idle boast, as the Kurds' history of struggle against Baghdad attests. And indeed, in the first few weeks of the Kurdish uprising, virtually all of northern Iraq fell to the insurgents with ease; by the end of March they had pushed to within 100 miles of Baghdad. Over 30,000 Iraqi soldiers and Kurdish *jash*, or progovernment Kurdish militia, were captured. Kurdish guerrillas, the *Economist* noted, "exude confidence." According to a study published in *Kurdish Life* some time after the war, "western analysts later disclosed that Kurdish insurgents 'found towns falling to them virtually without a fight'."[28] So why then, asks Saeedpour, did the Kurdish leaders so "precipitously [end] an uprising begun some four weeks earlier?"[29]

The question is revealing. With the international spotlight on Iraq, with more than 500,000 Coalition soldiers just over the border in Kuwait and Saudi Arabia and the combined air forces of NATO in Turkey and Saudi Arabia, Saddam Hussein was not likely to unleash chemical weapons against the Kurds as he had in 1987 and 1988. Then Saddam Hussein had been an ally, and the Western powers turned a blind eye his use of chemical weapons, whose manufacturing technology had been provided by Europeans and Americans. In 1991, however, Saddam Hussein had become the new "Hitler," in Bush's words. Moreover, as noted above, Kurdish forces had stood up against the full might of the Iraqi military for years in the 1960s and 1970s. With Saddam Hussein's military decimated by a Coalition aerial attack that in several weeks outstripped all the bombing of World War II, why did the Kurds choose to cut and run at this time?

Spokesmen for the Kurdish leaders argue that they were betrayed by the West and that they were outgunned, even though Saddam Hussein's heavy weaponry, the one clear strategic advantage Baghdad had over the Kurds, had been effectively destroyed by Coalition forces. Something, said a *New York Times* reporter interviewing Iraqi refugees returning to the safe haven in June 1991, was suspect about the leadership's explanations. "The Kurdish militia [PUK] knocked on our doors and ordered us to leave town or join them," one Kurdish refugee from Sulimaniye told him. "They said the Iraqi army was coming to kill the Kurds. But when people refused, they threatened to burn our houses and cars." Another refugee told newsmen the PUK soldiers spread rumors of Iraqi attacks. "Some of us were forced at gun point to leave our homes, but others heard the rumor and left out of fear."[30] Yet those who stayed said there had been almost no fighting in the city. "Given the rapprochement between Ozal and the Iraqi Kurdish leadership, and the nature of the plan for Iraq," concludes *Kurdish Life*:

> it is difficult to view the mass exodus of Kurds to the north [that is, Turkey] as entirely spontaneous. Prior to the Gulf crisis, Iraqi Kurds had taken on the Iraqis when their military and air forces were intact. This time they [Kurdish leaders] actively encouraged the exodus.[31]

The seemingly unplanned, pell-mell evacuation of Iraqi Kurdistan, then, may have been neither, though given the recent and horrifying experiences of the *anfal* campaign there is good reason to believe that the Iraqi Kurds, if not their leaders, were justifiably terrified at the prospect of a Baghdad counterattack. They may not have needed much encouragement or warning from anyone before fleeing the region. "If you have forgotten Halabja [site of the largest chemical attack against the Kurds in 1988]," a member of Iraq's ruling Revolutionary Command Council warned the Kurds of Sulimaniye in January of 1991, "I would like to remind you that we are ready to repeat the operation."[32]

Both the Turkish government and the Iraqi Kurdish leaders blamed the flight on those fears. The KDP called the evacuation a "tactical withdrawal" intended "to spare the lives of innocent civilians and spare the cities total devastation." Meanwhile, Ankara said the Iraqi counterattack was part of Baghdad's "deliberately orchestrated" plan to get rid of "two unwanted minorities, Kurds and ethnic Turks known as Turkomans."

OPERATION POISED HAMMER

Nevertheless, by the end of June 1991, most of the refugees had filtered back to the region above the 36th parallel, protected by some 11,000 Coalition troops (half of whom were American) in southern Turkey and northern Iraq. Their leaders meanwhile pursued negotiations with Baghdad. While the two sides discussed a wide range of issues, including all-Iraq elections, there was, in fact, only one real point of contention according to Barzani: the southern border of the autonomous zone. The Kurds wanted Kirkuk included; Baghdad refused. It is interesting to note this emphasis on boundaries by the Kurds, which for them outweighed the issue of the degree of sovereignty to be shared between the autonomous region and Baghdad. Did it mean that the federal relationship between Baghdad and the autonomous region did not really matter, since the Kurds expected to form an independent state before they had even established an autonomous region, and thus wanted the maximum amount of territory included within it?

Meanwhile, the Coalition, including Turkey, was hammering out an agreement to form a rapid deployment force based in Turkey to protect the autonomous region. This eventually became Operation Poised Hammer. Eager to remove their troops from northern Iraq, Coalition leaders began to pressure the Kurdish leaders, who made it clear they wanted a guarantee of continued international support before they signed any agreement with Baghdad. The Coalition agreed to a symbolic trigger force of about 500 UN guards. Still, negotiations between the Kurds and Baghdad remain bogged down. While Iraq's offer of amnesty, abrogation of all emergency laws and the release of Kurdish political prisoners was hailed by the Kurds, they refused to consider Saddam Hussein's power-sharing agreement since, they said, it left the ultimate authority to appoint governors for the region under Baghdad's control.

In mid-July, fighting broke out again between Iraq and the Kurds. On July 20, Kurdish forces under the command of Talabani's PUK launched a successful attack on the region around Sulimaniye, the center of the PUK's sphere of influence before the Gulf War. The attack occurred just days after the final withdrawal of American troops from northern Iraq. "We're just a phone call away," Coalition commander US Army General Jay Garner reassured the Kurds, as he crossed the Habur River into Turkey, the last Coalition soldier to leave.[33] Adding to the strangeness of the affair, the attack seemed to go almost unopposed by Saddam Hussein. Baghdad blamed it not on the Kurds but on Iranian infiltrators, and Kurdish forces were careful not to fire on government buildings or officials. Suspicions arose that the whole thing had been arranged among the Coalition, Baghdad and the PUK; and indeed, Talabani had always been the Kurdish leader most amenable to cooperating with Baghdad. According to this theory, the seizure of Sulimaniye was arranged to allow Talabani to reassert his authority over the major city in his sphere of influence, in exchange for some undisclosed future concessions to Baghdad.

If there was such a deal, it had fallen apart by the autumn. In early October, Saddam Hussein launched an offensive against Sulimaniye, but failed to seize the city. Frustrated at the negotiating table and on the battlefield, but fearing Coalition interference if he launched a new military assault, Saddam Hussein tried a new tactic: economic pressure. According to the Iraqi Kurdistan Front, Baghdad began reducing gasoline deliveries and food supplies in late October. While Kurds tried to rally international support against these latest Iraqi moves, there is reason to believe Kurdish leaders were exaggerating the situation, and may have even been exacerbating it for their own profit. "Piles of pilfered United States army rations are stacked in the local market [of Zahko]," the *New York Times* reported in December, "and thousands of gallons of cheap Iraqi diesel fuel are sold to Turkish truck drivers while Kurds wait days outside gas stations for a few gallons of gasoline. . . .

> In every conflict, it seems, there comes a time when refuse of war is for sale, larceny and intrigue are in the air and it's good business to traffic in human misery.[34]

While the *Times* correspondent did not say who was conducting this traffic, the presence of thousands of *peshmerga* indicated that control of the city's market in smuggled goods—smuggling was a traditional tribal economic activity—was in the hands of the rebel leaders. As the most eventful year in Iraqi Kurdish history came to an end, negotiations with Baghdad remained stuck, while the safe haven's poor suffered economic want. More ominously, a new and potentially dangerous rift had appeared among Kurdish leaders Barzani and Talabani, traditional rivals yoked in a common cause by the uncommon events of 1991.

TURKEY: WAR AGAINST THE PKK (1990–1995)

IN THE SOUTHEASTERN PROVINCES

While the Gulf War represented an opportunity for Iraqi Kurds, it was a mixed blessing at best for their Turkish cousins. While some of the harshest, and most difficult to enforce, restrictions on Kurdish cultural expression were lifted as a consequence of the war, the PKK was suddenly confronted with another enemy: Iraqi Kurdish *peshmerga*. As noted above, the Turkish government and Iraqi Kurdish leaders had worked out a deal in the months following Iraq's invasion of Kuwait. The Turks would support an autonomous region in northern Iraq in exchange for Iraqi Kurd assistance in rousting PKK guerrillas from the area. This move, of course, represented a dramatic turnaround in Turkish policy, which had hitherto been adamantly against autonomy for Iraqi Kurds. The reversal, however, is understandable when considered in the context of Turkey's six-year-long war with the PKK.

In March of 1990, some five months before the invasion of Kuwait, the guerrilla war in Turkish Kurdistan had taken an ominous turn for the government: it sparked massive and ultimately violent demonstrations in towns and cities across the country. On March 14, around the time of the Kurds' most important holiday, *New Roz*, or New Year's, some 5,000 Kurds demonstrated against the government's attacks on Kurds during the funeral of a guerrilla in Nusaybin. When government troops opened fire, killing one man (a young girl was also killed in the ensuing stampede), the demonstrations spread across Turkey. Over 1,000 people were arrested in Istanbul and Ankara. But the center of the spontaneous uprising was in the Kurdish town of Cizre.

When half the population of the city of 30,000 marched in protest, Turkish soldiers opened fire, wounding hundreds, who were refused treatment in government hospitals. This did not stop the protests. Demonstrators destroyed Turkish flags and statues and burned government and ruling party offices. According to American political scientist Paul White, "Turkish authorities reacted vigorously," declaring a "state of war," cutting off food supplies and imposing hefty fines on domestic "publications carrying reports deemed to be unhelpful to security forces." The foreign press was kept out altogether. "There didn't even have to be a leader of the protests," explained Nusaybin's mayor, who was fired by Turkish President Turgut Ozal for his comments. "Everything has come to the point of explosion from the inside, because of bad politics, state terrorism, and torture."35

In the aftermath of the protests, the government cracked down hard. State prosecutors asked for sentences in excess of 10 years for demonstrators, and the government announced plans to relocate Kurdish inhabitants away from border areas. "A buffer zone is to be created with strips of 'no man's land' averaging at least 600 meters in width," the Turkish daily *Hurriyet* reported. Over 10,000 Kurds lived in the 32 villages scheduled for demolition. Facing protests from the European Community, which the Turkish government has been eager to join for decades, the plan was halted.

More significant, however, was the Kurdish reaction. The absence of opposition in the Turkish parliament, even from parties on the left nominally sympathetic to the Kurds, permitted Ozal to bypass parliament when he issued the emergency legislation; the PKK's decade-old denunciation of parliamentary politics seemed well-taken by Kurds. "It is not surprising," concludes White, "that Turkey's Kurds are back to relying on purely Kurdish political forces." As if to underscore its position, the PKK, which then numbered some 10,000 guerrillas, increased its armed activity in the wake of the demonstrations. Over 160 people, according to Ankara, were killed in battles between PKK guerrillas and the Turkish military in April and May alone. In short, at the time of the Kuwaiti invasion, Turkey was facing a potential *intifada* in Kurdish towns and cities, and a guerrilla war in the countryside.[36]

The PKK, had been operating out of bases in northern Iraq for years. Supported nominally by Iran during its war with Iraq, the PKK had forged a tacit friendship with Iran's ally in Iraqi Kurdistan, Talabani's PUK. The PKK bases, however, were located in Barzani territory that abutted the Iraqi-Turkish border. As noted above, Ankara and Baghdad had a working agreement allowing Turkish forces to attack PKK bases in northern Iraq. Thus, Barzani's KDP was often the target of attack as Turkish warplanes and soldiers went after any Kurdish guerrillas they could find. Ideological differences added to the tension between the two groups. The PKK was then even more of a radical Marxist-Leninist group than it is today, and had nothing but contempt for Barzani (a contempt that was reciprocated), whom they saw as the kind of conservative and traditional tribal leader so detrimental to the cause of Kurdish nationalism and socialism. There was clearly no love lost between the two groups when Barzani actively aided the Turkish military in destroying PKK bases in northern Iraq before, during and after the Gulf War. "They [the KDP] are both weak so they talk," Ocalan told the *Christian Science Monitor* in August, 1991.

> We refuse this agreement [between Iraqi Kurds and the Turkish government]. They negotiate with Turkey . . . and Turkey is our enemy. Early this year, they came to this camp [in Lebanon]. Their words are good, but they speak too much. They are tribal leaders and only work for themselves.[37]

IN NORTHERN IRAQ

In October 1991, the Turkish military began its largest assault on PKK bases in northern Iraq since the Iran-Iraq War. Attacking from both land and air, the Turkish government announced that over 4,000 of its soldiers had crossed into the safe haven. Turkish planes dropped napalm on rebel camps and mines were sown along the border. "We are going to annihilate them," Turkey's military chief of staff told reporters.[38] The invasion, the official government pronouncement declared, was in response to recent PKK attacks on Turkish border towns and military outposts. The government also claimed, in an assertion backed up by Western diplomats and Iraqi Kurdish leaders, that Saddam Hussein was arming the PKK as revenge for Turkish cooperation with the Coalition during the Gulf War and its alliance with Iraqi Kurdish rebels since. The former claim was confirmed by Ocalan, though he said the aid had ceased with the end of the Gulf War. The Western press agreed. "A year ago they were little more than a rag-tag terrorist band, now they have become a viable guerrilla army," a Western diplomat told the *New York Times*, in an assertion of earlier PKK capacities that even the Turkish government would find hard to credit.[39]

While the PKK had launched a major guerrilla offensive that killed 17 soldiers some weeks earlier, and Saddam Hussein certainly was capable of arming his enemy's enemy, many observers suspected political motives for the Turkish assault. Parliamentary elections were scheduled for the Sunday following the opening of the assault, and Ozal was facing serious criticism from the right for his inability to crush the PKK. Ironically, one of the strongest showings in the election was made by the all-but-openly Kurdish nationalist People's Labor Party, which took up to 70 percent of the vote in parts of Turkish Kurdistan and gained 22 seats in the 450-seat assembly. Nor was criticism of the ruling party's Kurdish policies confined to Kurdistan and the right. "Discontent with those policies," the *Wall Street Journal* noted, "can be seen at funerals for soldiers killed in the southeast (nearly 100 have died this year), where crowds gather carrying signs with legends such as 'enough is enough'." This discontent was not changing the government's position, however. "There can be no negotiating with terror," said Ozal. More ominously, Turkey's chief of staff proclaimed that "if we avoided democratic niceties, we could finish this off in six months."[40]

The Turkish invasion was also angering both relief workers and Iraqi Kurdish leaders in the safe haven, as hospital workers near refugee camps in northern Iraq reported at least a dozen civilian dead. "Turkey is a member of NATO and a member of the allied coalition supposedly protecting Iraqi Kurds," said a KDP official. "We protested to the MCC [Military Coordination Center] that Turkey is bombing our villages, but we have no response."[41] Nor were they likely to get any. "I'm concerned that the United States did not intervene or even protest at these Turkish bombings," an American relief worker in the northern Iraqi city of Zahko said. "Somebody had better get on the phone to Washington and tell them that six months of good work here will count for nothing if this foolishness doesn't stop." In fact, the *Wall Street Journal* noted, "the US and Britain quietly support Turkey against the PKK rebels."[42] As the *Washington Post* noted, "NATO allies have largely accepted Turkey's contention that the PKK is a separatist terrorist organization."[43]

Mending fences with Iraqi Kurdish leaders was important if the Turks wanted to maintain their cooperation in keeping PKK guerrilla bases out of the safe haven. Following the attacks, Turkey agreed to work more closely with Iraqi Kurdish leaders to avoid such problems in the future. In the summer of 1992, Turkey also began to talk of establishing a "buffer zone" three miles wide inside the Iraqi border. "There is no authority in north Iraq," Turkish Prime Minister Mesut Yilmaz told the *Washington Post*, "The PKK are crossing the border. We can't stay disinterested. Turkish military planes will attack anyone who comes into the area."[44]

In the fall of 1992, Turkey's payoff came. On October 4, Turkish forces and Iraqi *peshmerga* launched their long-expected "final offensive" against PKK bases in northern Iraq. Turkey had two contradictory concerns. It wanted to eliminate the PKK, but it also had to worry about international reaction to an invasion of Iraq, just two years after Baghdad's attack on Kuwait. At first, it tried to keep the campaign under wraps, but that proved impossible. By the end of the second week of fighting, Turkey admitted publicly that its soldiers had entered the safe haven.

Coalition commanders already knew of their presence and approved it. NATO commander US Army General John Shalikashvili, now head of the Joint Chiefs of Staff, called the PKK a "terrorist organization" that "must be dealt with swiftly" and said Turkey's permission for the use of its air bases was "vital for the protection of Iraqi Kurds against Iraqi President Saddam Hussein." Increasingly Turkey was taking over the offensive. "It's not easy for the *peshmerga*," said a Turkish official, "Kurds are killing Kurds."[45]

But Talabani tried to place the blame on the PKK, calling Ocalan "a madman" leading his people into catastrophe:

> The PKK were poisoning the atmosphere in [Iraqi] Kurdistan and giving Kurds a bad name in the West, where the name Kurd was becoming associated with terrorism and violence. The problem was imposed on us.

In fact, as news began to filter out by late October, Western criticism was directed at the Turks and the Iraqi Kurds, rather than the PKK. Middle East Watch issued a report condemning the two forces, and when news footage showed a German-built armored car used by the Turkish military to drag a PKK guerrilla to his death, the German government demanded an explanation. Despite professed worries about Western perceptions, Talabani was more concerned with Turkish policy. "Cooperating with Ankara against the PKK is very important for us," he explained to the *Washington Post*, "to take the last card in the hands of Turkey for opposing Iraqi Kurdistan's self-autonomy."[46]

By the end of the month, Iraqi Kurds felt they had done their duty by Turkey. Barzani issued an ultimatum to the PKK: pack up and leave within 24 hours or face a renewed assault. Both the Iraqi Kurds and the PKK were claiming victory. "They [the PKK] are seeking a way out," KDP's Hoshyar Zibari noted. Ocalan disagreed. Referring to a postponed meeting of Iraqi opposition groups, he noted:

> they [the Iraqi Kurds] had hoped to defeat us by October 23 [the scheduled date of the meeting], but the failure of the *peshmerga* and the lack of success of the Turkish offensive has resulted in the postponement of this meeting. The fact that the Turkish army entered the fray in the last few days proves that the collaborators were unable to deliver the goods.[47]

Indeed, both the Iraqi Kurds and the Turkish military began trying to cover their tracks. Contrary to earlier statements, Gures insisted the Turks had no intention of creating and occupying a security zone inside the Iraqi border. "We don't say they [the Turkish forces] will remain in northern Iraq permanently," he said, "but our security has first priority." By the end of the month, however, the Turks seemed to be changing their minds and again began floating the idea of a permanent buffer zone inside the Iraqi border. Barzani and Talabani, meanwhile, were issuing protests to NATO, complaining that Turkish expansion of the operation "was without our knowledge, without our approval." But, as one Iraqi *peshmerga* deserter noted, "is it only now that they realize that the intervention of the Turkish armed forces is a flagrant violation of their sovereignty . . . now [that] they are convinced that the PKK has been rendered ineffective? Why not on the first day?"[48]

IRAQ: CIVIL WAR IN THE SAFE HAVEN
(1994–1995)

Iraqi Kurdish participation in Turkey's war with the PKK, as noted above, was part of the *quid pro quo* behind Ankara's support for the safe haven. The deal, admitted to the press in roundabout ways by both sides, was, according to a number of observers, tacitly approved and even encouraged by the Coalition, especially the Americans. According to this viewpoint, the Americans would maintain a presence in a critical region of the Middle East, justified by the continuing threat against the Kurds by Saddam Hussein, whom the Coalition had left in power in the wake of the Gulf War. But the deal sidestepped one very critical component: was the safe haven temporary or permanent? And if it were going to be permanent, what exactly would its status be?

Obviously, each participant in this trilateral deal had its own agenda, which paralleled the others' in the short run, but had the potential to diverge radically over time. The Turks were of two minds about the duration of the safe haven, an ambivalence traceable to their sudden change of policy on Iraqi Kurd autonomy shortly after the invasion of Kuwait. On the one hand, the prospect of *peshmerga* help in routing the PKK in northern Iraq was an enticing one, and one which, undoubtedly, Ozal used to convince hard-line opponents. But the thought of a permanent autonomous Kurdistan in neighboring Iraq, or worse, the establishment of a Kurdish state, was unacceptable. Ideally, what the Turks wanted was cooperation against the PKK in the short run and, for the long term, a settlement between the Iraqi Kurds and Saddam Hussein which would maintain Iraqi sovereignty over the northern part of the country. The US government was looking farther down the road: a long-term presence in the region to keep an eye on

Baghdad and, more importantly, Tehran. Thus, an unsettled situation in Kurdistan and Saddam Hussein ruling in Baghdad would be in its interest.

The Iraqi Kurds were looking at the situation within a historical framework that encompassed centuries of struggles against outside dominance. For them, the safe haven was a preliminary stage in the establishment of an independent Kurdish state, though they were careful not to say so for fear of jeopardizing Turkish and Coalition support. Nevertheless, whatever Baghdad's objections and offers, that, primarily, is what has kept the government and the Kurds from reaching a final settlement in the years since the establishment of the save haven. As noted above, borders are part of the problem. The borders of the safe haven and the 1974 autonomy agreement between the Kurds and Baghdad, the legal basis, say Kurdish leaders, for their current rule, do not coincide. The safe haven includes territory that is not primarily Kurdish, and the autonomy region under the 1974 agreement does not include large areas of Iraqi Kurdistan. But while Kurdish leaders admit this stumbling block, a more troubling issue remains under the table, and that is the status and future of the autonomous region itself, whatever its dimensions.

In 1986, during the Iran-Iraq War, Tehran had brokered a KDP-PUK reconciliation. The Iraqi Kurdistan Front (IKF) also included several smaller parties, including the Kurdistan branch of the Iraqi Communist Party, and was intended to coordinate Kurdish-Iranian military action against Baghdad. The IKF was crushed in the waning days of the Iran-Iraq War and the *anfal* campaign, remaining all but moribund until the March 1991 uprising in Kurdistan. It was the IKF that negotiated with Saddam Hussein after the Gulf War and assumed military and political leadership in the safe haven after the withdrawal of Iraqi troops and administrators in the summer and fall of 1991. While the IKF is composed of leaders from eight parties, each with a veto over decisions, the real power, to paraphrase Mao, comes from the barrels of the *peshmergas'* guns under the command of Barzani and Talabani. Their deal with Turkey, for example, was made without the authority of the IKF, which, in fact, opposed it.

While the Front quickly took over and remanned former Iraqi administrative offices, it was also moving to establish democratic legitimacy for its authority. Kurdish leaders were caught in a dilemma. They well understood the importance the US and the West publicly placed on democratic institutions, but they also knew that openly establishing what might be taken for a permanent state government in northern Iraq might offend their Western and Turkish allies. Moreover, neither Talabani nor Barzani had any experience of or, some would say, interest in democratic government. A kind of syndicalist approach to local rule, for example, was attempted in January 1992, when labor, student, women's and other organizations elected members to an advisory council in the Dohuk province near the

Turkish border. But this idea was quickly scotched when the IKF announced assembly elections for May.

There are many troubling details about this exercise in electoral democracy. Violence marred the weeks leading up to the election. Amnesty International reported voter intimidation by the *peshmerga* of both the KDP and the PUK in their respective regions. And since the elections were held without international observers—indeed, they were held without Coalition approval—estimates of the numbers of people voting are not completely reliable, though the IKF said about 1.1 million participated. (Interestingly, the few outside observers who came to the safe haven left before the elections—delayed for 48 hours because the official ink used to stamp the hands of those who had already voted was tampered with—could take place.) Not surprisingly, the PUK and the KDP took the lion's share of the vote. In the parliamentary vote, the KDP received approximately 45 percent of the vote and PUK about 44 percent, with the Islamic party taking 5 percent and the remainder divided among four other parties and independent candidates. In the elections for an executive, Barzani received about 48 percent to Talabani's 45. Clearly, the Kurdish electorate was evenly divided between the two main parties and a runoff election for executive would be needed.

It never happened. Instead, an agreement, in contravention of election rules, was worked out between Talabani and Barzani. Both sides would take 50 seats in the 105-member parliament, with the other five distributed to Islamist and Christian parties. The executive branch would be ruled by a "high committee" of two, Talabani and Barzani, and the various cabinet positions, ministries, media facilities and military would be shared by both sides. It was a coalition government, down to the very cameramen in the region's TV studios. But, says Saeedpour, there is something suspicious about a democratic election without a runoff.[49] In fact, tribal politics still seemed to be in force, despite the democratic facade. Both parties/tribal confederations continued to control their own regions like fiefdoms and, in the state institutions where they had to come together, they divided them like tribal fiefdoms as well. The arrangement proved to be a disaster.

As examined in Chapter Three, the rivalry between Jalal Talabani's PUK and Massoud Barzani's (and, before him, his father Mustafa Barzani's) KDP was not new. There had always been disputes over territory and political disagreements over how to deal with Baghdad. But Baghdad's threatening presence was also a reason to unite, a common enemy that threatened the Kurdish people generally and the two leaders specifically. With the creation of the safe haven that threat was temporarily removed. Barzani and Talabani had a shared interest for a time: resistance to any agreement with Baghdad that would formalize the Kurds' autonomous status and preclude the possibility of an independent state.

Nevertheless, rifts between the two leaders emerged almost immediately after the creation of the safe haven. It began in May, 1991, in the aftermath of the Kurdish exodus from Iraq, when Talabani went to Baghdad and was photographed hugging Saddam Hussein. The immediate motivation for the visit was to sound out Saddam Hussein on an autonomy agreement. Barzani, who, as a rule, prefers not to leave his enclave in northern Iraq, took a wait-and-see attitude, according to the *Christian Science Monitor*, though he sent his nephew to the talks.[50] At that time, Talabani, whose record of flip-flops on Kurdish autonomy and statehood is legendary in the region, was seeking a *modus vivendi* with Saddam Hussein. The safe haven idea had only recently been broached and the Coalition commitment to it had not yet solidified.

By October 1991, with Operation Poised Hammer established, Talabani had switched to a hard-line approach. But Barzani understood the costs of a confrontational approach with Baghdad; it meant an agreement with Turkey which would allow Turkish incursions into his enclave and a commitment on his part to fight the PKK. Already Barzani was complaining of Turkish incursions and casualties among his own fighters and people. Meeting with local tribal leaders that same month, Barzani was advocating caution and a more conciliatory approach to Baghdad. "If there is a peaceful way to reach an agreement, we will never think of any other way," he told reporters, adding that negotiations with Baghdad were the only course authorized by the IKF. "I am calling for elections, free elections among all of the Kurdish parties in Kurdistan to see which party gets more votes" and which approach to Baghdad should be taken. This was a direct challenge to Talabani.[51] Barzani also seemed to be the more conciliatory leader over internal safe haven politics as well. Most Kurds and most outside experts agreed that Barzani would have been the likely winner of the runoff election. His decision to call off the elections, while questionable on democratic grounds, was a concession to Iraqi Kurdish unity.

The general smoothness of the elections gave the Iraqi Kurds reasons for hope and the Barzani-Talabani decision to share power was greeted with celebrations across the autonomous zone. But while a political crisis seemed to have been averted, an economic one loomed. Iraqi Kurdistan is not a poor region even without the oil resources of Kirkuk that remained in Baghdad's hands. It is rich agriculturally and contains an infrastructure that, by third-world standards, is rather advanced. Nevertheless, the safe haven was struggling economically, for several reasons. First, the Coalition did not exempt the region from its sanctions against Iraq, knowing that what went into the safe haven was likely to make its way across the porous frontier into Iraq proper. Meanwhile Baghdad imposed its own sanctions, including the cutting off of government salaries and invalidation of Iraqi currency in the safe haven.

Worse than the sanctions, however, was the black market in Kurdistan itself. As Western journalists noted, there was plenty of gasoline and consumer items available for those who had the money. In addition, much of the Western relief to the region ended up on the black market as well. The large numbers of PUK and KDP *peshmerga* in and around the markets in Kurdish towns and cities made it clear that the parties were eagerly profiting off the situation. A KDP report issued in early 1995 provides a history of PUK pilfering: 175,000 Deutschmarks for health care items from the Berlin Physicians' Association, $750,000 from the Austrian parliament for schoolbooks, etc. The PUK has yet to issue a report but it undoubtedly would list similar corruption by the KDP.

The impact on the Kurdish people was tragic. In the countryside, things were not quite so bad, since people could live off the land. But in urban areas, the *New York Times* reported, Kurdish families were desperate. "Those who once had homes, modern appliances, and furniture have sold them all to put food on the table," an Iraqi Kurd wrote. "Men who once drove cars, wore expensive watches, took their families on vacations, now find themselves at a sidewalk selling what little they have left: a few dishes, a blanket, an old radio, or a couple of shirts."[52] Meanwhile, party leaders were making enough money to pay the *peshmerga* who controlled the black market.

Throughout 1993 and early 1994, the economic and political situation continued to deteriorate in the safe haven. A climate of fear had descended on the area, as terrorist bombings and assassinations escalated. Both Kurds and international relief workers were targeted. The Kurds blamed Baghdad, and Baghdad claimed the violence was caused by intra-Kurdish rivalries. No one can say for sure, not even Amnesty International, which investigated the situation during that time. Baghdad had the motive: destabilization of the safe haven; but subsequent events, specifically the civil war that broke out between KDP and PUK forces in the spring of 1994, suggested Kurdish responsibility. *Hawkar*, a Kurdish newsletter published in Britain, blamed the violence on the KRG's "lack of power and credibility," caused, in turn, by a "lack of international recognition" of the KRG government. But internal problems, it said, could not be entirely blamed on the international community. Going to heart of the dilemma facing the safe haven government, *Hawkar* noted that:

> while it is widely accepted that tension and rivalry [between the PUK and the KDP] would be damaging, no democracy is viable without an opposition. The KDP/PUK marriage of convenience has meant that healthy, constructive parliamentary opposition has been pushed to one side. Finally resources necessary to consolidate the new government are non-existent.[53]

In fact, the government's instability and financial difficulties were one and the same. Both parties were clearly siphoning off the government's main sources of income: international aid and customs duties. On May 1, 1994, the crisis came to a head, when PDK and PUK forces attacked one another across a broad front. In February 1995 a cease-fire was declared by the two sides, but was broken in July. To put an end to the fighting, the United States and Turkey sponsored peace talks in Dublin, Ireland, in August. The talks, which lasted into September, failed to produce agreements on two key issues, government revenues and control of the provisional capital, but did result in a renewal of the cease-fire.

Yet the situation remains tense. "It's madness," one UN official said during the fighting. "They all admit the folly of what they are doing, but do not stop. The Kurds are committing suicide." Or maybe just their leaders are. There is evidence of a growing disgust among Iraqi Kurds with their leadership and with the fighting, most of which involves *peshmerga* forces with civilians caught in the middle. The disenchantment began with Barzani's and Talabani's decision to cooperate with the Turkish govern-ment in their struggle with the PKK. The fighting has added to it. "The KDP-PUK brawl [has] disillusioned Kurdish people with their govern-ment," says a US official who worked in the safe haven from May 1993 to July 1994:

> It awakened local populations to political realities, and positively undermined the blind loyalty they once held to their political leaders. While maintaining traditional and tribal values, Kurdish people are beginning to show signs of modern political consciousness. During the May [1994] conflicts, towns and cities demonstrated against the fighting. People publicly criticized the Kurd-ish government, and demanded that officials be held accountable for their actions.[54]

This assessment may be premature and overly optimistic. But it calls to mind Sartre's dictum about the capacity for political and social progress: "Only when people become conscious of the group process can they transcend it."

UPDATE: TURKEY AND IRAN (1995–)

The situation in Turkish Kurdistan is also deteriorating, but in an entirely different way. Organizationally, there is no serious challenge to the PKK; it remains the only viable Kurdish nationalist movement in Turkey. While it is impossible to poll Turkish Kurds on the issue (Ankara would never permit it), it appears that the PKK is winning the hearts and minds of the Kurdish people, though to what extent and for what reasons remain unknown. "For better or worse," said a Turkish Kurdish lawyer, a self-pro-claimed opponent of the PKK, "the PKK is the only group in Turkey fighting for the Kurdish identity and many people have supported it for this reason."[55]

Repeatedly, the government talks of final assaults and thousands of dead PKK guerrillas. The PKK says the same about state security personnel and village guards. After every engagement, both sides proclaim victory. Then the cycle begins anew, with more soldiers, more guerrillas and more casualties. The winter of 1994–1995, however, saw a change in government strategy. For the first time, the Turkish military maintained its forces in the field during the winter months, when much of the mountainous region is bitterly cold and roads become impassable due to heavy snows. It recognized that the winter hiatus had allowed the PKK to regroup, recruit and rearm.

Moreover, the scale, and, some would argue, the audacity, of Turkish military operations in northern Iraq grow. While the government claims that incursions are limited to a 25-mile-deep swath along the border, Turkish jets have been reported attacking targets over a hundred miles deep in the safe haven. The government is also broaching the idea of a buffer zone again. Meanwhile, Baghdad, Tehran and Iraqi Kurdish leaders have voiced vigorous protests, the last claiming that the vast majority of victims are Iraqi Kurd civilians. The Turkish government denies this accusation, saying it has conducted intensive preinvasion reconnaissance to determine which encampments belong to the PKK. Nevertheless, relief officials in the area have confirmed Iraqi Kurd reports, saying that Turkish jets destroyed five Iraqi Kurd refugee villages along the Turkish border. Why Turkey would attack Iraqi Kurd civilians is a matter for speculation. Aside from possible military or political motives, racism may play a part as well. Turkish generals have been quoted to the effect that as far as they are concerned "a Kurd is a Kurd."

Meanwhile, after a telephone briefing by Turkish Prime Minister Tansu Çiller following Turkish operations in the safe haven in early 1995, President Clinton expressed "understanding for Turkey's need to deal decisively" with the PKK. Turkish President Suleyman Demirel assured Saddam Hussein that his government respected Iraqi territorial sovereignty and would pull its troops out as soon as the operation had achieved its objectives, a promise put into question by Turkey's talk of buffer zones. The government and the PKK have issued contradictory assessments. A PKK spokesman said that the operation had failed to intimidate Kurds on either side of the Turkish–safe haven border:

> [Çiller] claimed that 1994 would be a decisive year marking the crushing of our struggle . . . [yet] the military balance has changed in our favor and in many areas even the Turkish civil administration is no longer able to function. . . . The genocide and destruction of 4,000 Kurdish villages [has] only strengthened our people's determination to fight for freedom and human rights.[56]

But from the Turkish prime minister came this statement: "We expect to clear out this area and rip out the roots of the [PKK] terror operations aimed at our innocent people. Utmost effort is being made not to harm civilians."[57] A number of experts believe the Turkish government effort is doomed to fail. The PKK, taking advantage of Ankara's weeks-long preoccupation with invasion preparation, slipped most of its guerrillas back into Turkey. Other observers say that the invasion may be a large-scale ploy by elements within the military tired of the war and interested in negotiating with the PKK. According to this logic, the military had to invade to prove its toughness first.

While Turkey has refrained from attacking Turkish Kurds in northern Iraq since May, fighting has broken out between Barzani's KDP forces and the PKK in August and September, with both organization's blaming the other side and proclaiming victory in clashes that killed several hundred fighters on both sides.

Finally, what of the Iranian Kurds in the 1990s? There has been little discussion of events there because, compared to the situation in Iraq and Turkey, Iranian Kurdistan has been relatively, though not completely, quiescent since the end of the Iran-Iraq War. In 1989, it will be recalled, the Iranian government assassinated A. R. Ghassemlou, leader of the Kurdish Democratic Party of Iran, while ostensibly negotiating with him in Vienna. Ghassemlou's successor and political heir, Sadeq Sharafkandi, led Iranian Kurds until his assassination in a Berlin restaurant on September 17, 1992. Tehran denied any responsibility for the murder.

While there is almost no doubt that Tehran ordered the assassination of Ghassemlou, there may be some truth in Tehran's protestations of innocence in the Sharafkandi assassination. Iranian Kurds under both Ghassemlou and Sharafkandi generally remained aloof and apart from Kurds in Iraq and Turkey (though, as socialists, Ghassemlou and Sharafkandi sympathized with the goals, if not the methods, of Ocalan's PKK). This aloofness is part of a long tradition of Iranian Kurd separateness dating back, says historian Mehrdad Izady, to the divisions between the Ottoman and Persian Empires. "The [KDPI] message has remained the same for 47 years," Sharafkandi explained in an interview on French radio in 1992:

> Allow me to repeat once more that Iran is our problem. We naturally have relations with the political parties in Iraqi Kurdistan and Turkish Kurdistan. Each party, in conformity with the principle of non-interference in the internal affairs of others, is free to choose its fate according to the conditions prevailing in its country.[58]

This kind of talk, along with Sharafkandi's socialism, upset and offended the Iraqi Kurdish leaders who have sought to establish their hegemony over Iranian Kurds for decades; it was a goal pursued by the elder

Barzani during the Mahabad Republic. In fact, of all Kurdish leaders, Ghassemlou and Sharafkandi were always the most willing to work with the central government in establishing Kurdish autonomy and cultural rights.

Sharafkandi's successor, Mustafa Hejri, is a different story. From the very beginning he established Iranian Kurdish bases in northern Iraq. In March of 1993, Tehran attacked the bases from the air, explaining that they were going after "counter-revolutionary elements who had infiltrated Iranian soil from inside Iraq." The KDPI protest seemed a long way from the rhetoric of Sharafkandi and Ghassemlou. This is "an aggression against the movement of the Kurdish people in Iraqi Kurdistan, the political organization in Iraqi Kurdistan and the Kurdish people in Iraqi Kurdistan."[59]

The United States, while condoning Turkish air attacks against PKK bases in Iraq (and, by implication, Iraqi Kurd civilians), denounced Iran's much more limited incursions. "They shouldn't be there," a State Department spokesman told newsmen in March, 1993. "They shouldn't be bombing people and they shouldn't be in the no-fly area." In Iraq on April 22, the KRG organized a mass demonstration in Arbil, protesting the "antihuman" actions of the Iranian regime. Asked if he would agree with Iran's request to help root out Iranian Kurdish bases on Iraqi Kurdish territory (as he had done for Turkey), Barzani equivocated. "The [KDPI] takes account of our circumstances, and Iran is not Turkey," he told newsmen. "Our Iranian brothers are in agreement with us on not using Iraqi Kurdistan as a staging post to carry out operations and launch attacks against Iran."[60]

Hejri, however, freely admitted that this was not so. Interviewed in Arbil, the KRG capital, he told an English newswoman, "we send people over from here to take part in special operations, but we do so *secretly* because we don't want to make problems for the Iraqi Kurds [emphasis added]." In a joint press conference with Iraqi Kurdish leaders in June of 1993, he once again complained about victimization of *Iraqi* Kurds by Iran.[61] The situation would be comical if it were not so tragic for Kurdish civilians in both Iran and Iraq.

Hejri imagined he was using the Iraqi Kurds for his own advantage, but was actually being used by them. Recognizing that unilateral assaults on Iranian Kurds in Iraqi Kurdistan would not do the trick as long as the KDPI was protected by Iraqi Kurds, Iran sent a mission to meet with the Iraqi Kurdish leaders in July 1993. They were seeking a deal similar to Turkey's, and used a morally convincing argument. According to *Middle East International*, "the delegation reminded Iraqi Kurdish officials that Iran had provided them with 'invaluable help' through the 1980s and deserved to be treated 'at least as well' as the Kurds' traditional tormentors, the Turks."[62] The argument struck home. KDPI bases were moved away from the Iranian border, and party members received orders not to approach the border areas or to engage in any provocative acts against Iran. But later that same month, Iraqi Kurdish forces took part in defending Iranian Kurds against another Tehran attack, though they tried to sugar the pill by declaring that they had taken "a moderate stand . . . against Iranian shelling . . . [as they had] never wanted to terminate the bilateral relations of the two sides [that is, Iran and the KRG]" which, they said, "serves . . . the interests of the two sides."[63]

Frustrated by this equivocation, Tehran has pursued its anti-Kurdish strategy on two fronts. It continues to attack KDPI bases in the Iraqi safe haven, but it has also begun to pursue diplomatic means to rid itself of the Kurdish rebels. Since 1992, Iran, Turkey and Syria have been involved in a series of delicate negotiations concerning regional cooperation on Kurdish and other issues. Turkey wants Syria and Iran to discontinue their support of the PKK. Syria has maintained support for the PKK as a negotiating chip with Turkey over water rights to the Euphrates River. (Since the completion of the Ataturk Dam in 1992, Turkey has alternatively threatened to deny Syria water or flood Syria by releasing waters if it did not stop supporting the PKK.) Iran wants a *quid pro quo* with Turkey: Iran would drop its support of the PKK in exchange for Turkish pressure on the Iraqi Kurds to stop supporting the KDPI. In late 1993 and early 1994, the deal seemed to be working, at least as far as Turkey was concerned. Iran turned over 28 members of the PKK (including 10 corpses) to Turkish officials. Ankara even asked Tehran for approval to bomb PKK bases suspected to be on Iranian territory, a request which Iran has not agreed to. Iran, however, has yet to see any benefits from the negotiations, and continues to attack KDPI bases in Iraq from the ground and air.

KURDISTAN INTO THE TWENTY-FIRST CENTURY

As the twentieth century closes, the Kurds remain the largest ethnic group in the world without a state of their own, caught in one of the cruelest paradoxes of our age. As the function, power and significance of the nation-state dwindles in the coming century, the Kurds continue to struggle for a decreasingly meaningful political goal.

Whatever the future of the Baath regime in Baghdad, the Kurds of Iraq are unlikely to move backward in their century-long quest for statehood, though there are, of course, possible scenarios in which that might happen. The continuing civil war in the safe haven could very well draw in Baghdad's forces under the guise of peacekeeping and establishing order. Obviously, that is not likely in the short term, with the US and Coalition forces poised in Saudi Arabia, Kuwait and Turkey. For now, as discussed above, it serves US and Turkish (as well as Israeli and Saudi) interests to maintain Saddam Hussein and the safe haven. The US presence in the region needs a humanitarian justification as much as a strategic one, just as the Gulf War did. The safe haven may have been forced onto the West, or it may have been part of its strategy from the beginning, but now that it exists, it will not be abandoned in the short term. The enemy still rules in Baghdad.

But stranger realignments of forces have occurred before. It is not impossible to imagine a situation in which Saddam Hussein returns to the fold of Western allies, where he resided from the collapse of the shah to the invasion of Kuwait, a decade when Western arms dealers and Western governments helped build what was called during the Gulf War, with a great deal of exaggeration, the "fourth-largest military in the world." The increasing potential for radical Islamist politics in the region may make Saddam Hussein's more secular and nationalist form of government seem appealing once again to the West. There is always the possibility of an Islamist revolution in Iraq in which, with the Kurds gone, Shiites now outnumber Sunnis, although there has been little indication of it thus far, given the Baath party's totalitarian control over the population.

The essential issue in the safe haven in the coming years will be the growing divergence of interests among the US, Turkey and the Iraqi Kurds. Turkey wants the safe haven to be temporary; the US sees it lasting into the indefinite future and seeks to maintain the UN sanctions against Iraq as part of that strategy. Superpower muscle is flexed when necessary. In March, 1995, during a Security Council debate over extending the sanctions, the US cited Saddam Hussein's many "palaces" as an indication that the Iraqi leader was not hard-pressed enough to change his aggressive policies and intentions; this thin argument won the day over the growing protests of the international community, including many members of the Gulf War Coalition such as France, Germany, Italy, Spain and Canada. As for the Iraqi Kurds themselves, they see the safe haven as an interim step on the road to statehood.

Yet, while Iraqi Kurdistan gets more attention in the West, the situation in Turkey is likely to be the real trouble-spot in the near future for several reasons. First, there is the size of the Kurdish population. Iraq's Kurds number 3.5 million; Turkey's includes at least three to four times that number. Despite their more limited gains so far, the PKK is the most serious threat to the territorial integrity of any of the three countries with major Kurdish populations. While Iraq's Kurds established an autonomous region, they did so only under the protective umbrella of Turkey and the West. And in their current civil war, they have proved themselves once again unable to transcend the old tribal divisions that have plagued them throughout their history.

Not so the PKK. While the Turkish government continues to dismiss the organization as a small group of terrorists, the government's own actions belie its public statements. Turkey currently has some 300,000 to

400,000 troops in southeastern Turkey, and its March 1995 attack against PKK bases in the safe haven was its largest ever. The outcome of this latest campaign is uncertain, but recent history suggests that it is as unlikely to succeed as earlier offensives have been. The PKK is a disciplined and ideologically dedicated revolutionary organization, with at least 15,000 guerrillas and, despite US and Turkish claims to the contrary, a great reserve of sympathy and outright support in the Kurdish countryside and, increasingly, among the urban Kurdish population.

The second reason the Turkish-Kurdish struggle is likely to take center stage in coming years is the importance of Turkey itself. While Iraq has the oil reserves, Turkey, or rather, Turkish Kurdistan, has the water, a resource many believe will be the likely focus of conflict in the Middle East in the coming century.[64] As important, however, is Turkey's strategic position. Turkey has taken the place of the shah's Iran as the pillar of US strategy in the Persian Gulf and the Muslim world generally. This gamble on Turkey makes sense at one level. There are really no other options for an active superpower. Egypt is torn by Islamist dissent; Saudi Arabia is stable, but it lacks the manpower and military to do the job.

At another level, though, Turkey looks like a risky bet. Not only is the government facing a major guerrilla war in the southeast, but it is also being increasingly confronted by Islamist militants among its Turkish-speaking population as well. The wave of violence as the government faced off against these militants in the early part of 1995 may be a prelude to far graver confrontations in the future. Sunni militants have increased attacks on members of the Alawite sect, which comprises a third of Turkey's population. When Alawites protested these attacks in March of 1995, police opened fire, killing 25 people (the government claims 16 were killed).

In fact, Turkey has all the makings of an Islamist revolution. Its economy, due in part to the costs of the Kurdish war, is in collapse. Estimated costs of conducting the war are put at about $7 billion annually, contributing to Turkey's $70 billion foreign debt, which, after Brazil's and Mexico's, is the highest in the world, despite write-offs of portions of it during the Gulf War. Shantytowns ring the major cities and unemployment hovers around 25 percent, by official measurements. In nationwide elections in 1994, the Islamist Welfare Party took 20 percent of the vote.

And despite protestations by Turkish government officials and their Western backers, Turkey is not the model of a secular state that they claim it to be. The secularism and modernism evident in the major cities is a veneer. The early history of the Turkish state should be recalled here. Not only was Turkey the home of the Muslim caliphate as late as the 1920s, but Ataturk, the great secularizer of modern Turkey, was forced to rely on Islamic propaganda to rally his people, including Kurds, in his struggle to drive the British and Greeks from Anatolia in the years following World War I.

As for the war in Turkish Kurdistan, things look equally bleak for the the Turkish government and its Western backers. To make a comparison used by the Turkish generals themselves, Turkey has an internal Vietnam on its hands. The very methods used by the Turks, with their strategic hamlets, free-fire zones and village guards, bear an uncanny resemblance to those of the Americans in Vietnam. And like the Americans and their artificial South Vietnamese state, the Turks are losing the struggle for the hearts and minds of the Kurdish people. Moreover, the Turkish military seems caught up in the same strategic blunders their American counterparts made in Vietnam. They believe the war can be won with ever-more sophisticated technology and ever-greater application of force, as their March 1995 Cambodia-like incursion into northern Iraq demonstrates. As one American expert on Turkey noted, their military was created and their generals trained within the context of outdated NATO priorities, that is, to confront an invasion from the Soviet Union. While in recent years the military has altered its strategy somewhat to deal with guerrilla warfare, as the US did in Vietnam, the emphasis remains on conventional methods, with one exception, the pursuit of an alliance with Iraqi Kurds. Turkey hoped to pit Iraqi Kurd against Turkish Kurd, but the current civil war in Iraqi Kurdistan is quickly sinking that idea.

In general, there is little reason to think that the government will change its approach in the future. With the war in Kurdistan, a weak civilian government under Prime Minister Tansu Çiller, ambitions in the former Soviet republics of central Asia and its new role as the centerpiece of US strategy in the Middle East, the Turkish military—the real power in the country, according to many—is aggressively reasserting itself. In fact, says *Atlantic Monthly* analyst Robert Kaplan, the Turkish military has organized a "quiet coup" in the country, whose impact has been felt in all sectors of government, from parliament to the judiciary.[65] Recently six Kurdish parliamentarians were imprisoned for supporting Kurdish rights, a crime punishable under the 1992 terrorism act, which defines such advocacy as "threatening the indivisibility of the Turkish nation."

Moreover, the military understands Turkey's new importance to the West and has ideas of its own about a pan-Turkic sphere of influence in central and southwest Asia. This will make the government less likely to follow the US lead in the future, despite America's massive contribution to Turkey's military machine. Ankara's recent rapprochement with Iran may be a sign of things to come, says political scientist Robert Olson. Traditionally, in Turkish history, the hard-line–soft-line cycle in the government's approach to Kurdish nationalist aspirations has always shifted to the former under military regimes. As Turkey enters a military-dominated phase, there is no reason to expect that pattern to change. Meanwhile, the war continues to bankrupt the economy.

Only in Iran does a relative peace seem to reign in Kurdistan, and that peace may be a deceptive one. True, Kurdish nationalist organizations and the Kurdish liberation movement were shattered by the Islamic government during the Iran-Iraq War. But as noted above, Iranian Kurdish separatists have regrouped in the safe haven where they, unlike the PKK, are receiving the support of Iraqi Kurds. Iran has launched several assaults against them, though these are minor compared to Turkey's. Nevertheless, the government in Tehran complains that the Iranian Kurds are receiving aid from Turkey and the West. It is also conceivable that the Islamist government may not always enjoy the support it does now among the Iranian people. Revolutions as intense as the Islamist one in Iran have been challenged and overturned in the past. A breakdown of governmental authority, a militant antigovernment movement within Iran, another war with Iraq or a civil war would create conditions ideal for another cycle of Kurdish nationalist militancy.

Clearly the Kurdish struggle will continue. A struggle that has gone on for centuries and that has become increasingly nationalistic with each passing year is unlikely to change course simply because local governments and the international community would like it to do so. There has been too much conflict, hatred and suspicion to think that the Kurds can live peacefully in a single state under the sovereign authority of Turks, Arabs or even Persians, unless forced to do so. Whether the solution to this historical dilemma, if one is to be found, will take the form of autonomy, federalism or statehood is anyone's guess.

And finally, what of the prospect of Kurdish unity across national borders, the dream of every Kurdish nationalist since Prince Sharaf Khan of the sixteenth century? It is not likely, at least not in the near future. The ideological chasm between the PKK and the Iraqi Kurds, for one thing, is too great to be bridged. But as Iraqi Kurdistan descends into civil war and chaos, there is always the possibility of a struggle from beneath, against the tribal leaders and against tribalism itself. Moreover, the two main geopolitical forces that have emerged at the end of what historian E. J. Hobsbawm calls the "short twentieth century" may work in the Kurds favor. Technology and market forces are breaking down the kinds of national boundaries that have divided the Kurds since the end of World War I. At the same time, the current wave of ethnic politics and warfare in the Balkans, the Caucasus and central Asia suggests that the Kurdish struggles may have arrived at a crucial moment.

While the possibility of a transnational Kurdish movement may send shivers down the spine of government leaders in Ankara, Baghdad and Tehran, it is unlikely to happen anytime soon. The words of William Hay, a British administrator in the Mandate of Iraq, seem as useful to keep in mind today as they were when written 75 years ago:

[the Kurds] are not a political entity. They are a collection of tribes without any cohesion, and showing little desire for cohesion. They prefer to live in their mountain fastnesses and pay homage to whatever Government may be in power, as long as it exercises little more than a nominal authority. The day the Kurds awake to a national consciousness and combine, the Turkish, Persian, and Arab states will crumble to dust before them. That day is yet far off.[66]

NOTES

[1] This is not the place to go into Baghdad's reasons for invading Kuwait, though there is cause to wonder what Saddam Hussein was thinking when he upset the region's delicate balance of power by raising the issue of territorial integrity. Some of Hussein's grievances with the Kuwaitis were genuine, and he was no doubt encouraged both by his close relationship with the West during the Iran-Iraq War and by the Bush administration's nonreaction to Iraqi military gestures and rhetoric in the months leading up to the invasion.

[2] *Washington Post* (August 26, 1990), p. A35.

[3] *Ibid.*

[4] "The Gulf between Rhetoric and Reality," in *Kurdish Life*, No. 10 (Spring 1994), p. 1.

[5] *Washington Post* (August 16, 1990), p. A35.

[6] Thompson, Peter, "Turkey and the U.S. Strategic Vision," in *Kurdish Life*, No. 11 (Summer 1994), p. 3.

[7] *Ibid.*

[8] *Christian Science Monitor* (April 26, 1991), p. 7.

[9] Quoted in Thompson, *op. cit.*, pp. 4–5.

[10] "While Washington Sleeps, Ankara Dreams," in *Kurdish Life*, No. 5 (Winter 1993), pp. 4–5.

[11] National Public Radio, "All Things Considered" (January 9, 1991).

[12] "Rhetoric and Reality," pp. 2–3.

[13] Quoted in Thompson, *op. cit.*, pp. 4–5.

[14] *Washington Times* (October 17, 1986), p. 7.

[15] "On the Turkish Attack Against Guerrilla Bases in Iraqi Kurdistan," unpublished press release, May 29, 1983, Kurdish Cultural Institute, Brooklyn.

[16] London *Observer* (April 7, 1991), p. 5.

[17] Kurdistan Human Rights Project, *Freedom of the Press in Turkey: The Case of Özgür Gündem* (London: KHRP, 1993), p. 5.

[18] "Rhetoric and Reality," p. 4.

[19] *Washington Post* (February 17, 1991), p. A43.

[20] "Rhetoric and Reality," p. 4.

[21] *Ibid.*, p. 3.

[22] *Ibid.*

23 *Washington Post* (March 22, 1991), p. A29.

24 *Los Angeles Times* (May 15, 1991), p. 22.

25 *Ibid.*

26 Saeedpour, Vera Beaudin, interview with author, March 14, 1995.

27 *Ibid.*

28 "Rhetoric and Reality," pp. 6–7.

29 Saeedpour, interview, March 14, 1995.

30 *New York Times* (June 9, 1991), p. 10.

31 "Rhetoric and Reality," p. 6.

32 *Washington Post* (January, 1991), p. A18.

33 *Gazette Telegraph* (Colorado Springs) (July 16, 1991), p. A7.

34 *New York Times* (December 13, 1991), p. 9.

35 White, Paul, "The March 1990 Uprising in Turkish Kurdistan and Its Effects on Turkish Politics," in *Kurdish Times*, vol. 4, No. 1–2 (Summer-Fall 1991), pp. 97–106.

36 *Ibid.*

37 *Christian Science Monitor* (August 13, 1991), p. 4.

38 *News-Times* (Danbury CT) (October 26, 1991), p. 7.

39 *New York Times* (November 6, 1991), p. 1.

40 *Wall Street Journal* (November 13, 1991), p. 11.

41 Kurdistan Info Centre, "Turkish Cross-Border Raids Anger Iraqi Kurds," unpublished press release, October 16, 1991.

42 "While Washington Sleeps," pp. 3, 5.

43 *Washington Post* (June 26, 1992), p. A19.

44 "Washington Sleeps," p. 5.

45 *Ibid.*, pp. 1–2.

46 *Ibid.*, pp. 3–4.

47 *Ibid.*, p. 3.

48 *Ibid.*, pp. 3–4.

49 Saeedpour, interview, March 14, 1995.

50 *Christian Science Monitor* (May 8, 1991), p. 8.

51 *New York Times* (October 26, 1991), p. 9.

52 Reprinted in *Kurdistan Review* (April 1994), p. 8.

53 "Thought Waves," *Hawkar: Newsletter of Hawkarani Kurdistan*, No. 14/15 (January/February 1994), p. 4.

54 "Rhetoric and Reality," pp. 7–8.

55 Reuters on-line wire service, C-reuters@clarinet.com, November 25, 1994.

56 Xulum, Kani, interview with author, November 21, 1994.

57 Reuters on-line wire service, C-reuters@clarinet.com, March 20, 1995.

58 *Ibid.*, pp. 3–4.

59 *Ibid.*, p. 4.

60 *Ibid.*

61 *Ibid.*

[62] *Middle East International* (July 21, 1993), p. 3.

[63] *Ibid.* (August 11, 1993), p. 3.

[64] "Middle East Water—Critical Resource" in *National Geographic*, vol. 183, No. 5 (May 1993), p. 1.

[65] On "MacNeil/Lehrer Newshour" (March 21, 1995).

[66] Hay, William R., *Two Years in Kurdistan; Experiences of a Political Officer, 1918–1920* (London: Sidgwick & Jackson, Ltd., 1921), p. 35.

GLOSSARY

agha (Kurdish) Tribal chief.

Ahmad, Shaikh (Iraq) Elder brother of Mustafa Barzani and early leader of the Barzan tribal confederation.

Alevis (Kurdish) A syncretic cult among Kurds, also known as Alawites among Turkish-speaking people (see Cult of the Angels).

Algiers Accord An agreement reached in 1975 between the shah of Iran and Iraqi president Saddam Hussein, whereby the shah agreed to cut off support for Iraqi Kurdish rebels in exchange for Iraqi territorial concessions.

Anfal (Arabic) "Spoils of war." Saddam Hussein's campaign to break Kurdish resistance after the Iran-Iraq War.

Arbil (Iraq) The current "capital" of the Kurdish autonomous region.

Armenia (Turkey/Armenia) A nation of Christian peoples, once a part of Turkey and the Soviet Union. Traditionally, northern areas of Kurdistan have overlapped Armenian territory.

Assyrians (Iraq) A Christian minority in northern Iraq, also known as Nestorians.

Autonomy Agreement, March 11, 1970 (Iraq) Offered by the Baath government and accepted by Mustafa Barzani.

Azadi (Kurdish) Freedom Party. Founded in Turkey in the 1920s by former Hamidiye leaders and urban Kurds (see HAMIDIYE).

Azerbaijan (Iran/Azerbaijan) A nation of Muslim people in northern Iran and the former Soviet Union. The Soviet area is now independent.

Baath (Iraq/Syria) Arabic for "resurrection." Founded in the 1940s, the Baath Party is a socialist and nationalist party ruling Iraq and Syria.

Baban (Ottoman) One of the last emirates of the Ottoman Empire, it was situated in what is now Iraq (see EMIR).

Barzan (Iraq) The largest tribal confederation in Iraq.

Barzani, Massoud (Iraq) Leader of the Barzani tribal confederation and the Kurdish Democratic Party, he is the son of Mustafa.

Barzani, Mustafa (Iraq) Former leader of the Barzanis and the Kurdish Democratic Party until his exile to the US in 1975.

Cult of the Angels Syncretic cult that combines worship of ancestors and various elements of Islam and other monotheistic faiths.

Demirel, Suleyman (Turkey) Conservative Prime Minister from 1965–1971 and 1991–1993.

Dervish A member of an Islamic mystical order.

diwan (Turkish/Kurdish) Tribal court.

Diyarbakir (Turkey) Largest city in Turkish Kurdistan.

emir Leader of an emirate or principality.

209

Faisal, King (Iraq) The former Emir of Mecca who was placed on the Iraqi throne by the British, he ruled from 1930–1941 (see MANDATE).

Ghassemlou, A. R. (Iran) Leftist intellectual and leader of the Kurdish Democratic Party-Iran until his assassination in 1989.

Halabja (Iraq) Site of Iraq's largest chemical attack against the Kurds in 1988. Some 5,000 people were killed.

Hamidiye (Ottoman) Cossack-like force of Kurdish mounted regiments led by tribal chiefs. Originally intended to protect Ottoman borders, it was often used against internal enemies of the empire and Kurdish rivals like the Armenians.

jash (Kurdish) "Little donkeys." Kurdish militia who serve the state government.

Kemal, Mustafa (Turkey) Also known as Kamal Ataturk, Kemal established the modern Turkish state in the wake of World War I.

Khani, Ahmad (Kurdish) Author of the seventeenth-century Kurdish epic *Mem o Zin.*

Khoyboun (Kurdish) Independence. A nationalist organization founded in 1927.

Kirkuk (Iraq) An oil-refining city on the southern edge of Iraqi Kurdistan.

Komala (Kurdish) "Rebirth." Formed in 1942, the party ruled the Republic of Mahabad.

Kurdish Democratic Party (KDP) (Iraq) One of the two main parties of Iraqi Kurdistan (see BARZANI).

Kurdish Democratic Party-Iran (KDPI) The main political party of Iranian Kurdistan **(see** GHASSEMLOU).

Kurdish Workers' Party (PKK) (Turkey) The revolutionary party and guerrilla movement of Turkish Kurdistan (see OCALAN).

Lausanne, Treaty of (1923) Superseded the 1920 Treaty of Sèvres, giving most of Kurdistan to Turkey.

Mahabad, Republic of (Iran) An independent Kurdish state founded in Iran in the 1940s.

Mahmud, Shaikh (Iraq) Leader of a series of Kurdish revolts in the 1920s and 1930s.

Mandate of Iraq A League of Nations-authorized British government, it functioned from 1920–1932.

Medes An Indo-Aryan people who entered Kurdistan in the eighth century B.C., they had a major impact on the development of Kurdish culture.

Menderes, Adnan (Turkey) Populist President from 1950–1960.

Mossadegh, Mohammed (Iran) Leftist Prime Minister from 1951–1953, overthrown by CIA.

Mosul (Iraq) Once a province of the Ottoman Empire, it was made part of Iraq after World War I (see SÈVRES).

Motherland Party (Turkey) Liberal nationalist party (see OZAL).

Ocalan, Abdullah (Turkey) Founder and current leader of the Kurdish Workers' Party.

Operation Poised Hammer Post–Gulf War operation to protect the Kurdish safe haven by Coalition warplanes.

Operation Provide Comfort Post–Gulf War operation to provide relief aid to Iraqi Kurdish refugees in Turkey.

Ottomans An empire that ruled over much of the Middle East and Kurdistan from the fifteenth century until the end of World War I.

Ozal, Turgut (Turkey) Liberal Prime Minister from 1983–1989 and President from 1989–1991.

Pasdaran (Iran) Revolutionary Guard of the Islamic Republic.

pasha (Ottoman) A military and civil governor.

Patriotic Union of Kurdistan (PUK) (Iraq) One of the two main parties in Iraqi Kurdistan (see TALABANI).

peshmerga (Kurdish) It means "those who face death." Traditional Kurdish guerrillas.

Qasim, Abd al-Karim (Iraq) Leftist military ruler from 1958–1963.

Qazi Muhammed (Iran) Leader of the Mahabad Republic.

qazi (Kurdish) Judge.

Safavids (Iran) Rulers of the Persian empire from the sixteenth to eighteenth centuries.

safe haven An autonomous Kurdish zone established in northern Iraq after the Gulf War.

Said, Shaikh (Turkey) Leader of a Kurdish revolt in the 1920s.

Sèvres, Treaty of (1920) The post–World War I peace treaty dividing the Ottoman Empire, it included implicit promises of a Kurdish state (see LAUSANNE).

shaikh (Kurdish) A religious and political leader of a tribal confederation.

Sharaf al-Din (Kurdish) Prince of Bitlis and author of the first history of Kurdistan, the *Sharafnama*.

Simko (Iran) Agha Ismail. Kurdish tribal chief and rebel leader in the 1920s.

Sulimaniye (Iraq) Major city in the eastern part of Iraqi Kurdistan.

Sultan Abdulhamid II (Ottoman) Leader of the Ottoman Empire in the late nineteenth century and founder of the HAMIDIYE.

Sultan Abdulmejid (Ottoman) A reform leader of the Ottoman Empire in the mid-nineteenth century. Land privatization, under the Land Act of 1859, was inaugurated during his reign.

sultan (Ottoman) Also known as the Sublime Porte, the absolute ruler of the Ottoman Empire.

Sykes-Picot Agreement (1916) Named after the British and French negotiators, it secretly divided up the Ottoman Empire among the British, French and Russians (see SÈVRES).

Talabani, Jalil (Iraq) Founder and current leader of the Patriotic Union of Kurdistan Party.

Tudeh Party (Iran) The Communist Party of Iran.

Ubaydullah, Shaikh (Ottoman) Leader of a Kurdish revolt in the 1880s.

umma (Arabic) The Islamic community of believers.

vilayet (Ottoman) Province.

BIBLIOGRAPHY

Abrahamian, Ervand, *Khomeinism: Essays on the Islamic Republic*, Berkeley: University of California Press, 1993.

*al-Khalil, Samir (pseud.), *Republic of Fear: The Politics of Modern Iraq*, Berkeley: University of California Press, 1989.

Amjad, Mohammed, *Iran: From Royal Dictatorship to Theocracy*, New York: Greenwood Press, 1989.

Arfa, Hassan, *The Kurds: An Historical and Political Study*, New York: Oxford University Press, 1966.

Bois, Thomas, *The Kurds*, Beirut: Khayats, 1966.

Bonner, Raymond, "A Reporter at Large: Always Remember," *New Yorker*, September 28, 1992.

*Bruinessen, Martin van, *Agha, Shaikh and State: The Social and Political Structures of Kurdistan*, London: Zed Books, 1992.

Bulloch, John and Harvey Morris, *No Friends but the Mountains: The Tragic History of the Kurds*, New York: Oxford University Press, 1992.

CARDRI (Committee Against Repression And For Democratic Rights In Iraq), eds., *Saddam's Iraq: Revolution or Reaction?* London: Zed Books, 1986.

*Chaliand, Gerard, ed., *A People Without a Country: The Kurds and Kurdistan*, New York: Olive Branch Press, 1993.

Coan, Frederick, G., *Yesterdays in Persia and Kurdistan*, Claremont, Calif.: Saunders Studio Press, 1939.

Cottam, Richard, *Nationalism in Iran*, Pittsburgh: University of Pittsburgh Press, 1964.

Edmonds, Cecil J., *Kurds, Turks and Arabs: Research in North-Eastern Iraq, 1919–1925*, London: Oxford University Press, 1957.

*Farouk-Sluglett, Marion, and Peter Sluglett, *Iraq Since 1958: From Revolution to Dictatorship*, London: KPI, 1987.

Ghareeb, Edmund, *The Kurdish Question in Iraq*, Syracuse, N.Y.: Syracuse University Press, 1981.

Ghassemlou, Abdul Rahman, *Kurdistan and the Kurds*, Prague: Publishing House of the Czechoslovak Academy of Sciences, 1965.

Gunter, Michael, *The Kurds of Iraq: Tragedy and Hope*, New York: St. Martin's Press, 1992.

Hay, William R., *Two Years In Kurdistan; Experiences Of A Political Officer, 1918–1920*, London: Sidgwick & Jackson, Ltd., 1921.

Helsinki Watch, *Freedom and Fear: Human Rights in Turkey*, New York: Helsinki Watch, 1986.

Helsinki Watch, *State of Flux: Human Rights in Turkey* (December 1987 Update), New York: Helsinki Watch, 1987.

Hitchens, Christopher, "Struggle of the Kurds," *National Geographic*, August 1992.

Hotham, David, *The Turks*, London: John Murray, 1972,

International Journal of Kurdish Studies (formerly *Kurdish Times*), Brooklyn, N.Y.: The Kurdish Heritage Foundation, 1986.

*Izady, Mehrdad, *The Kurds: A Concise Handbook*, Washington, D.C.: Taylor and Francis, 1992.

Jawad, Sa'ad, *Iraq and the Kurdish Question*, London: Ithaca Press, 1981.

Jwaideh, Wadie, "The Kurdish Nationalist Movement: Its Origins and Development" (unpublished dissertation), Syracuse, N.Y.: Syracuse, 1960.

Kurdish Life, Brooklyn, N.Y.: The Kurdish Heritage Foundation, 1991.

Lazier, Sheri, *Into Kurdistan: Frontiers Under Fire*, London: Zed Books 1991.

Longrigg, Stephen, *Iraq, 1900 to 1950: A Political, Social, and Economic History*, New York: Oxford University Press, 1953.

McDowall, David, *The Kurds: A Nation Divided*, London: Minority Rights Publication, 1992.

Middle East Watch, *Genocide in Iraq: The Anfal Campaign Against the Kurds*, New York: Human Rights Watch, 1993.

Millingen, Frederick, *Wild Life among the Kurds*, London: Hurst and Blackett, 1870.

Powell, E. Alexander, *By Camel and Car to the Peacock Throne*, New York: The Century Company, 1923.

*Rich, Claudius, *Narrative of a Residence in Koordistan* (two volumes), London: James Duncan, 1836.

Schmidt, Dana Adams, *Journey Among Brave Men*, Boston: Little, Brown and Company, 1964.

Soane, Ely Bannister, *To Mesopotamia and Kurdistan in Disguise (1907–1909)*, Holland, N.Y.: Armorica Book Co., 1979 (reprint of 1912 edition).

Sykes, Mark, *The Caliph's Last Heritage: A Short History of the Turkish Empire*, London: Macmillan, 1915.

Vryonis, Speros, *The Turkish State and History: Clio Meets the Grey Wolf*, Thessalonika, Greece: Institute for Balkan Studies, 1991.

Wilson, Arnold, *Loyalties in Mesopotamia, 1914–1917*, London: Oxford University Press, 1930.

*Especially recommended.

INDEX

Entries are filed letter by letter.
Page references followed by "g" indicate glossary.

A

Abdulhamid II, Sultan 42, 211g
Abdulmejid, Sultan 39, 211g
Aflaq, Michel 116
Aftenbladet (Swedish newspaper)
  160
aghas (chiefs) 80–82, 209g
  in electoral politics 92
  Iran 31
  nontribal Kurds 84
  under Ottomans 40
  tribal functions 86, 87, 89, 91
  Turkey 49
agriculture 88, 89–90, 112,
  117–118, 125
Ahmed, Shaikh 55, 56, 209g
Alevis (Alawites) (sect) 203, 209g
Algiers Accord (1975) 27, 61,
  130, 209g
Amjad, Mohammed 67, 121, 124
Amnesty International 158, 165,
  194, 196
ANAP *see* Motherland Party
anfal campaign (1988–1990)
  61–63, 209g
  characterized as genocidal 150
  motivation for 10, 117
  refugees from 71, 99, 131
  tactics of Iraqi government 30,
    63, 162
Anglo-Iraqi Treaty (1930) 113,
  115
Anglo-Persian Oil Company 118,
  120, 125
Ankara Journalist Association
  142, 160
Ararat, Mount (Turkey) 76

Arbil, Iraq 166, 200, 209g
Arfa, Hassan 67
Ariç, Nizamettin 145
Armenia 43, 84, 85, 88, 209g
Assad, Hafez al- 132
Associated Press (news service)
  163, 165
Assyrian Democratic Movement
  (Iraq) 21
Assyrians (ethnic group) 20, 54,
  56, 84, 85, 209g
Ataturk, Kamal (Mustafa Kemal)
  culture and society 8
  democracy not pursued by
    47–48
  economic development 112
  establishment of modern Turkey
    43, 44, 45
  Islam used by 92, 203
  Kurdish militia dissolved by 93
  nationalism 106–110, 145
Ataturk Dam (Turkey) 112, 143,
  201
Autonomy Agreement (Iraq,
  1970) 21, 209g
Ayaz, E. Nevzat 178
Ayyubids (dynasty) 37
Azadi (Kurdish) Freedom Party
  (Turkey) 45, 93, 209g
Azerbaijan 25, 66, 209g

B

Baath Party (Iraq) 21–22, 59–61,
  115–117, 209g
Baban (Ottoman emirate) 209g
Baghdad Pact (1955) 57, 58, 122

Bani-Sadr, Abolhassan 24, 69, 123
Barraclough, Colin 160
Barzani, Ahmed 83
Barzani, Massoud 209g
  democracy not pursued by 193
  elections of 1992 19, 194
  income from tariffs and customs 151
  Iran-Iraq War 61
  Iraqi relations 168, 186, 195
  Kuwait invasion as opportunity for 176, 177
  Talabani rivalry 19–20, 150–152, 165–166, 170, 187, 194–195, 197
  tribal base of power 6, 82, 147
  Turkish relations 149, 157, 165, 181, 191, 192, 197
  vision of Kurdish state 97
Barzani, Mustafa 209g
  escape to Iran after 1975 fighting 61
  Iranian aid to 130
  Iraqi relations 57, 58, 60, 169
  Mahabad Republic 56, 65, 66
  tribal politics 86
  U.S. statehood proposed by 128
Barzani (tribal confederation) 20, 55, 59, 209g
bazaaris (retailers) 24, 120, 123
Bazzaz, Abd al-Rahman al- 59, 60
Besikçi, Ismail 108, 110, 145
black market 196
Bois, Thomas 90
brigandage 78, 88
Britain
  Iranian relations 65, 120
  Iraqi mandate *see* Iraq
  Iraqi relations 57, 96, 114, 115
  nationalism promoted by 138
  Turkish relations 27, 44
Bush, George 27, 101, 128, 162, 184

C

Canada 202
censorship 22, 110
Chaliand, Gerard 69, 81, 94
Chamchamal, Iraq 165
charisma 20
chemical weapons 31, 63, 161
Christian Science Monitor (newspaper) 51, 179, 189, 195
Çiller, Tansu 17, 18, 111, 198, 204
circumcision 91
civil war, Kurdish (Iraq, 1994-95) 5–6, 30, 192–197 *see also* Kurdish Democratic Party; Patriotic Union of Kurdistan
Cizre, Turkey 188
climate 75
Clinton, Bill 4, 27, 198
coal deposits 76
Communist Party of Iran *see* Tudeh Party
Coon, Carleton 137
Corbin, Sam 143
Correct Way Party (DYP) (Turkey) 17
Cult of the Angels 209g *see also* Alevis
culture, Kurdish 145–147
Cursel, Cemal 48

D

Dashnak (Armenian independence organization) 46
death squads 16, 48, 111
Defense and Economic Cooperation Agreement (United States/Turkey, 1980) 178
Demirel, Suleyman 17, 18, 19, 111, 146, 198, 209g
Democracy Party (DEP) (Turkey) 19, 158
demography 76–78
  Iran 120
  Iraq 113

Turkey 106
dervish 209g
Desert Storm and the Kurdish Uprising 184–185
detribalization 80, 84, 92
diaspora 101–103, 140
Diodorus (Greek historian) 155
diwan (tribal court) 86, 91, 209g
Diyarbakir, Turkey 209g
Dowson, E. 53
DYP *see* Correct Way Party

E

Eagleton, William 66
Economist (British magazine) 98, 184
economy
    Iran 125–127
    Iraq 117–119
    tribal 88–90
    Turkey 112–113, 142–145
Edmonds, C. J. 54
Egypt 115
electrical power 112
Elphinston, W. G. 47
emir 209g
Epic of Gilgamesh 36
European Convention for Prevention of Torture 158
European Union (European Community) 4, 111, 188
Evren, Kenan 17

F

Fahd, King of Iraq 118
Faisal, King of Iraq 54, 56, 113, 210g
Faistauer, Renata 171
farming *see* agriculture
Farouk-Sluglett, Marion *see* Sluglett, Peter and Marion Farouk-
fatwa (judgment) 127
feuds, tribal 86

Financial Times (London newspaper) 50, 159, 179, 180
foreign debt
    Iran 127
    Iraq 119
    Turkey 203
France 4, 27, 44, 202
Free Officers' Association (Iraq) 57, 58

G

GAP *see* Greater Anatolia Project
Garner, Jay 186
gecekondu ("night-built houses") 102
Germany 4, 27, 103, 161, 191, 202
Gezmis, Deniz 94
Ghareeb, Edmund 114
Ghassemlou, A. R. 210g
    assassination of 34, 153, 171, 199
    autonomy as goal 171, 200
    elections of 1980 70
    Iran-Iraq War 70
    Iraqi relations 62, 67, 130, 131
    Khomeini opposed by 97
    leadership tradition 154
    Mahabad Republic 66
    on World War I 43
GNP *see* gross national product
Gokalp, Zia 43
"golden age" 37
government *see specific country* (*e.g.*, Turkey)
Great Britain *see* Britain
Greater Anatolia Project (GAP) 9, 18, 112, 143, 144
Greece 44, 132
gross national product (GNP)
    Iran 120
    Iraq 113
    Turkey 106
guerrilla warfare 155 *see also peshmerga*

Gulf War (1990) 13, 27, 29, 119, 176–178
Gures, Dogan 164, 192

H

HADEP see People's Democracy Party
Halabja, Iraq 31, 63, 161, 210g
hamidiye (Kurdish mounted regiment) 42, 43, 45, 85, 93, 210g
Hamilton, A. M. 86
Hamzali, Turkey 159
Hawkar (Kurdish newsletter) 151, 196
Hay, William 41, 205
Hazleton, Fran 115
Hejri, Mustafa 35, 153, 172, 200
Helsinki Watch 101
HEP see People's Labor Party
history 36–74
Hobsbawm, E. J. 205
Hotham, David 43, 137
Hottinger, Arnold 142
human rights abuses see also anfal campaign; chemical weapons; torture
   Iraq 10
   Iraqi Kurds 166
   Turkey 19, 27, 139, 145, 156, 157, 159
Human Rights Association of Turkey 181
Human Rights Foundation of Turkey 51, 158
Human Rights Watch 31, 145, 150, 159, 162
Hurriyet (Turkish newspaper) 188
Hussein, Saddam
   anfal campaign (1988–1990) 62, 63, 71, 117
   Baath Party 116
   cultural policy 10
   Desert Storm and the Kurdish uprising 184, 185
   economics 119
   Iran-Iraq treaty of 1975 61, 130
Iran-Iraq War 7, 61, 123, 131
   Kurdish-Iraqi peace agreement of 1970 60
   Kuwait invasion 177, 178
   nationalism 117
   Operation Poised Hammer 186, 187
   political participation in Iraq 21, 23
   safe haven 170, 193, 195
   tactics 161, 162, 163, 166
   Turkish relations 184, 189, 190, 198
   U.S. relations 128, 202

I

identity, Kurdish 78–79
IKF see Iraqi Kurdistan Front
Independence Treaty (Iraq, 1932) 55
infant mortality rate 77
Inonu, Ismet 48
internal colony 9, 89, 113
International Monetary Fund (IMF) 127
Iran 2, 120–127, 121
   cultural policy 13–14
   demography 76, 77, 120
   diaspora of Kurds 103
   economy 15
   future of Kurds in 205
   history 63–71
   Iraqi Kurds backed by 26, 130, 131
   negotiations 34–35, 170–172
   politics and government 14, 23–25, 97–98, 152–155
   recent developments 6–7
   refugees 99, 100
   tactics 31–32, 166–167
   tribal functions 87, 92
   Turkish relations 132, 197–201
   Western alliances 27
Iran-Iraq War (1980–1988) 70–71

domestic politics (Iran) 25,
123–124
economics (Iraq) 119
Kurdish alliances during 130,
131
tactics (Iran) 32
tactics (Iraq) 29, 161
Iraq 2, 113–119, *114*
British mandate 27, 52–55, 80,
96, 113, 117, 127–128, 210g
cultural policy 10–11
demography 76, 77, 113
diaspora of Kurds 102, 103
economy 12–13
future of Kurds in 201, 202
history 52–63, 56–57
Iranian relations 26, 130, 131
negotiations with Kurds 33–34,
168–170
politics and government 11–12,
19–23, 96–97, 147–152
recent developments 5–6
refugees 98, 99, 100
safe haven 176–187, 192–197
tactics 29–31, 161–166
tribes and tribal confederations
80, 82
Turkish relations 4, 26, 132
U.S. relations 27
Iraqi Communist Party 193
Iraqi Kurdistan Front (IKF) 21,
150, 169, 181, 193, 194
Islamist Party (Iraq) 20, 21
Islamist Welfare Party (Turkey)
19, 96, 203
Ismail, Shah 98
Israel 26, 130
Italy 202
Izady, Mehrdad
on early history of Kurdistan
36, 38, 39, 42, 46, 109
on Iranian-Kurdish relations 97,
199
on Kurdish nationalism 63, 136
on nontribal Kurds 84
on population growth 76
on tribal politics 83, 96

Izmir *see* Smyrna

J

jash (Kurdish progovernment militia) 56, 86, 155, 184, 210g
Jews 84
Jwaideh, Wadie 40, 41, 53, 64,
80, 83

K

Kamal, Hussein 23
Kandemir, Nuzhet 140, 142,
143, 144
Kaplan, Robert 111, 204
KDP *see* Kurdish Democratic Party
KDPI *see* Kurdish Democratic
Party of Iran
Kemal, Mustafa *see* Ataturk, Kamal
Kendal, Nizzan 40, 42, 49, 77,
93, 108, 111
Khani, Ahmad 136, 210g
Khashan, Hilal 102
Khomeini, Ayatollah Ruhollah
economy 126
Ghassemlou assassination or-
dered by 34
Iran-Iraq War 62, 70–71, 124
Iraqi aid to Kurds claimed by
131
Islamic rule 24
Kurdish autonomy resisted by
32, 68–70, 153, 170
pre-revolutionary preaching
122–123
Khoyboun (Kurdish) Inde-
pendence (organization) 46,
210g
Kirkuk, Iraq 210g
Kurdish attacks on 62, 131
negotiations over 170, 186
relocation of Kurds from 59, 98
Turkish claims on 179–180, 182
komala (Organization of Revolutionary Toilers of Iranian Kurdistan) 98

Komala ("Rebirth") Party (Iran) 65, 210g

KRA *see* Kurdish Regional Administration

Kurdish Committee for Diffusion of Learning 93

Kurdish Cultural Institute 142

Kurdish Democratic Party (KDP) (Iraq) 19–20 *see also* Barzani, Massoud; Barzani, Mustafa
  black market 13
  PUK conflict and cooperation with 5, 30, 62, 130, 150–152, 164–166, 170, 194–197
  tribal focus of 15, 102–103

Kurdish Democratic Party of Iran (KDPI) 23, 97–98 *see also* Ghassemlou, A. R.
  autonomy as goal 14
  intra-Kurdish policy 14
  Iraqi Kurd manipulation of 7, 200
  under Islamic Republic 6, 34, 69–70, 124, 152–154, 172, 201
  leftist secular nature of 103
  Mahabad Republic *see* Mahabad, Kurdish Republic of
  politics 15
  under shah 67–68
  tactics 31–32, 166–167

Kurdish (language) 7, 8, 10, 13, 52, 181

Kurdish Life (publication) 150, 166, 180, 181, 184, 185

Kurdish National Front (Iraq) 62

Kurdish Regional Administration (KRA) 151

Kurdish Workers' Party (PKK) (Turkey) 16–17, 49–52, 94–95 *see also* Ocalan, Abdullah
  economic policy 10
  founding of 49
  Iranian support for 132, 201
  Iraqi Kurd collaboration against 129, 149, 183
  negotiations 32–33
  organizational form 15
  political goals 8, 9, 141, 142
  prohibition on dialogue with 19
  refugees 101
  Syrian support for 130
  tactics 28, 158–160
  tribal functions 87, 90
  Turkish war against 3–4, 26, 139, 155–158, 167, 180, 187–192, 197–199, 202–203

Kurdistan *see specific topics* (*e.g.,* climate); *groups* (*e.g.,* Kurdish Workers' Party); *key figures* (*e.g.,* Ocalan, Abdullah)

Kurdistan Human Rights Project 156

Kuwait, Invasion of (1990) 176–178

L

Land Code (Ottoman Empire, 1859) 40

land reform
  Iran 15, 25, 125
  Iraq 118
  Ottoman Empire 41–42
  PKK's support of 10, 90

language *see* Kurdish

Lausanne, Treaty of (1923) 44, 210g

Lawrence, T. E. (Lawrence of Arabia) 54

Lazier, Sheri 140

League of Nations 54, 56, 113

Lebanon 16, 26, 129, 130

Libya 26, 130

literacy rates 77

Local Languages Act (Iraq, 1931) 55

Longrigg, Stephen 81, 85, 113

Los Angeles Times (newspaper) 140, 182

M

Mahabad, Kurdish Republic of 14, 31, 32, 56, 65–66, 128, 210g
Mahmud, Shaikh 55, 210g
Mahmud II, Sultan 39
Makiya, Kanan 116
March 11, 1970, accords (Iraq) *see* Autonomy Agreement
Marcus, Aliza 95, 111, 141, 142, 144
McDowall, David 46, 60
Medes (Indo-Aryan people) 13, 37, 210g
Mem o Zin (Ahmad Khani) 136
Menderes, Adnan 110, 112, 210g
Merawdli, Kamal 95
Mesry, Fouad Majied 151
Middle East International (publication) 200
Middle East (publication) 51, 62, 144
Middle East Watch (organization) 18–19, 191
Millingen, Frederick 40, 41, 81, 84, 88, 89
Milliyet (Turkish newspaper) 100, 179, 181
missionaries 138
Mitterrand, Danielle 168
Mossadegh, Mohammed 67, 120, 210g
Mosul, Iraq 109, 179, 210g
Motherland Party (ANAP) (Turkey) 17, 50, 180, 182, 210g
mountains 1, 3, 75
Mount Ararat uprising (1929-1932) 46
Muhammed, Muhammed 56
Muhammed, Qasi 65
mujahideen (left-wing Islamic Iranian militants) 23, 70, 123, 124, 167
Mustafawi, Hadji 171

N

napalm 156
Naqshabandi (Dervish order) 82
Nasser, Gamel Abdel 115
National Council of Resistance (Iran) 70
National Democratic Front (NDF) (Iraq) 131
nationalism
  Iran 120–124
  Iraq 113–117
  Kurdish 135–138
  Turkey 106–110, 138–142, 145
National Public Radio (United States) 180
NATO *see* North Atlantic Treaty Organization
negotiations *see specific country* (*e.g.,* Iran)
Nestorians *see* Assyrians
New Roz (Kurdish New Year) 188
New Statesman (British publication) 100
Newsweek (magazine) 95, 98
New York Times (newspaper)
  Iran 68, 69, 92
  Iraq 100, 151, 182, 185, 187, 196
  Turkey 51, 190
Nisan, Mordechai 113, 152
no-fly zone 4, 163
nontribal Kurds 83–84
North Atlantic Treaty Organization (NATO) 111
Noury, Ihsan 46
Nuri, Said 56
Nusaybin, Turkey 188

O

Observer (London publication) 181
Ocalan, Abdullah 211g
  economic policy 144
  founding of PKK 49

independence denied as goal by
4, 33, 141, 142
Iraqi Kurds criticized by 182,
183
reformist Kurdish politicians
scorned by 9
terrorism condoned by 160
traditional allegiance to 94, 95
Turkish war against the PKK
167, 189, 191
writings sold openly 146
oil industry
Iran 15, 76, 125, 126
Iraq 12, 21, 57, 76, 117, 118,
119
Olson, Robert 46, 204
OPEC see Organization of Petroleum Exporting Countries
"Operation Desert Shield" 130
"Operation Poised Hammer"
163, 186–187, 211g
"Operation Provide Comfort"
211g
Organization of Petroleum Exporting Countries (OPEC) 126
Organization of Revolutionary
Toilers of Iranian Kurdistan see
Komala
Ottoman Empire 37–39, 40,
42–43, 106, 211g
Ozal, Turgut 211g
cultural policy 18, 52, 145,
146, 181, 183
on diaspora of Kurds 102, 140
Iraqi Kurds cooperation with
181, 182, 183, 192
politics 17, 111
refugees 99, 100
Turkish rights to Kirkuk 179,
180
war against PKK 33, 50, 180,
188, 190

Pahlavi, Shah Mohammed Reza
14, 27, 65, 66–68, 120, 122, 125
Palme, Olaf 160
Paris-Match (publication) 98
Parthian Empire 37
Pasdaran see Revolutionary Guards
pasha 211g
Patriotic Union of Kurdistan
(PUK) 19–20 see also Talabani,
Jalal
black market 13
Islamists challenge to 21
KDP conflict and cooperation
with 5, 30, 62, 130, 150–152,
164–166, 170, 194–197
KDPI relations 97
refugees 185
tribal focus of 6, 102–103
People's Democracy Party
(HADEP) (Turkey) 158
People's Labor Party (HEP) (Turkey) 158, 190
Persian Gulf War See Gulf War
personal names 7
peshmerga (Kurdish guerrillas)
211g
Iran 14, 23, 31, 32, 70
Iraq 13, 20, 30, 56, 61, 63, 165
Mahabad Republic 65
nontribal Kurds 84
tactics 155
tribal leaders use of 82
petroleum see oil industry
PKK see Kurdish Workers' Party
place-names 7
political organizations 92–98
political participation 15–27
population 76–77, 106, 113, 120
Powell, E. Alexander 113
PUK see Patriotic Union of Kurdistan

P

Pahlavi, Reza Shah (Reza Khan)
64, 120

Q

Qaderi-Azar, Abdullah 171
Qadiri (Dervish order) 82

Qasim, Abd al-Karim 57–59, 85, 115, 116, 118, 211g
qazi (judge) 211g
Qazi Muhammed 211g

R

Radi, Selma al- 119
Rafsanjani, Ali Akbar Hashemi 25, 34, 62, 124, 127, 153, 172
Rassoul, Fadhil 171
rebellions *see also key figures (e.g., Ocalan, Abdullah); specific groups (e.g., PKK)*
  Iran 23, 31, 32, 67, 92, 120 *see also* Mahabad, Kurdish Republic of
  Iraq 34, 56, 184–185
  Ottoman Empire 41–42
  Turkey 44, 45–47, 92
refugees 98–101
Reuters (news service) 181
Revolutionary Guards (Pasdaran) (Iran) 32, 69, 211g
Rich, Claudius 82, 95
Richard Lionheart 37
Roman Empire 37
Roosevelt Jr., Archie 65, 66
Rushdie, Salman 127
Russia 39, 63, 85, 138

S

Saeedpour, Vera Beaudin 144, 151–152, 166, 183–184, 184, 194
Safavids (dynasty) 38, 63, 211g
safe haven 150–152, 192–197, 211g
  economy 13
  elections 19
  future of 201–203
  Iranian Kurd bases in 23, 32, 131, 153, 201, 205
  Iraqi pressure on 31, 163, 164
  Islamists 21
  nontribal Kurds 84

tribalism 79, 87
Turkish relations 109, 129, 156–157, 189–191, 198
Sahraroudi, Mohammed Jaraf 171
Said, Shaikh 45, 46, 83, 211g
Salah ud-Din (Saladin) 37
Saudi Arabia 26
SAVAK (Iranian secret police under Shah) 122
SAVAMA (Iranian secret police under Islamic rule) 171
sayyid (holy man) 82
Schmidt, Dana 58
schools 101–102
Sèvres, Treaty of (1920) 53, 54, 128, 211g
Sezgin, Ismet 165
shaikhs 40, 41, 49, 82, 89, 211g
Shalikashvili, John 191
Sharaf al-Din 136, 211g
Sharafkandi, Sadeq 34–35, 154, 172, 199, 200
Sharafnama (history of Kurdistan) 136
sharia (Islamic law) 123, 154
Shiite Muslims 13, 22, 25, 92, 113
Simko (Agha Ismail) 64, 211g
Sinjar, Iraq 163
Sluglett, Peter and Marion Farouk- 58, 59, 99, 114, 116, 118
Smyrna (Izmir) (Turkey) 44
Soane, Ely 53, 78
Socialist Party of Kurdistan (Turkey) 16
Society for the Defense of Freedom (Iran) 25, 124
Soviet Union 21, 27, 32, 57, 65–66, 128
Spain 202
"spoils of war" campaign (Iraq) *see anfal* campaign
Stalin, Josef 75
Sulaiman, Azad 151
Sulimaniye, Iraq 163, 186, 187, 211g
sultan 211g

Sunni Muslims 13, 25, 68, 91, 92, 113
"sun theory of language" 108
Sykes-Picot Agreement (1916) 44, 53, 211g
Syria 6, 16, 26, 76, 115, 129–130, 132, 201

T

tactics 28–32, 155–160
Talabani, Jalal 212g
  allegiance to 147
  Barzani rivalry 19–20, 59, 150–152, 165–166, 170, 187, 194–195, 197
  democracy not pursued by 193
  Desert Storm and the Kurdish uprising 184
  Iran-Iraq War 61–62, 130
  Iraq: tactics 163
  Iraqi negotiations with 168–170
  Islamist attacks on 151
  Kuwait invasion as opportunity 176
  Kuwait invasion as opportunity for 177, 178
  political goals 97, 148
  Sulimaniye attack 186, 187
  tribal basis of power 6
  Turkish relations 181, 182, 191, 192
  U.S. relations 149, 177
  views on Kurdish unity 149
Talabani (tribal confederation) 82
Taurus Mountains (Turkey) 76
tax-farming 39
terrorism 160
Thompson, Peter 178, 183
Time (magazine) 98
Toperi, Kaya 180
topography and climate 75–76
torture 22, 51, 146, 158
tribes and tribal confederations 6, 79–83, 86–92, 96
Truman Doctrine 110
Tucker, W. F. 46

Tudeh Party (Communist Party of Iran) 23, 24, 98, 120–122, 124, 212g
Turcomans (Iraq ethnic group) 179
Turkey 2, 106–113, 107
  cultural policy 7–8
  demography 76, 77, 106
  diaspora of Kurds 101, 102, 103
  economy 9–10
  future of Kurds in 202–204
  Gulf War and aftermath 178–184
  history 43–52
  Iranian relations 6
  Iraqi Kurds supported by 129
  mid-1990s 3–5
  Middle East alliances 26, 132
  negotiations 32–33, 167–168
  politics and government 8–9, 16–19, 93–96
  recent developments 197–201
  refugees 98, 99, 100, 101
  tactics 28–29, 155–160
  tribes and tribal confederations 80, 87
  war against the PKK 138–147, 187–192 see also Kurdish Workers' Party
  Western alliances 27
Turkish Workers' Party 94, 111

U

Ubaydullah, Shaikh 41, 42, 83, 128, 212g
umma (community of believers) 69, 124, 136, 212g
United Arab Republic of Egypt and Syria (UAR) 115
United Kingdom see Britain
United Nations 27, 62, 71, 100, 119
United States
  Iranian relations 27, 127, 128
  Iraqi relations 57, 119, 164
  Kuwait Invasion 177

missionaries from 138
safe haven 192, 201–202
Turkish relations 4, 156, 178,
181, 183, 200, 203

V

van Bruinessen, Martin
on Hamidiye 42
on Iranian Revolution 152
on Kurdish emirates 40
on Kurdish nationalism 102
on Shaikh Said 46
on tribalism 83, 86, 87, 90
Vanly, Ismet Sheriff 56, 61
Vietnam War 204
vilayet (province) 11, 40, 212g

W

Wall Street Journal (newspaper)
190
Washington Post (newspaper) 50,
140, 176, 181, 182, 190, 191
water 112, 203

White, Paul 188
"White Revolution" (Iran) 15,
67, 122, 126
Wilson, Arnold 55
women 17, 21, 78
World War I 42–43

X

Xulam, Kani 50, 95, 160

Y

Yilmaz, Mesut 190
Young Turks 42, 43, 93, 106, 138

Z

Zagros Mountains (Iran) 53, 63,
76, 98
Zahedy, Fazlollah 122
Zahko, Iraq 166
Zaken, Moti 168, 169
Zibari, Hoshyar 176, 191
Zibari (tribal confederation) 58